MARCHING FOR UNION

*A Civil War Soldier's Walk
across the Reconstruction South*

RANDY BISHOP

STACKPOLE
BOOKS
Guilford, Connecticut

Published by Stackpole Books
An imprint of The Rowman & Littlefield Publishing Group, Inc.
4501 Forbes Blvd., Ste. 200
Lanham, MD 20706
www.rowman.com

Distributed by NATIONAL BOOK NETWORK

British Library Cataloguing in Publication Information available

Library of Congress Cataloging-in-Publication Data available

ISBN 978-0-8117-6988-4 (cloth : alk. paper)
ISBN 978-0-8117-6989-1 (electronic)

♾™ The paper used in this publication meets the minimum requirements of American National Standard for Information Sciences—Permanence of Paper for Printed Library Materials, ANSI/ NISO Z39.48-1992.

To John Thompson,
the man who introduced me to the story of Gilbert Henderson Bates and
encouraged me to compile a record of the travels and endeavors of the veteran.

Contents

INTRODUCTION

GILBERT HENDERSON BATES WAS BORN FEBRUARY 13, 1836, IN SWEET-
water, New York, a community of Livingston County. An article written
decades later reported that Bates was "descended from two of the oldest
colonial families of New England."[1]

In the ensuing years, Bates moved to Albion, Wisconsin, situated
in the vicinity of Edgerton. Bates secured a position as a laborer and
worked on a farm. Known locally as "Tobacco City U.S.A.," Edgerton,
Wisconsin was the hub of southern Wisconsin's tobacco industry. The
municipality also served as the location of more than fifty tobacco warehouses. Albion, in Dane County, was a relatively new town; the area's first
settler, Freeborn Sweet, had arrived just two and a half decades earlier,
in August 1841. Aside from being the setting of a significant number of
churches, Albion soon gained a solid reputation as an area retail center
with a wagon and blacksmith shop, general store, a hotel, and a harness
shop. A steam mill served as a site for sleigh and wagon manufacturing
and provided employment for community residents.[2] It is safe to assume
that a number of these establishments served the needs of Bates.

Little information exists in relation to the childhood or youth of Gilbert Henderson Bates, but the onset of the American Civil War increased
the amount of recorded evidence for Bates and his family. As the years
progressed, three of his brothers were reported as joining the military as
members of the Federal forces during the War Between the States.[3]

Gilbert Henderson Bates enlisted in the 1st Wisconsin Heavy
Artillery September 17, 1864. Interestingly, the Roster of Company H
lists Bristol, Wisconsin as his residence. As a member of Company, or
Battery, H, Bates quickly rose to the rank of sergeant. Battery H, along
with Batteries E, F, G, I, K, L, and M, were ordered to Washington, D.C.

While in the nation's capital, those units, all of which were organized during either September or October 1864, were attached to the Third Brigade of Brigadier General Gustavus Adolphus DeRussy's Division, Twenty-Second Army Corps. The batteries maintained that assignment until December 1864. From that point until late June 1865, the batteries were components of the Fourth Brigade.[4]

On June 26, 1865, Sergeant Gilbert Henderson Bates and his fellow members of the Fourth Brigade, also a section of the Twenty-Second Army Corps, were mustered out of service. Of the 2,163 men who had served in the ranks of the First Wisconsin Heavy Artillery Regiment at various points of the American Civil War, eighty-three had died. Four enlisted men had been killed in military actions, while two officers and seventy-seven enlisted men succumbed to a variety of diseases.[5]

Information indicates that Gilbert Henderson Bates returned to his Wisconsin farm after the war. Waiting for him was his wife, Anne Noe Bates, whom he had married December 23, 1863. In addition to Anne, Bates was reunited with his daughter Hattie, who had been born in Edgerton on January 9, 1865.[6]

A period newspaper article recorded that Bates, "at the close of hostilities . . . went home, and after . . . some reverses in business . . . deprived him of nearly all [of his money] . . . [he] purchased five acres of good, deep, rich soil and went into the grape culture."[7]

The financial and personal circumstances described to this point were the issues surrounding Gilbert Henderson Bates as the fall of 1867 arrived. The notoriety Bates was to earn lay in the near future. The events in which he would soon participate had lasting effects upon him for the remainder of his life and toward his reputation to this day.

CHAPTER ONE

Bates and His Bet

MULTIPLE SOURCES STATE THAT GILBERT HENDERSON BATES WAS A staunch Democrat. An Illinois newspaper, the *Ottawa Free Trader*, recorded that Bates, "all his life, as well as before and after the war, was a democrat." The *Daily Phoenix*, a publication based in Columbia, South Carolina, proclaimed that Bates was "a Democrat from principle, [and] remained true to the party during all the conflict." Reinforcing the political affiliation of Bates, the majority of documents, period and modern, simply state that Bates was a Democrat.[1]

The genesis and premise of the pilgrimage in which Gilbert Henderson Bates would participate and gain accolades and notoriety rest upon his political views. Bates noted in his autobiography that he was a "resident of the State of Wisconsin, a soldier in the Federal Army during the war to suppress the Rebellion, a Northern man in every sentiment." He added that he "never sympathized with those of my fellow townsmen and neighbors who declare the Southern people to be devoid of honor and worth, but have always believed that at the close of the war the South gave up their cause, and honestly resolved . . . to be true to the Government and the flag."[2] It is noteworthy that his opinion of his Southern countrymen, based upon his recollections as well as those of numerous recorded comments of the time, were not the most commonly declared among the citizens of the Northern states in the period immediately following the American Civil War.

Bates further elaborated upon the varied sentiments after the war by penning, "This . . . was firmly planted in my breast, and the continual

3

assertions made by my friends that every white man in the South is disloyal and treacherous, and a bitter enemy of the Government, filled me with indignation and sorrow."[3]

Precisely preceding the November 1867 Wisconsin gubernatorial election, in which the Republican incumbent, Lucius Fairchild, the Democratic challenger, faced John James Tallmadge, the former mayor of Milwaukee, Gilbert Bates allegedly visited the Post Office in Edgerton, Wisconsin. Legend holds that Bates was hampered in his immediate goal to return home as "some accident delaying the train, he waited for a while . . . only to remember . . . he wanted a pipe."[4]

Bates did not note the issue of the pipe in his recollections of the day, but an *Edgefield Advertiser* article not only recorded that aspect of the incident, but also claimed that Bates had documented the date of the event as December 14.[5] Therefore, some of the particulars of the incident must be viewed with scrutiny.

A period publication proclaimed, "a common clay pipe, priced one penny . . . stepping in for his pipe . . . [Bates] . . . found the usual knot of politicians hold high debate, the great them being, of course, Reconstruction."[6]

Gilbert Bates affirmed, "Most of 'em was rampant Rads; had never been in the war and didn't know anything about the feelings of the Southern people. . . . I directed most of my conversation with one man." Bates continued, "He remarked, 'Sergeant, the Southerners are rebels yet. They are worse now than they were during the war. They hate the Union flag. No man dare show that flag anywhere in the South, except in the presence of our soldiers.'"[7]

Various sources note similar, but distinctly varied, remarks from Bates. One reported that Bates argued, "No . . . part of them gave up in good faith and are well disposed now to the Union." Yet another article recorded Bates as saying, "You are mistaken; I can carry that flag myself from the Mississippi all over the rebel States, alone and unarmed, too."[8]

The response of the protagonist, according to Bates in comments from his memoirs, was, "It is an absurdity, they would cut your heart out before you could get ten miles from Vicksburg, and your flag would be torn in pieces and trampled in the dust."[9]

A subsequent recollection of Bates recorded that the man with whom he continued conversing countered, "Whoo! Why don't you believe that if the troops were to be withdrawn that the flag would be torn down and trampled underfoot almost before the blue coats could get out of sight?" As he completed that phase of his argument, the gentlemen said to Bates, "Why . . . they're just like the Injuns on the plains. They're just like the Comanches by nature. They possess no generosity."[10]

Gilbert Bates discounted the claims of his assailant, and he countered with his own solid attitudes. Bates said, "Sir, this is not so . . . these words of yours express . . . [those] of thousands in this State and . . . through the North. They do a great wrong. I am sure such sentiments have no foundation, and I can prove it to you and everybody else." Perhaps the strongest statement Bates could offer in relation to his opponent's views was then uttered; Bates stated, "The Southern people are just as willing to live in the Union as we are."[11]

Evidently, witnesses to the conversation maintained that Southerners were outlaws "who did not hesitate to take the life of any man, white or black, suspected of Unionism." One source recording the event added that a vocalization during the altercation was "the people of the South . . . abhorred the American flag . . . no loyal man could live safely among them."[12]

Gilbert Bates told a reporter the following year, "I was in a bad humor that day. . . . I am generally in a good humor, but I got a little angry." Bates offered his quickly devised response to his counterparts by saying, "I'm a poor man and can't afford to leave my family . . . if you'll give me a dollar a day for them, I'll go to Vicksburg . . . without money, and then through the South with the flag, unarmed."[13]

Another individual who wrote of the event explained, "The sergeant . . . declared that he, an ex-soldier of the Union army, could march through the South with the Union flag exposed, without a cent in his pocket, and not only escape bodily harm, but receive hospitable treatment from the Southern people, upon whom ignorant radicalism was heaping so much abuse."[14]

Witnesses evidently became active participants; Bates recalled, "So, after some more talk, they drew up the writings there in regular lawyer form, and we agreed on it." Bates added that "pretty soon" his opponent urged Bates to back down from the bet. Bates noted that his challenger then pleaded, "Give it up! You won't get ten miles from Vicksburg."[15]

Those who were in attendance joined the instigator in attempts to persuade Bates to forego participating in the proposition. An evident brief change in the mindset of the man who initially insinuated that the trip would end in failure said that Bates "would never get to Washington" and that Bates would "be wiped out." Bates remarked that his antagonist became self-centered in adding, "then all the neighbors would blame him for it."[16]

A neutral party reporting the incident penned, "A purse-heavy radical offered to bet a certain amount that Bates would be killed if he undertook the journey; and in the event of the sergeant's death, agreed to pay the sum to the fool-hardy young man's family. The banter was accepted by the sergeant."[17]

Bates stated, "It was no use. I was determined to go, and just here . . . [he] looked as firm as if he was at his gun ready for action."[18]

The contract Bates entered stated,

> *To enter Vicksburg without money and carry the United States flag from there to Washington on foot, through all cities and town, and by all collections of people, and carry the flag unfurled. Of nights and during storms to furl the flag, provided I passed no such cities or towns, and by no such collections of people. And not to travel by night and at all times to be unarmed. To employ, if I wished, one person as guide, but to have no person or persons to protect me day or night, though any might accompany me who desired voluntarily. One dollar a day to be paid my family in case I got to Washington, but if the flag was insulted or I, while bearing it, the one dollar a day to be forfeited.[19]*

Bates wrote additional information in his personal recollections of the event: "It was finally agreed between us that, if I carried the flag through from Vicksburg to Washington on or before the 4th day of July . . . he was to pay me one dollar a day while I was engaged in the undertaking. If I failed, or was compelled to return, I was to get nothing for my trouble." Gilbert Henderson Bates revealed that his determination was strong in adding, "My Radical friend felt safe on these terms, and never for a moment thought I would make the venture, but he was doomed to disappointment."[20]

Perhaps the mindset of Bates was best recorded in an article from the December 31, 1867 issue of the *Western Democrat*. The commentary cried out, "Sergeant Bates became indignant. . . . He loved the old flag too well to think that there was any section of our country where it would not be respected."[21]

Another article, one from the February 16, 1868, edition of the *Daily Phoenix*, explained, "The sergeant is a poor man . . . devoid of conceit, and perfectly honorable in his conduct."[22]

The self-assuredness and courage Bates possessed were noted in a manuscript that recalled the situation under which Bates accepted the wager associated with the march. The writer documented, "[Bates] was advised that it was a hazardous task, and that he should have his life insured, but he would rely for his insurance, upon the good sense and loyalty of the Southern people. He believed that the people of the South would respect the flag . . . he stated he was not acting for any party, for the flag only."[23]

An additional ambition Gilbert Bates held, according to a Wisconsin reporter, was the financial well-being of his family. In an article titled "The Flag March from Vicksburg," an individual inscribed, "Bates is a young man with a family, and somewhat in close circumstances, but he thereupon made a proposition . . . for the support of his family."[24]

In a more nationalistic view, Milton Lomask stated in 1965, almost a century after the march, that the goal Bates held was to "disprove the belief, widely held in the North, that disloyalty to the Union was still rampant below the Potomac and that a man could not take the Stars and Stripes onto Southern soil without being murdered."[25]

It is logical to think that as Gilbert Henderson Bates prepared for his journey, his personal goals for the trip were at the forefront of his mind. It was written that he was convinced "the American people had three great and all-important objects to attain [and] in which every citizen should feel a personal interest." Elaborating upon this theory, it was noted those interests were "First, peace to the community, state, and nation; second, the restoration of fraternal relations between the two great sections of the country; and, third, the creation and maintenance of a great national brotherhood based upon knowledge, industry, and loyalty."[26]

The news of Bates and his march made the papers as far away as California. Although it was on the fourth page of the *Shasta Courier*, the article was sent from Milwaukee, Wisconsin, and indicated the pride many people felt for Bates. It said, "A novel wager was laid between a citizen and a soldier . . . and will soon enter upon it. . . . The risk and undertaking is a great one, requiring some pluck and more muscle."[27]

From a negative or critical standpoint, an article in the *National Republican*, a Washington, D.C., publication, belittled Bates and his efforts. Titled "Perilous Pedestrianism," the article contained, in part, "Sergeant Geo. H. Bates . . . will leave Vicksburg . . . and intends to enter Washington the 4th of July. If Sergeant Bates undertakes that job, it will be a safe thing to bet that he will be a dead man with a bullet through his brain before reaching the Ohio River or Mason and Dixon's line. He will never see another 4th of July."[28]

The variety of causes and interests Gilbert Henderson Bates held dear would certainly serve as motivational factors throughout his unparalleled journey. The polarized political arenas in which he lived and chose to make his mark upon history and endeavored to create unity among the citizens of the recently reconciled United States provided a unique setting for his wager. National fame, as well as criticism and accusations, were to be his rewards during and in the years following his accomplishment.

CHAPTER Two

Bates Leaves Home for Vicksburg

Modern students of the facts surrounding Gilbert Henderson Bates and his activities that preceded the onset of his historic march are left with little concrete evidence. Bates did not mention such situations in his personal account of the journey. Therefore, his departure from his Wisconsin home serves as the situation upon which the sojourn begins.

However, in the days foregoing his exit from Wisconsin, Gilbert Bates announced a facet of his journey. Bates said, "I will fit myself out with a large United States flag, and I will carry it to Vicksburg. At Vicksburg I will unfold the flag to the breeze and will carry it on foot across the country to Washington." Bates described the intended efforts for the remainder of his journey by saying, "The flag shall be plainly in view to all, and I will go alone and unarmed, and without a cent in my pocket when I leave Vicksburg."[1]

Bates wrote that he left the confines of his "quiet home" on January 14, 1868, in order to "fulfill an unheard-of undertaking." Prior to the onset of his march, Bates penned, "Many of my friends had admonished me to desist from such a hazardous enterprise, not to throw my life away in some Southern swamp while trusting in the loyalty and kindness of the rebels."[2]

The confidence, calmness, and enthusiasm evidently overtook the enormity of his journey as Bates stated, "I apprehended no violence from the Southern people, and set out for Vicksburg without fear or trembling."[3]

A South Carolina publication, the *Daily Phoenix*, was quick to offer the itinerary Bates had established. The writer of an article in the

February 16, 1868, edition reported, "He will travel from Vicksburg to Jackson, thence to Montgomery, Alabama; thence to Milledgeville, Georgia; thence to Columbia, South Carolina, thence to Raleigh, North Carolina; thence to Richmond and thence to Washington."[4]

The well-publicized route Bates planned to follow was also provided in the *Daily Milwaukee News*. A reporter for that periodical expounded upon the tour's destinations and recorded, "His line of march is from Vicksburg to Jackson . . . and into Washington, to arrive on or before the fourth of July."[5]

As word of the wager Bates had entered spread across the nation, a significant number of Wisconsin cities made offers to provide the aforementioned flag to him. Bates graciously declined the offers and confidently proclaimed, "No, thanks; Vicksburg will take care of that."[6]

In a report from the *Cairo Democrat*, Cairo, Illinois, Bates was reported to be in Cairo "en route to for Vicksburg." Although the article proclaimed that Bates was a Federal veteran, it erroneously claimed that he "was one of the first to enter the service and was one of the last to leave it."[7]

Perhaps, if accurate, a strong motivational factor for Bates undertaking the march is seen in the report from the *Cairo Democrat*: "As a matter of course, he became a target at which all the radicals in his neighborhood aimed their abuse. He was vilified and persecuted by men who had talked war but never shouldered a musket."[8]

As he progressed toward Vicksburg, Bates passed through Memphis, Tennessee. He recalled the impact of his stopover in the Bluff City in writing: "At Memphis certain parties learned the object of my undertaking, and when I reached Vicksburg everyone was aware of it. Every man, woman, and child knew that my purpose was to prove that the Southern people revered the flag, and everywhere the greatest curiosity was manifested to see the man who was willing to attempt the proof."[9]

Bates certainly knew some of the history of Mississippi, and he had likely encountered some of its citizens during wartime. Mississippi draft officials used 1864 county reports to tabulate more than 67,000 of the state's men had served the Confederate military in the first three years of the American Civil War.[10] Several significant military engagements had also taken place in Mississippi between 1861 and 1865. Besides Vicksburg, other settlements including Corinth, Brice's Crossroads, Tupelo, Raymond, and Port Gibson had seen significant clashes that yielded wide-ranging numbers of casualties and destruction.

In addition to Mississippi serving as the site for battles and campaigns, Jefferson Davis, the first and only President of the Confederate States of America, moved from Kentucky to Mississippi as a child. Davis had represented the state during the Mexican-American War, during which he was wounded. He had served Mississippi in various political offices, including the U.S. Senate. At the end of the American Civil War, Davis was imprisoned for two years, having been indicted for treason.[11] These past incidents and situations had to have entered the mindset of Bates as he neared the state's border.

Mississippi was enduring Reconstruction during the time Bates reached the state's borders. Federal troops were occupying many areas of the South during that postwar era, and Mississippi was no exception. In January 1865, Congress proposed the Thirteenth Amendment, abolishing slavery. That same year, Mississippi instituted "An Act to Confer Civil Rights on Freedmen, and for Other Purposes." The act, with Mississippi being the first state to do so, abolished the full rights African Americans had just attained. Two years later, Congress passed the Fourteenth Amendment, which granted citizenship to former slaves. Another 1867 law of Congress was the first Reconstruction Act, dividing the South into five military districts.[12] The tension between the Northern and Southern sections of the nation was strong, and Bates intended to do what he could to diminish that.

While states in the Upper South, such as Tennessee, represented areas where freed slaves constituted a minority of the population, Mississippi was similar to Lower South states where freedmen comprised the majority of citizens. Fifty-five percent of Mississippi's population was African American, and the state's version of the Black Codes attempted to "replicate slavery."[13]

Provisions of the Black Codes in Mississippi's Act to Confer Civil Rights on Freedmen included punishment of African Americans who committed "any breach of Old South etiquette." Those transgressions encompassed African Americans avoiding being disorderly, idle, or using "insulting gestures." A special license was required for blacks to preach the Gospel or own guns.[14] Thus, Gilbert Bates battled pressures that appeared overwhelming as he entered the Magnolia State.

Gilbert Bates arrived in Vicksburg on January 24, 1868. His attire was a subject of concern among the residents, and the reaction Bates received was filled with concern. A period publication recorded that in Vicksburg Bates "was somewhat detained by the 'rebels' who not only gave him an ovation, but found fault with the shabbiness of his clothes, and presented him with a splendid new velvet walking suit."[15]

Noting the appearance of his gifted clothing and affirming his stature, a period article said of Bates, "He is dressed in a suit of black velvet . . . He is thirty years of age, is 5 feet, 6 ½ inches high and weighs 142 pounds. He has a wife and two children."[16]

Equally impressive as his receipt of a new suit of clothes was another gift a group of Vicksburg residents gave Bates. A newspaper article described the endowment, given to him later in his visit, as "a beautiful silk flag."[17]

Bates's reminiscences of the offerings was more detailed. He penned, "I entered into Vicksburg in the evening, dressed in coarse, heavy clothing, with cow-hide boots and a slouch hat. My personal appearance was anything but prepossessing, and would scarcely have justified a hotelkeeper in trusting me for a night's lodging."[18]

Gilbert Bates had met Frank Howard before entering the confines of Vicksburg. Mr. Howard had been intrigued over the fact that the agreement's articles held that Bates was to make his trek without any funds. Therefore, according to Bates, Mr. Howard "kindly invited me to the Prentiss House, and agreed to settle for all my bills."[19]

A postwar article titled "The Prentiss House" held that the structure had been built around 1842. An early proprietor, a Mr. Simmons, held the position several years, but "at the breaking out of the war he was, very appropriately, made a Confederate quarter-master, with the rank of major." After the American Civil War, Mr. Simmons served as the manager of another hotel in Vicksburg, and he was described as "old and broken in health and fortune."[20]

The Prentiss House, situated along Levee Street, was noted as "never [possessing] the slightest pretensions to architectural beauty." It was observed that "the old hotel suffered greatly during the war, but was refitted at the close of hostilities and reopened by its manager, General McMakin. . . . It had seen its best days, however, and . . . it sank into insignificance by degrees."[21]

The Prentiss House was recalled as having once "enjoyed the patronage of the wealthy planters of the Lower Mississippi Valley." An article written a decade before the outbreak of war exclaimed, "The Prentiss House is truly a delightful place. . . . No bill of fare is needed at the dinner table . . . from roast beef to pickled onions . . . the clatter of knives and forks . . . English peas . . . fresh venison, the best in the world."[22]

Unfortunately, the location where Gilbert Bates spent the night in Vicksburg did not receive positive comments from a local reporter who inscribed, "That once famous hotel, the Prentiss House . . . its glories are all in the past tense."[23]

CHAPTER THREE

Vicksburg

THE VICKSBURG, MISSISSIPPI THAT GILBERT HENDERSON BATES visited in early 1868 was a town that had experienced and endured extreme
hardships less than five years earlier. Situated along the east bank of
the Mississippi River, the port settlement was the location of a forty-
seven-day-long siege that had ended with the July 3, 1863, surrender of
Confederate General John Pemberton to federal troops under the command of General Ulysses Simpson Grant. Residents of the community
who endured the siege, as well as the besieged Confederate troops, had
regularly resorted to eating mule meat, rats, and other items typically
considered inedible in order to remain alive.[1] The willingness of Gilbert
Henderson Bates, a federal veteran of the War Between the States, to
enter Vicksburg so soon after the siege clearly indicated his bravery and
determination.

The 1860 U.S. Census recorded that Vicksburg had a population of
4,591 people. Despite the hardships of war, the 1870 U.S. Census showed
a major increase in population. That year, the number of people residing
in Vicksburg had grown to 12,443.[2] It stands to reason that since Gilbert
Bates reached Vicksburg in 1868, the number of citizens he encountered
would have likely been closer to the larger number than in 1860.

Contained within articles that chronicled Bates as he reached Vicksburg are comments related to random offers individuals made to the
Federal veteran. One article declared, "Letters have been received by him
from prominent gentlemen living in the cities on his march, inviting him

to be their guest when he passes through, and tendering him a guard of honor."[3]

A second article, one from a Wisconsin-based newspaper, added additional information to the scenario by asserting, "Bates has received letters from the South urging him to make the attempt and . . . assurances that an escort of honor composed of veteran Confederate soldiers will volunteer to accompany him from Vicksburg to the Alabama border."[4]

Bates recalled that on the morning following his first night spent in Vicksburg, he was the recipient of a hero's welcome. The mayor of Vicksburg, as well as what Bates saw as "all the prominent men of Vicksburg" contacted Bates. At that location, Bates was presented the flag that a group of Vicksburg ladies "volunteered to make." Bates went on to explain, "I never witnessed such enthusiasm, such an abundance of attention as were shown by the people of this city."[5]

Gilbert Bates added, "Soldiers who had served in the rebel army were eager to grasp my hand and encourage me; and Northern soldiers, my former comrades, were no less friendly and interested . . . my clothing was sent to my home in Wisconsin."[6]

The former Federal soldier enthusiastically declared, "I remained in Vicksburg four days. I was the guest of the City, entertained in the kindest manner by the citizens, treated with the honors of a prince, and, at the same time, with the affection due to a friend."[7]

On his last day in Vicksburg, Bates was given his flag during a public ceremony at the Prentiss House. The 11:00 a.m. presentation was heavily attended. Bates inscribed, "There was an immense crowd of people present. . . . Colonel Partridge spoke on behalf of the ladies in presenting the banner. The same hands had made flags for the rebels during the war . . . [and] now gladly worked for me, the stars and stripes, my avowed object was to wave that flag before their eyes in their own country."[8]

Bates was certain the creation and presentation of the U.S. flag would affirm to the world that the people of the South were submitting to those against whom they had once battled with a sense of "nobleness and sincerity to their defeat," and that they once again held dear "the glorious emblem against which they once arrayed themselves in war."[9]

Ironically, as Bates explained, his march would be longer than that of William Tecumseh Sherman, the Federal general whose infamous "March to the Sea" had laid waste to vast areas of the South only four years earlier. Bates was quick to note a stark contrast between the march he was to begin soon and that of Sherman.

Gilbert Bates compared the two marches by writing, "When [Sherman] made the march, he carried the sword in one hand and the torch in the other. The flag of the Union was then the emblem of death and ruin to the Southern people." Bates continued, "I was to pass over much of his line of march; to tread the battlefields which were trodden by his army, and pass through the cities that were burned by his men." Bates concluded, "but in my hand the war being ended, the same flag was to be the emblem of peace and friendship and good will to the South."[10]

As Bates left the Prentiss House, his accompaniment included "the Mayor, Col. Brown, and the Marshall, Capt. Fisk, and an immense crowd of people." The crowd made their way toward the Washington House, a frontier residence constructed in 1822, prior to Vicksburg's incorporation. The Washington House was located in the oldest neighborhood in Vicksburg and served as the setting where Bates was introduced "to a great many ladies and gentlemen, residents of the city."[11]

After participating in a reception that Bates described as "cordial," a procession was formed for the purpose of attending Bates as he made his way from Vicksburg. Bates remarked, "The Mayor and Councilmen were on horseback, and headed the procession. They were followed by a [brass] band of music. Behind them, I marched, carrying the flag."[12]

A crowd that was estimated to number in the thousands, some on foot and others mounted, joined the group as they made their way from the confines of the Vicksburg city limits. The mass made its way to the Pemberton and Grant Monument, where a pause in the march was held. According to the National Park Service, the original stone marker that designated the location where Confederate General John Pemberton met Union General U. S. Grant to discuss the terms of surrender had initially been intended to serve as a grave marker. However, federal soldiers had taken possession of the stone and used it as a monument. By the time

Bates visited the site a few years after the war, the original marker had become "heavily damaged by relic hunters and vandalism."[13]

At the monument, referred to in an Arkansas paper as "The Grant and Pemberton," the crowd gave three cheers for "Sergeant Bates and the United States flag" before beginning to disperse. There were requests made that Bates shake hands and listen to encouraging words from members of the crowd. Bates also remembered that "Nearly every hand offered me money, but I did not take [it]." Bates added that he was "much affected by the kindness of these people." His words expressed the mixed feelings he possessed: "The war had left them with almost nothing, and yet they wished to give me of their scanty store."[14]

Bates attempted an abandonment of Vicksburg, but people clung so closely to him that he found it impossible to set out on his journey. He wrote, "The Mayor, seeing my difficulty, directed the crowd to open and give me way. I lost no time in moving off."[15]

As Gilbert Bates marched from the monument, he noticed, "the road rises over a hill. On reaching the summit, I turned and waved my flag. This was the signal for a new outburst of enthusiasm."[16]

Mixed emotions are evident in the words Bates wrote about the moments that followed: "Cheer upon cheer arose, till it almost awakened the dead echoes of the cannon that had roared about the spot in 1863. Such cheers I had never heard before. I moved . . . and soon was obscured by the hill from the gaze of my friends." The isolation Bates faced numerous times in the ensuing months also crept into the situation. "I could still hear the music of the band . . . as it died away in the distance. Not without a certain feeling of sadness, I pursued my solitary way."[17]

The words of Bates were reinforced in a Washington, D.C., paper from the day after his departure. It said, "Gilbert H. Bates, of Wisconsin . . . started from Vicksburg yesterday . . . an immense crowd, headed by the Mayor and Common Council and many prominent citizens, accompanied him some distance, and bade him farewell with good wishes."[18]

A second publication, based in Richmond, added, "Sergeant Gilbert H. Bates . . . who made a lot to carry the stars and stripes from Vicksburg to Washington . . . started hence alone at 11 o'clock a.m. today. An immense crowd . . . bade him farewell, with many good wishes."[19]

Soon after Bates left Vicksburg, another period paper noted the same. The publication, the *Memphis Daily Appeal,* recorded the proposed route Bates was to follow. It stated, "Bates started on his walk from Vicksburg. . . . From Jackson he will strike for Brandon . . . Meridian, Selma, Montgomery, etc."[20]

Even the humorist Mark Twain acknowledged Bates. Twain penned, "The Mayor and a large portion of the population of Vicksburg ushered him out of that city with grand demonstration." Twain then added a seldom-noted aspect of the journey by writing, "[Bates] proposes to sell photographs of himself at 25 cents apiece . . . and convert the proceeds into a fund to be devoted to the aid and comfort of widows and orphans of soldiers who fought in the late war, irrespective of flag or politics."[21]

CHAPTER FOUR

Vicksburg to Jackson

As GILBERT BATES STRODE FROM THE CONFINES OF VICKSBURG, Mississippi, he found his route, for several miles, took him "over hills and valleys," in a continuous southerly direction. Bates also acknowledged that that course of movement continued until he reached the Vicksburg and Meridian Railroad. That particular rail line had been in operation since the January 28, 1867, reorganization of the Southern Railroad of Mississippi. The Vicksburg and Meridian Railroad contained approximately 141 miles of track.[1]

The railway Bates encountered had seen its construction begin in 1833 with earthwork beginning at Vicksburg. The first train car carried passengers on the track in May 1838. However, Federal troops under officers such as Benjamin Grierson, U. S. Grant, and William Sherman had burned stations and depots along the way.[2]

An evaluation of the condition of the Vicksburg and Meridian Railroad came from the president of what was the Southern Railroad in the fall of 1865. Morris Emanuel was quoted as saying, "At the close of the war we were left to contemplate its blighting effect on our road and property, as evidenced by our tracks torn up, crossties burned, rails bent, twisted and broken, bridges and culverts destroyed, depots burned, cars destroyed, and locomotives and all other machinery in a damaged condition without a dollar in the treasury, with nearly $1,500,000 of unpaid debts that had matured during the war, besides upwards of $500,000 of unpaid interest coupons, making a total of more than $2,000,000 of indebtedness past due."[3]

A modern history of the Vicksburg and Meridian Railroad relates, "The route between Jackson and Vicksburg was almost a solid battleground. The broken uplands in Hinds and Warren counties were scenes of numerous skirmishes and several important battles. . . . During the great conflict between the North and South this historic line of railroad was the objective of the contending armies and the scene of many stirring battles. At the close of the struggle it was little more than a streak of blackened ruin and wreckage."[4] It was along this devasted track, and with the residents of communities along its route, that Bates would make the early steps of his journey.

Gilbert Bates elaborated upon his dependency on the Vicksburg and Meridian Railroad by saying, "It became apparent, early in my enterprise, that it would be impossible for me to take the wagon roads. They were in a fearful condition, exceedingly muddy . . . and by no means direct."[5]

With few options remaining, Bates determined that he would have to follow the rail lines at least as far as Selma, Alabama. His rationale: "This plan would enable me to meet with more people, and would afford much better walking."[6]

Each station on the line, "however small," according to Bates, enabled him to find "many persons waiting to receive" him. Bates also said, "Frequently they would come out from towns and villages three and four miles, in order to walk the distance with me in returning."[7]

The fact that Bates left Vicksburg, Mississippi, for future locations in his march gained attention of the press in Nashville, Tennessee. A four-line snippet about Bates noted his name, hometown, and purpose of the march. Appearing on the second page of the publication, it also pointed out the date on which Bates moved from Vicksburg. Sadly, the short mention of Bates fell between two similar write-ups about Georgia's secretary of state being removed from office and another concerning the factions of the Radical Party in Louisiana.[8]

An article that was lengthier, but far more unfavorable of Bates, was printed in a Dodgeville, Wisconsin, paper. It criticized Bates: "Among all the humbugs of the day, the biggest is Sergeant Bates, who is now on a tramp from the Mississippi to the sea . . . it is a very nice way to raise the wind, but an exceedingly poor way to demonstrate the loyalty of the section of country through which he traverses. Had he started on his mission without a great flourish of trumpets, there might have been some significance of his feat. As it is, there is none whatever."[9]

Bovina, Mississippi, located approximately seven miles east of Vicksburg, was the first post-Vicksburg stop for Bates; he arrived in Bovina at 3:00 p.m. Snow began to fall during what Bates recalled had been "a quite cool" afternoon. A man who resided in Bovina supplied Bates with a heavy overcoat that Bates remarked "proved of great comfort to me."[10]

An interesting aspect of this phase of the trip occurred when Bates reached the Big Black River, the scene of a major 1863 confrontation, at 5:00 p.m. Bates called for the ferryman "with no little trepidation. The citizens of Vicksburg had told me that this ferryman of the Big Black would never allow any one to cross in his boat without paying fare." Bates had no money, and when the ferryman noticed the velvet pants of his patron, he informed Bates that he was aware of his identity. With that said, the ferryman said to Bates, "You may cross here a thousand times if you want to, and no charge."[11]

Bates soon reached the Kidd's Plantation where the proprietor, a Mr. Cordevent, invited him to stay for the night. Bates reminisced, "Here could be clearly seen the ravages of war . . . articles of furniture destroyed in the most wanton manner. This plantation is as fertile as any in Mississippi, but . . . the labor of [freed slaves] . . . [had cost Cordevent] fifty thousand dollars."[12]

Mr. Cordevent blamed the loss of labor and his financial problems on "the teachings of the Freedmen's Bureau, and tended to make the two races, white and black, suspicious and distrustful of each other. . . . After a lengthy conversation, I was glad enough to retire to rest."[13]

On the next morning, January 29, 1868, Gilbert Bates recalled, "I left the Kidd Plantation about 9 o'clock and continued my journey. About four miles from Smith Station, the passenger train was stopped . . . and the passengers rushed to see me. This was a pleasant surprise."[14]

From the information Bates imparted, passengers began offering him money, but he refused. Bates also said, "The conductor, however, thrust three dollars into my pocket, saying that I would need it for postage stamps in writing home. My protest was of no avail."[15]

As the train left him behind, Bates followed its path along the tracks. In a short time, Bates reached Edwards Station, Mississippi, where "a large crowd was assembled." Edwards, as the settlement came to be known, was located twenty-eight miles west of Jackson, Mississippi and fifteen miles east of Vicksburg. Edwards Station, formerly known as Amsterdam and Edwards Depot, had begun as a plantation settlement that was named for Richard Edwards. The depot had been burned at the hands of Federal soldiers in 1863, but the structure was rebuilt nearby. The postwar years had seen the area transformed into a commercial center where some twenty thousand bales of cotton were shipped to other destinations each year.[16]

"A delegation from the town of Raymond" approached Bates and urged him to visit their town. Raymond "lay away" from the route Bates intended to travel, causing him to graciously decline their offer. Bates penned, "They were sorry that I could not accept their invitation."[17]

Raymond, Mississippi, chartered in December 1830, is thought to be one of the oldest towns in the state. It served as the county seat for Hinds County and was the location of several "large and beautiful homes." Although some of the homes had been destroyed during the Civil War, some of the plantations that occupied the area were Waverly, Belcher House, Phoenix Hall, Shelton House, and Southern Cedars.[18]

Raymond had also been the location of a six-hour battle on May 12, 1863. The struggle had pitted federal forces of General James McPherson against Confederates under the command of General John Gregg. Over one thousand total casualties were inflicted upon the participating armies. Many homes, as well as the courthouse, churches, and schools, were transformed into hospitals. The period after the War Between the States had caused Raymond to endure difficult times. An area historian wrote, "All of the plantations were financially ruined . . . the business district was also destroyed. . . . Business owners . . . were forced to seek their fortunes elsewhere."[19] Despite deep destruction that was present at the time, Bates was invited to visit the town.

His initial impressions of the hospitality prevalent in the area caused Bates to note, "Everyone seemed to welcome me and the flag with open arms. The greatest cordiality prevailed everywhere, and almost an excess of generosity. Here, I was compelled to accept more money, eleven dollars and a half."[20]

Bates explained that the receipt of the eleven and a half dollars outside Raymond, Mississippi "was so distasteful" that he became determined to avoid taking any more funds during his march. He proclaimed, "I put the money in an envelope and sent it home. This was the last that I received during the whole march from Vicksburg to Washington."[21]

The mindset Bates held in regard to money differed from what Mark Twain felt about the federal veteran. Twain had earlier stated that Bates was going to sell photographs for twenty-five cents and send the money to widows and orphans. However, Twain's words became more offensive toward Bates in the early days of the Federal veteran's famed march. Twain avowed,

And then, I suppose, when he gets a good round sum together for the widows and orphans, he will hang up his flag and go and have a champagne blow-out. I don't believe in people who collect money for benevolent purposes and don't charge for it. I don't have full confidence in people who walk a thousand miles for the benefit of widows and orphans and don't get a cent for it. I question the uprightness of people who peddle their own photographs, anyhow, whether they carry flags or not. . . . But this fellow will get more black eyes down there among those unreconstructed rebels than he can ever carry along with him without breaking his back. I expect to see him coming into Washington . . . on one leg . . . with one eye out and an arm gone. He won't amount to more than an interesting relic by the time he gets here. . . . Those fellows down there have no sentiment in them. They won't buy his picture. They will be more likely to take his scalp.[22]

Nonetheless, Bates managed to come within three miles of Jackson, Mississippi, the state capital, where he gained the fellowship of a local resident. The duo noted "a crowd of negroes, who seemed to be waiting on the railroad track for some purpose or other." Bates recalled that the assembly of freedmen were silent as he approached them, then one of the group inquired of the identify of Bates and his "countryman" companion.[23]

According to an account Bates compiled, his recently gained cohort "replied that I was the biggest Yankee officer in the land, and that just a mile and a half behind me were hundreds and thousands of soldiers" who were entering the area to arrest all lazy individuals of color. The remark must have proven believable, as "with this they all scampered, like struck hares, at full speed, into the woods." Bates used this event to add, "Negroes everywhere seemed idle, and restless, discontented, as if waiting for some unknown thing to occur . . . they knew not what."[24]

The *Daily Clarion*, a newspaper published in Jackson, Mississippi, made a prediction concerning Bates. The short article noted, "Gilbert H. Bates, on his walk from Vicksburg to Washington City, stopped at Clinton last night and may be expected in this city today at 10 o'clock."[25]

CHAPTER FIVE

Jackson, Mississippi

GILBERT HENDERSON BATES ARRIVED IN THE MISSISSIPPI CAPITAL OF
Jackson around 3:00 p.m. on January 30, 1868. Bates was regretful when
he discovered that his arrival had been expected earlier that morning. He
contritely composed the following, "The Mayor and all the city authorities, and hundreds of citizens, had assembled to meet me; but I was so
much behind time that they began to give me up."[1]

The *Ottawa Free Trader*, published in Ottawa, Illinois, incorrectly
noted in its coverage of the event, "we next hear from him at Jackson
. . . where he was welcomed by a large crowd who went out several miles
on foot and in carriages to meet him, and being conducted to the State
house, received a formal reception in a speech by the mayor."[2]

A trio of papers, the *South-Western* from Shreveport, Louisiana,
the *New Orleans Republican*, and Richmond, Virginia's *Daily Dispatch*
recorded, "Sergeant Gilbert H. Bates, the pedestrian, arrived here at noon
today, and was kindly received by the citizens. He reports nothing but
kind treatment thus far on his journey, and will start eastward at 9 o'clock
a.m. tomorrow."[3]

The *Evening Argus*, from Rock Island, Illinois, added the following in
its February 3, 1868 issue: "There is a feat of walking now in progress in
this country which is eminently honorable to the performer engaged in it,
and with which our readers will become acquainted. . . . Bates has started
on this trip . . . simply to show the radicals that Southerners can respect
the flag of the Union when it is emblematic of a truly national desire to

promote peace and disarm sectional hatred . . . the Southern press speaks of the enterprise in terms of warm commendation."⁴

It is interesting to note that Bates arrived in Jackson the same day as former Confederate president Jefferson Davis. A Richmond periodical noted, "Hon. Jefferson Davis and Mrs. Davis arrived here last night, and are guests of Governor Humphreys. Today a large number of citizens called to pay their respects. Mr. Davis appears in excellent health."⁵

Jackson, Mississippi, named in honor of Andrew Jackson, had been established in 1821. The city had long been a center for economic, political, and social activity in the state. While the population reached 3,191 in the 1860 census, the number increased during the months preceding the American Civil War. Ten years later, 4,234 people were recorded in the census.⁶ The capital Gilbert Bates visited in early 1868 more closely reflected the latter number.

Bates also encountered a metropolis that had experienced the ravages of war. Like many of the areas Bates visited as he crossed the state of Mississippi, Jackson had seen large numbers of soldiers passing through its confines. Additionally, Jackson was the setting for "a great deal of war industry . . . textile, weapons, and ammunition factories and arsenals."⁷

Citizens who enthusiastically greeted Bates had suffered significantly during the war. A modern historian has noted that various prices increased as some items became less plentiful. For example, a pair of boots rose to a price of $125.00, while sugar cost $3.50 a pound. The price of tea escalated to $7.00 per pound, and a watermelon cost $25.00. In November 1862, an ammunition factory had exploded; the result was approximately forty workers, largely women and children, killed.⁸ People who had dealt with such situations were those who opened their city to Bates.

A battle in May 1863 added additional insult to the residents of Jackson. Part of the city was later burned, and the rail line toward Vicksburg was cut. When military governor Brigadier General Joseph Mower ordered that Jackson be neutralized as a Confederate transportation, industrial, military, and political center, the destruction became more widespread. Federal General William Tecumseh Sherman said of the devastation, "the arsenal buildings, the Government foundry, the gun carriage establishment, including the carriages for two complete six-gun batteries, stable, carpenter and paint shops were destroyed."[9]

The rail lines, a major lifeline of Jackson, were also heavily damaged during the war. It was stated that the railroads "4 miles east of Jackson, 3 south, 3 north, and 10 west," were useless. Moreover, General Sherman reported, "Jackson, as a railroad center or Government depot of stores and military factories, can be of little use to the enemy for six months."[10]

While modern historians often debate the accuracy of the term "Chimneyville," which a newspaper applied to Jackson as an indication of the heavy concentration of burned structures, comments from residents of the city note its level of demise. A preacher proclaimed, "My thresholds . . . were spared the stain of blood, but theft and ravage, and wanton destruction marked every room in the house and every article on the premises." A citizen claimed that Jackson was a "miserable wreck" and possessed "a deplorable aspect."[11]

In 1865, federal troops captured Jackson for the fifth and final time of the war. That seizure of the capital city was said to have "put Mississippi and its government out of the war for good. . . . Mississippians from all over the state saw Jackson as their symbolic center, and its capture had a devastating psychological effect on the people." An additional aspect, according to a modern historian, was "the continual recapture of the city, almost at the whim of the Federals . . . showed the people of Mississippi that their state and . . . government could no longer protect them."[12]

Gilbert Bates reminisced about his arrival in Jackson, writing that he "went to the Benton House quietly and took my dinner. Very soon it was known that I was in town, and a carriage was sent for me. I declined the carriage, and, unfurling the flag, I walked in the center of the street to the Capitol. An immense crowd . . . received me with great enthusiasm."[13]

A similar account appeared in a local paper and said, "After dining at the Benton House, he came up Capitol Street . . . carrying a beautiful silk flag. He was met and welcomed by a large crowd at the Capitol gate, and from there conducted to the Convention Hall."[14]

The Mississippi State Convention was under way when Bates arrived in Jackson. It was recorded that within the Convention, "Mr. Compton moved that the Convention adjourn to meet Sergeant Bates, who was expected to arrive in the city during the next ten minutes."[15]

The *Daily Clarion*, based in Jackson, stated, "Bates . . . was met and welcomed by a large crowd at the Capitol gate, and from there conducted to the Convention Hall. . . . On entering the Hall, and upon the motion of Mr. Woodman . . . Bates was conducted to the secretary's desk and related the origin and object of his expedition."[16]

Bates was invited to visit the convention. He accepted the offer "and was introduced to the delegates amidst thunders of applause from the floor and . . . crowded galleries." He received a welcoming address from a local politician and was invited to "become the guest of the city."[17]

An Illinois newspaper noted, "Of course, during his brief stay there, he had the best the city afforded, and more than he would take was pressed upon him to help him on his way."[18]

As if the applause and warm welcome were not enough to embarrass the relatively shy Bates, he was called upon to make a speech. Reportedly, Judge Potter, an official at the meeting, "remarked, substantially, 'Sergeant Bates, we welcome you to the Capitol of Mississippi. We are here to receive you and the flag you bear as a herald of peace and union to the Southern people. You may be assured that you are received, and that you will leave with our hearty good will. We believe that your exploit will show to the North that your confidence in the honesty of the Southern people is well founded. We owe you thanks that you have undertaking this great labor for the conviction of some of your doubting fellow-citizens.'"[19]

The subsequent remarks from Judge Potter included, "'The Southern people desire, sir, peace, hearty brotherhood and perpetual union under the Constitution as our fathers framed it. . . . I feel assured you, on your long journey, will find the Southern citizen everywhere will welcome you to what remains of his home.'"[20]

Bates recalled that he used a few words to explain the "object of his mission" to the interested spectators. An elderly judge followed up the words from Bates, and Bates said the judge "made a good speech, marked with cordiality towards me and for the flag."[21]

The duo of addresses was followed with multiple handshakes and introductions. Bates alleged, "I . . . shook hands until my arms were more fatigued than my legs." A majority of the delegates requested that Bates leave his flag in the Capitol; this appeal he granted.[22]

On his return to his hotel, Bates ran into groups of Confederate veterans "who were eager to greet me and offer me assistance. They were very pleasant and friendly. It was strange enough to find them now so friendly, who a few years ago were fighting the North." Summing up the impact of his visit thus far, Bates exclaimed, "It was a fact, however strange. Those men were my friends, although we had fought in armies opposed to each other."[23]

On the last day of January 1868, Bates awakened and traveled through the brisk morning air to the Capitol to retrieve his flag. He remembered, "A great many persons followed me, so that when I came out of the building, there was a large assemblage waiting to say a last word before my departure. They called on me for some remarks."[24]

Bates addressed the crowd: "Citizens of Jackson, for your demonstrations of friendship for me and respect for the flag of our country, I thank you. I am thus confirmed, in my convictions respecting the sentiments of the Southern people. Heaven be praised that these convictions have proven correct."[25]

Ending his speech in a somewhat foreboding manner, Bates uttered, "You will probably never see me again. I will pass from your sight, and from you . . . but this flag will remain with you forever. It is your banner; it is your hope and pride, as well as mine. I pray to God that before long it may wave over a happy and prosperous people who entertain no ill will toward each other, that from its waving folds only blessings may descend upon the citizens of our country."[26]

The crowd heavily applauded his statements, and Bates began his exodus from the Capitol. He once again found that doing so "was no easy matter." He elaborated, "Everyone seemed to take a lively interest in me, and wished . . . to shake hands; any many a time the eyes of grown men have filled with tears as I have clasped their hands."[27]

Bates recorded a summary of his impressions of the people he had met to that point: "The Southern people are warm-hearted . . . quick in gratitude as well as in resentment. They are not far different from the Irish nation . . . cordiality of the people was everywhere displayed."[28]

From Jackson to Meridian, Mississippi

Gilbert Henderson Bates left Jackson to the cheers and acco-lades of a massive crowd. In his journey to reach Meridian, Bates stated, "Nothing of importance occurred on my march."[1] Incidents he recorded in his memoirs warrant disclosure at this point of the text.

As he entered Lake, Mississippi, a settlement that is, incongruously, not on a body of water, Bates remarked that the scenery composed a "pretty place." At that location, Bates was given a horn drinking cup, a gift from a lady whose husband had made the chalice while a prisoner of war in a Northern facility.[2]

The memoirs Bates compiled indicate that the next location of any significance was a settlement known as Hickory, Mississippi. The town, settled a few years earlier in 1860, earned its name from Andrew Jackson's nickname of Old Hickory. Legend held that General Jackson's army had camped in the location as they returned to Nashville after their major victory in New Orleans in early 1815. Jackson's army crossed the Pot-terchitto River south of Hickory, and the location of that town, and the military road, are said to coincide with Jackson's campsite.[3]

The area around Hickory was home to Native Americans whose stone tools, broken pottery, and arrowheads were readily detectable. Swamps and upland timber were plentiful in the area and created a source of game and building materials. The nearby town of Chunky was the location of Shawnee chief Tecumseh's visit for recruiting Choctaw warriors to join his confederation, which was being organized to end encroachment upon their lands. Another chief, Pushmataha, forced Tecumseh from the area before the recruitment effort proved profitable.[4]

Around 1833, Lewis Bryan, through the Dancing Rabbit Treaty, had gained the rights to more than 1,600 acres. Bryan and his Choctaw wife had five children. Asberry English Gray, the town's first merchant, eventually held the rights to the land Bryan had owned, and Gray remained a prominent citizen of the town when Bates visited in February 1868. In fact, Gray had been the first railroad agent in the area from 1861 to 1866. Afterward, he held posts such as the probate judge of Newton County, sheriff of Newton County, and justice of the peace. At the time Bates visited Hickory, Gray was the town mayor and a merchant.[5]

The railroad Bates followed as he entered Hickory had reached the town in 1861, but the American Civil War delayed service to the public. Troop movement became a top priority, and the town benefited from that as the struggle progressed. Asberry Gray was the individual who had courted the Southern Railroad Company to run its tracks through Hickory; he set aside that land while he also laid off lots in the area.[6]

Bates must have been impressed with Gray's hospitality; his journal contains positive remarks. Bates pronounced, "I was very kindly entertained by Mr. A. E. Gray. About this time, February 3, it was raining continuously, and I was glad to remain in doors for a day or two."[7]

Entertainment was in abundance at the Gray home, according to Bates. Bates jotted, "One night, after I had retired, I heard the most formidable compound of sounds near my window. Looking out, I discovered fifty or more men near the house, about a dozen of them had fiddles of various sizes, which they were playing lustily."[8]

Bates continued, "I dressed with all possible haste . . . the house was opened and in they came. I soon found they were Confederate soldiers. Some had come forty miles to see me. A keg of whiskey was opened, and a jolly time we had. . . . We broke up pretty late, but in good spirits."[9]

The morning after the musical performance, February 5, 1868, Bates left Hickory. He walked to Meridian, Mississippi, where Mayor R. L. Henderson greeted the Federal veteran. Historical records indicate that Henderson also left office around the time Bates visited the town. Nonetheless, according to Bates, Henderson welcomed him to Meridian, "in the name of the citizens, and tendered me the hospitality of the city in a very handsome speech."[10]

The *Anderson Intelligencer*, a paper printed in Anderson Court House, South Carolina, contained comments on the treatment Bates received in Meridian: "He had reached Meridian . . . where he was warmly received and heartily welcomed. As he is championing the good character of the Southern people, he ought to be kindly and hospitably treated wherever he passes."[11]

Meridian, Mississippi had a small population in 1860; the community was incorporated in February of that year. By 1870, the population had reached 2,709 in the city's first census. The statistic is significant, especially when the incidents of war are considered. Federal General William Sherman would lead 25,000 troops from Vicksburg on February 3, 1864; the group would live off the land as they neared Meridian.[12]

Sherman's forces moved into Meridian on February 14, 1864. Sherman reported, "For five days . . . men worked hard and with a will in that work of destruction. . . . Meridian, with its depots, storehouses, arsenals, hospitals, offices, hotels . . . no longer exists."[13]

When the Federals departed Meridian, they left behind destroyed railroad tracks, bridges, locomotives, and basically "anything else they could find." A modern historian explained, "The Confederates were able to repair their railroads within a month. But the weak Confederate industrial base could not replace the locomotives, and that placed the Confederate forces in a critical situation."[14]

Headstones in the area still provide "somber reminders of the conflict." Confederates were interred at Rose Hill Cemetery, the Confederate Cemetery, and at a nearby burial location named Lauderdale Springs Cemetery.[15]

It was noted that "after the war, Meridian boomed. The railroads generated manufacturing and prosperity." The location of the city at the junction of two railroads "made Meridian a key link" in the future railroad impact upon the area. Sadly, for many years after the war, Valentine's Day was not viewed as a time for love and flowers in Meridian, but "as the anniversary of the day they lost everything."[16]

By contrast, and as an evident act of forgiveness for the war's impact, an open carriage was provided for Gilbert Bates. He rode through the town's street in it with his flag unfurled. Bates wrote, "I stopped before the hotel, the Jones House, and was alighted. On leaving the carriage I was forcibly reminded of a remark by some of my friends before I left Wisconsin.... 'You will meet somewhere a drunken Confederate soldier, and he will kill you.'"[17]

Interestingly, a Texas Ranger whom Bates described as "considerably the worse for liquor," held a position at the door of the hotel. The drunken ranger approached Bates with, "Sergeant, I want to take hold of you . . . I was a rebel once, and fought you Northerners . . . but I got whipped, and all of us got whipped . . . we have quit, and we intend to stay quit."[18]

Words of peace came from the ex-Confederate, who uttered, "The old flag is all right now, and I for one am willing to light for it against anybody, and I can lick . . . any man that dare insult this flag or you either. . . . Isn't that so?"[19]

Bates remarked that he exchanged some kind words with the Ranger and then, "I left him, ready to risk his life for me, and passed into the hotel."[20]

Additional acts of hospitality were described in a telegram that was published in the *Charleston Daily News*. The paper stated that Bates had arrived in Meridian a cold, wet, and thirsty man who had told his supporters he would like to "take a drink." In turn, Bates was "escorted to a saloon by an enthusiastic crowd of ex-rebels" who exercised a strong level of hospitality upon their visitor. The article noted, "The whole party took sugar and whiskey. Bates pronounced it good, and the party took another taste all around." Reportedly, Bates expressed a fondness for the mixture and "wanted to stand treat himself, but it couldn't be thought of."[21]

To avoid leaving Bates unfed, the "delegation of citizens, headed by the Mayor," took it upon themselves to fulfill his desire for food. It was recalled, "Oysters were ordered. Bates took a dozen raw and a dozen fried, with butter and pepper. The Mayor presented his guest with the freedom of the city. The barkeeper now treated. They all took whiskey and sugar."[22]

After the food and drinks were consumed, "Bates and the Mayor adjourned to the billiard room and played a friendly game, at intervals taking whiskey and sugar. After which, on account of the weather, they took a little whiskey and sugar."[23]

The next morning, February 6, Bates left Meridian, Mississippi. A large crowd accompanied him out of town. It was noted that as Bates trod down the Selma Road, he suddenly returned to the city and "took some whiskey and sugar." His fondness for the concoction must have preceded Bates; one man "gave Bates a bottle of whiskey, and an enterprising grocery merchant gave him two pounds of sugar, which he put in his pocket." With the acquisition of his beverage complete, Bates "left on the road for Selma."[24]

Approximately two miles from the city limits, Bates "met some Confederate soldiers, who were changing their residence in the hope of bettering their condition. They talked freely . . . and expressed fears for my safety."[25]

The rationale of the ex-Confederates became clearer as they elaborated, "Every white man in the South, except for the carpetbaggers, was my friend and would protect me; but I should keep a close eye on the carpetbaggers, or they might hire some . . . to shoot me in the woods, and then lay it on the Southern people." Bates assured the well-intentioned individuals that he had no fear, and he "bade them farewell."[26]

Interestingly, in this particular phase of his journey, Bates ran into a puppet of the Union League. According to the Abbeville Institute, the purpose of the decade-old League in post–Civil War America was "in the South to serve as rallying points for whites that had opposed the Confederacy." As former slaves entered the ranks of the organization, its goals became more centered upon registering blacks to vote. The Abbeville Institute contends, "The Union League recruited members with a cult of secrecy and exaggerated promises. Members were indoctrinated to believe that their interests were perpetually at war with Southern whites that were falsely accused of wanting to put blacks back into slavery." With that in mind, the former slaves were urged to support the Republican Party in order to maintain their freedom.[27]

Bates compiled a story for the *Daily State Register*, a Carson City, Nevada publication. The lengthy passage appeared in the May 13, 1871 edition, and provides insight into the latter portion of the Mississippi march Bates underwent. He elaborated, "Before getting out of Mississippi . . . I was being followed by a respectable and very intelligent looking negro . . . he was a spy and a tool of the Union League, and was to follow and act under instructions from the League in regard to me; he was to do me no harm, but if my object in going through the South was what the directors of the League asserted it to be, I was to be assassinated unless I would return to my Northern home when warned to do so."[28]

Bates continued, "I made him my friend, and arranged with him to take charge of my baggage, meeting me at such points as railroad communication would admit of . . . he assisted me to attend three secret meetings of the League in disguise at the risk of my life, how on two occasions . . . he saved me from serious harm and perhaps death from the . . . blood hounds of the League."[29]

CHAPTER SEVEN

Bates Ventures into Alabama

BATES APPROACHED THE BORDER OF ALABAMA, THE STATE WHERE Civil War battles in areas such as Mobile Bay, Spanish Fort, Fort Blakely, and Selma occurred during the conflict. The secession convention that subsequently led to Alabama leaving the United States and eventually serving as the location of the first Confederate capital city resulted in a pro-secession vote of sixty-one to thirty-nine. The state's official history website proclaims, "Throughout the war, Alabama escaped much of the terrible destruction that other Confederate states endured." However, the state supplied approximately 90,000 soldiers to the Confederacy.[1] Those facts remained fresh in the minds of many Alabamians as Bates neared his arrival.

At four o'clock on the afternoon of February 5, 1868, Gilbert Bates entered the state of Alabama. Having traveled approximately twenty-one miles from Meridian, Mississippi, Bates arrived at Cuba, Alabama, where he intended to spend the night.[2] There is no indication as to where he slept that evening; he did not make mention of a specific location.

Cuba, Alabama, is located along the western-central boundary the state shares with Mississippi. The town's history indicates that by 1850 the name Cuba had been applied to a post office that was located in the town Gilbert Bates would visit almost two decades later. In 1852, a major landowner, R. A. Clay, moved into the area and, using one hundred slaves, established a cotton plantation. Clay donated land to the Southern Railroad in 1861. The post office was moved to the rail line, and the resulting community became known as Cuba Station, and eventually Cuba.[3]

R. A. Clay partnered with a man surnamed Ferguson to begin a mercantile firm in Cuba. Stores, a Masonic lodge, and a hotel were soon built nearby, and the community grew. Fortunately, the town remained largely undamaged during the Civil War. A skirmish took place when military cadets and a Home Guard unit fought a detachment of Sherman's cavalry, but without making any impact on Cuba. In the latter stages of the conflict, federal soldiers gained control of a Confederate camp and remained in possession of the location until hostilities concluded.[4]

Bates offered little commentary about Cuba aside from an incident that happened after he left. He recalled traveling an estimated fifteen to twenty miles eastward from Cuba when he made contact with a group of African Americans. He remarked, "I met several negroes going to vote. ... I conversed with one ... and was amazed at his ignorance. He did not know for what he was going to vote, but said all he had to do was to go down and vote, and he would get forty acres of land and a pair of mules, because they told him so; and those mules were just what he wanted."[5]

The former Federal artilleryman continued,

I was convinced that bad men had been lying to these negroes ... to get them to come out and vote. The election continued for several days, and was quite a sickening affair. I often thought if my Radical friends at the North could have witnessed it as I saw it in Alabama, they would have lost all love for negro suffrage, and would condemn the men who enforce it on unwilling people against their will, and by military power. Such a loathsome mass of ignorance never before exercised political power in a civilized community. To my mind such a state of things is disgusting. I certainly never fought for any such object.[6]

At 5:00 p.m. on February 11, 1868, Gilbert Bates arrived at Selma, Alabama. A Jackson, Mississippi paper, the *Daily Clarion*, proudly pronounced the event: "There was a public meeting of the citizens of Selma ... in honor of Sergeant Bates."[7]

Selma, located on the banks of the Alabama River, had served as a major manufacturing center during the Civil War. Its population, according to the 1860 census, was 3,177. That number more than doubled by the 1870 census, with 6,484 people being counted.[8]

The city's major economic activity during the war, according the state's official history, was the Selma Ordnance and Naval Foundry, containing more than one hundred buildings, and employed 10,000 workers at one point. Cannons, four iron-clad warships, and other military items were produced at that location. The foundry was the second largest in the Confederacy, trailing the Tredegar Iron Works in Richmond, Virginia. By the end of the war, Selma was one of the last remaining industrial centers the Confederates controlled.[9]

A battle took place in Selma in early April 1865. Federals under the command of General James Wilson fought General Nathan Bedford Forrest's confederates. The earthen defenses in which Forrest's men served had been built two years earlier, and Forrest gained command of them a short time before the battle. The defenses were described as "8 to 12 feet high, 15 feet thick at the base, with a ditch 4 feet wide and 5 feet deep along the front. In front of this was a picket fence of heavy posts planted in the ground, 5 feet high, and sharpened at the top."[10]

An intense, day-long struggle on April 2, 1865, resulted in Forrest and others in his command, some of whom had to swim across the Alabama River under the cover of darkness, escaping a federal onslaught. Aside from some 2,700 men in gray being captured, an unknown number of casualties were inflicted upon the Confederates. However, the aftermath of the battle included many private homes and businesses being looted or destroyed.[11]

Within the arsenal property, "fifteen siege guns, ten field pieces, ten heavy carriages, ten caissons, sixty-three thousand rounds of artillery ammunition, three million feet of lumber, and ten thousand bushels of coal were destroyed." The state's official site for the Selma engagement adds, "The Battle of Selma decimated the city and was one of many Confederate setbacks in the spring of 1865 that ultimately resulted in the Confederacy's surrender."[12]

Adding additional insight into the setting that Gilbert Bates entered less than three years after the battle, it is noteworthy to read the words of a member of the victorious federal army. E. N. Gilpin of the Third Iowa Cavalry wrote of Selma, "Of all the nights of my experience, this is most like the horrors of war, a captured city burning at night, a victorious army advancing, and a demoralized one retreating . . . this Sunday night now nearly gone, will be remembered. If there is a merciful God in the heavens. He must be looking down upon this scene in pity."[13]

The year after the war, Selma became the county seat of Dallas County, and a courthouse was constructed. As Gilbert Bates approached the city limits, he was once again received with a welcome committee. Mayor R. M. Robertson headed a group that met Bates and escorted him to what Bates called the Trout House.[14]

As was becoming the norm for Bates, he recalled, "I was formally received. In the evening . . . numerous callers, many from the best people in the city. The following night a meeting was called in honor of the flag."[15]

At the meeting, Bates, "was conducted to the hall by a committee of gentlemen . . . found the building crowded with people from top to bottom. As I passed, flag in hand, there was a fearful demonstration of applause which continued until I took my seat upon the stage. Afterwards, I was introduced to the audience, when the storm of applause broke out again with renewed fury."[16]

Bates returned to his seat after speaking, and the crowd heard an address from former Alabama Governor Andrew Barry Moore, an intimidating sight, standing more than six feet in height and known for being well built. His wife and he had four children, and Moore secured the design of a flag following Alabama's convention to leave the Union. Moore's service as governor at the time of Alabama's secession adds interest and irony to his presence at the celebration for Bates.[17]

Following Governor Moore's speech, the crowd heard from another former Alabama Governor, Lewis Eliphalet Parsons. Having been the Governor from June 21 until December 13, 1865, Parsons was a member of the Douglas Democrats, a group who opposed the state seceding. Born in New York, Parsons moved to Talladega, Alabama in 1840, married a lady from Kentucky, and the couple had seven children. Parsons was a wealthy man, and he continued to maintain his legal practice until the final months of the Civil War.[18]

As a state representative, Parsons had advocated the use of slaves as Confederate soldiers and opposed the system of state militias. He was appointed provisional governor upon President Andrew Johnson's order, and served until December 20, 1865. Parsons resumed his Talladega law practice after leaving office and managed to lead the successful opposition of Alabama's readmission to the Union. The latter event would not take place until July 1868, months after Gilbert Henderson Bates visited the state.[19]

A third Alabama personality, Judge William Brooks, followed Parsons. Bates proposed, "These men are the true representative men of the South. A more patriotic assemblage could not be found in the North. They were enthusiastic in their adherence to the flag and the Constitution."[20]

The appreciation Bates and the U.S. flag received from the crowd was evidenced in a write-up: "At a public meeting of the citizens today, the following resolution was unanimously adopted, 'That we heartily each and every principle embodied in the Constitution of the United States: that we respect the flag of our Union as the symbol of these principles, and we pledge ourselves to support the one and uphold and defend the other.'"[21]

Once the meeting concluded, Governor Moore spoke with Gilbert Bates. Moore uttered, "Sergeant Bates, come home with me and sleep in my house, so that when you return North you can say that you have spent the night under the same roof as men who were once leading rebels, and that you got up in the morning safe and sound, and not a hair of your head injured." Bates added that Moore offered him money, but in keeping with his personal policy, Bates declined.[22]

A summary of the evening's events appeared in an issue of the *Charleston Daily News*. It said, "Sergeant Bates, the pedestrian . . . was publicly received at the Watts Hotel, in Selma, Ala., on Wednesday night, by a crowded night. Speeches were made . . . Many ladies were present."[23]

On the following day, Bates attended another political gathering and remarked it was "larger than the previous one." One of the aspects that made a positive impression upon Bates was that "No man whispered anything against the flag. My reception through all this country was most hearty." Bates, needless to say, obtained encouragement from his perception: "I was the object of untiring devotion everywhere."[24]

Bates projected a sense of racism in projecting, "The negroes said little or nothing; but the whites, I verily believe, had a sort of affection for me."[25]

In his journey toward the state capital of Montgomery, Bates had a layover near Benton, Alabama. The plantation where he stayed was known as White Hall; the proprietor was recorded as Mr. Joseph A. White. Bates remembered a kind reception from Mr. White and his wife, with Mr. White insisting "on my staying with them overnight."[26]

Benton, Alabama, was originally known as Maull's Landing, but the more recent name had been adopted after the 1834 incorporation. The namesake was Thomas Hart Benton, a South Carolina resident and veteran of the Battle of Horseshoe Bend and the Creek War. During the steamboat era, the town became a major trading post and grew quickly after a two-hundred-acre auction set aside lots that were also added to the town in 1855. By 1870, shortly after Bates visited the area, Benton had a population of 2,627.[27]

Accepting the offer to slumber at White Hall, Bates commented, "They entertained me elegantly. When I took my leave of them, I found that my flag was decorated with laurel wreaths. This was the work of Miss Sallie E. White."[28]

Bates recollected the situation he faced as he prepared to leave White Hall in authoring, "The ladies wished me a safe return to my family. Mr. White accompanied me a short distance on my way. He spoke of the unhappy condition of the country, of the necessity of forgetting and forgiving the past. He hoped for a union of all good men. North and South, a restoration of peace, and, moreover, a restoration of good feeling."[29]

In his conversation with White, Bates was told the Radicals had performed a great wrong and, "treat us hatefully . . . seek to degrade us . . . . make life unendurable . . . leave no reason to expect us to like them . . . tearing down civil government, and setting up military government over us, they . . . disenfranchise hundreds of thousands of intelligent men, and give the negroes the ballot."[30]

Bates took that conversation to heart; he had accepted the challenge to undertake the march after his encounter with a man whom Bates labeled as a Radical. The conversation with Mr. White not only impacted Bates, but also had an effect upon Mr. White. Bates concluded by saying that Mr. White "spoke feelingly, and when we parted, his eyes were filled with tears."[31]

As Bates traveled across Alabama, the *Manitowoc Tribune*, published in Wisconsin, his home state, updated his fellow statesmen on his travels. "With a great flourish of trumpets, it was announced some time ago that one Sergeant Bates of this state was about to walk from Vicksburg to Washington. . . . The object was to test the loyalty of the South. It is now announced by telegraph that Sergt. Bates is on his way and that he is not molested, but treated with great consideration."[32]

The article assumed a defiant tone: "The story of the wager is undoubtedly a fabrication. The whole affair is a very silly attempt at creating a sensation. . . . Bates goes through the South advertised in advance as having made a bet that he will not be assailed . . . we expect to find the Copperhead papers deeply impressed by the evidence of loyalty . . . the Southern people . . . manifest in refraining from lynching the man who claims to have made a bet on their good behavior."[33]

Chapter Eight

Montgomery

Gilbert Henderson Bates reached Montgomery, Alabama, on February 17, 1868. National newspapers announced the event; among those was the *Emporia News* of Emporia, Kansas. In an issue published four days after Bates arrived in Montgomery, the paper exclaimed, "Sergeant Bates . . . walking from Memphis to Washington, reached Montgomery . . . met a cordial meeting."[1] It is noteworthy that while the quotation is largely accurate, Bates did not begin his march from Memphis.

Bates elaborated, "Here I was met with a magnificent reception. The ladies of this city made . . . a beautiful pink sash, of fine silk, and ornamented with heavy gold. It was presented to me at a public festival, given to aid some charitable purpose, and is really a very beautiful sash."[2]

Printed the day after Bates arrived in Montgomery, an article in the *Alexandria Gazette* provided more about his reception. The write-up noted, "Sergeant Bates . . . was met by a large number of citizens in carriages decorated with United States flags, and by a band of music. About three thousand people turned out to hear the . . . speeches and welcome him."[3]

Another article stated, "The old flag was enthusiastically cheered. Hundreds of ladies, from windows, balconies, and verandahs on the principal streets waved their handkerchiefs to him as he marched along."[4]

Montgomery's history as a significant location in Alabama was older than the state itself. A major catalyst in the establishment of the site where Montgomery was founded and grew rested upon the fact that a significant Native American trade route, paths, the Alabama River, and streams crossed at the location. By 1822, the town, named for American Revolution hero General Richard Montgomery, had become the county seat of Montgomery County, named for Major Lemuel Purnell Montgomery, a casualty of the Battle of Horseshoe Bend.[5]

With the growth of Alabama, state legislators grew determined to move the state capital from Tuscaloosa. A local businessman, Andrew Dexter, set aside Goat Hill, a portion of his land holdings, for the site of a new state house. That offer became official in 1846 with the legislature's decision to move the capital to Montgomery. Fifteen years later, Montgomery served as the first capital of the Confederate States of America, and it served as such for three months. At that time, the capital of the Confederacy was moved to Richmond, Virginia.[6]

Montgomery was able to escape the effects of the Civil War for the majority of the conflict. A large number of the town's homes, as well as six hospitals, provided locations where sick and injured soldiers found relief. The relative peace Montgomery had experienced for most of the war was ended in April 1865 when retreating Confederates burned an estimated 100,000 bales of cotton before evacuating the city. The Federal troops remained in possession of Montgomery for two days. During that time the men in blue destroyed railroad cars, a train depot, the arsenal, rolling mills, and foundries.[7] The effects of the federal annihilation lasted for years; those could have had ramifications upon the reception the residents gave Gilbert Bates.

A Montgomery highlight for Bates, and an indication that the mindset of the citizens contained little animosity, was a speech given on behalf of the ladies of the city. A period publication stated that "All the speakers and marshals of the day were former Confederate soldiers."[8]

Continuing the content of other sources, another 1868 article elaborated,

Sergeant Bates . . . was bidden to feast at the municipal expense as long as he cared to stay there . . . these frantic ebullitions of joy were the work of ex–Confederate soldiers . . . there must be a great deal of heavy romancing in the Alabama letters that find their way into

Radical journals, and in the speeches that ring daily in the halls of Congress, according to which the ex-Confederates of Alabama are as venomous as ever they were to the old flag, and are marking for future vengeance every man of color who revives his fealty to it.[9]

Llewellyn Adolphus Shaver, an attorney who served more than two years in the Sixteenth Alabama Infantry, said to Bates, "You have undertaken to demonstrate to the country the fact that the South, when she laid down her arms at Appomattox and other points, did so in good faith, that her people are anxious, if possible, to observe the terms of that surrender, and that the charges of rebellious hostility on their part toward the Government are groundless."[10]

A vow was made: "Should you succeed in accomplishing this object and removing from the minds of our Northern brethren . . . prejudice which has doubtless been engendered against us, many instances by the slanderous politicians or vindictive scoundrels who seek our destruction, you have done more to reunite the several sections than a Radical Congress has been enabled to do by the Reconstruction measures of three years. Your object is highly patriotic, and whether achieved or not, your effort will entitle you to the gratitude of all true lovers of the country."[11]

The speaker continued, "Thus far you have been more than successful. You . . . travelled from Vicksburg to Montgomery, and have not only been unharmed by 'rebels,' but have, on the contrary, met with ovation after ovation, your progress has been one continued triumph."[12]

The conclusion of the speech praised Bates: "You have been everywhere enthusiastically greeted and hospitality entertained by ex-Confederate soldiers. It affords me much pleasure, at the request of the ladies of Montgomery, the mothers, wives, daughters, and sisters of ex-Confederate soldiers, to present you with this token of their approbation and esteem."[13]

Bates seized the opportunity to thank the ladies for their act of kindness. Afterward, he was "escorted to one of the leading hotels, and is the guest of the city as long as he remains."[14]

Bates remarked that his "sojourn in Montgomery was delightful," and that he "left it with reluctance." A proposed source of income for

Bates was selling photographs of himself. In turn, "Bates . . . realized about $500 from the rebels of Montgomery, from the sale of his photographs, and about $480 in the way of a donation from the same source. Nearly $1,000."[15]

The weather Bates encountered leaving Montgomery was primarily rainy and cold. He recalled the rains as "frequent, and my journey was rendered thoroughly disagreeable."[16]

Aside from the weather, an incident that took place during his stay in Montgomery caused Bates to pen, "While stopping at the European Hotel in Montgomery, Alabama, I was one evening a short time absent from my room. On returning to it . . . I found a communication which had been thrust under the door during my absence, and it was from the League . . . threatened me with certain death unless I furled my flag and returned to my home, giving up all further efforts in my attempt to deceive the people of the North in regard to the loyalty of the red-handed traitors of the South."[17]

As for the secrecy of the incident, Bates exclaimed, "I mentioned the matter to . . . General James Clanton, of Montgomery. [He] urged me to accept . . . an escort of ex-Confederate soldiers, who would see me and the flag pass safely through Alabama into Georgia. I refused."[18]

The Confederate general, James Clanton, to whom Bates referred, had been born in Georgia in 1827. His family moved to Alabama when he was a child, and his studies at the University of Alabama were cut short when he joined the U.S. Army to fight Mexico. After the Mexican-American War, Clanton became an attorney, but he left his practice to serve the Confederate States of America. Having seen action at Shiloh, as well as Farmington and Booneville, Mississippi, he eventually reached the rank of brigadier general. As Clanton resumed his practice after the war, he was an attorney at the time he served as a confidant for Bates. Sadly, an ex-Federal soldier would kill Clanton in Knoxville, Tennessee in 1871.[19]

An article expounded upon the positive properties of the impact Bates made upon the residents of Montgomery: "Instead of finding a rebel behind every tree ready to shoot him or tear the 'hated flag' out of his hands, finds the flag greeted with cheers wherever he shows it, and is living off the land. The only enemies he has thus far encountered are the carpetbagger politicians that infest the land."[20]

Soon after Bates departed the confines of the friendly reception he received in Montgomery, a satirical article in an Orange Court House, Virginia publication proclaimed, "If he comes this way with his flag, we in Virginia will not make any hullabaloo over him. We will trust him kindly, and, let him proceed with his flag."[21]

A similar article of a mixed nature appeared in the *Richmond Dispatch*. "The expedition of . . . the flag . . . is a very absurd affair, and come what may to him, should not be misinterpreted. It would not be surprising that some deranged man or fool, in a passion, might trounce him and damage the flag."[22]

The Richmond-based article continued, "Indeed, his proclamation is a banter, which may be considered a banter to someone besides Radicals. Thoughtless and mischievous persons might play a trick on him. . . . Radicals would raise a howl that would be reechoed from the shores of the Pacific as a preliminary to further persecutions of Southern people who would be no more responsible for what might happen to Bates than they are for the earthquakes at St. Thomas."[23]

Still more opinions included in the *Richmond Dispatch* article, "On the other hand, suppose that Bates reaches the termination of his route without molestation, as we conjecture he will, what will that prove? That we love Radicalism? That we regard that as the law and the Constitution? That we are ready to lick the hand that's raised to shed our blood? Nonsense. The South has not altered its opinion of the Constitution, and its attachment for it, since it was adopted. . . . It is loyal to the Government framed and administered according to that instrument."[24]

The conclusion to the editorial's content read, "It is ready and anxious to return such a government; and in that sense is truly loyal . . . opposed to the party that has destroyed both. . . . The latest generation . . . in this part of the Union there will be cherished an undying hate for that worst schism that ever cursed this land. Don't misrepresent Bates's trip."[25]

A contrasting mood was projected in a piece published in a Charleston paper, the *Daily News*. It said, "The wager of Sergeant Bates . . . is likely to be won. Our people had no quarrel with that flag. Indeed, some of the most thoughtful of the Southern statesmen, among whom Governor Wise was prominent, objected to giving it up. . . . The danger which besets the sergeant on his way is . . . of the good fellowship which must be encountered from . . . beginning to . . . end."[26]

The paper persisted, "There are other mixtures that . . . overthrow a soldier besides powder and ball . . . vastly more numerous is the number of travelers prostrated by the flask that bursts into beads and bubbles, than of those subdued by the flask that explodes with smoke and fire."[27]

The last words of the Charleston commentary specified, "Sergeant Bates will be certain to reach Washington in due time, unless he looks too frequently at the clouds through the muzzle of his pocket pistol. We earnestly wish the honest and truthful soldier a safe passage to his place of destination."[28]

A final observation on the visit Bates made to Montgomery was published in the *Evening Argus* in Rock Island, Illinois. It quantified, "Sergeant Bates . . . so far, received no harm. . . . In the Capital of Alabama, where the Constitution was framed which the radicals have so recently rejected, he was met enthusiastically."[29]

"The demonstration amounted to an ovation. . . . The same scene was enacted at Selma . . . enthusiasm for the old flag was displayed . . . the same hearty good-will toward the government was expressed. Not only was the pedestrian fed and lodged with all hospitality and honor, but the democratic club of the city called a meeting to welcome him," constituted the bulk of the second paragraph.[30]

Speaking of some individuals who had expressed fellowship toward Bates, the article noted, "They said that if ever the flag were insulted or trampled upon, the South would be the first to defend it; they welcomed it as the emblem of our common country, destined to wave over a united nation, whose glorious future was only limited by the bounds of the continent."[31]

The termination of the exposé encompassed praise for an eventual goal Bates held in visiting Montgomery and other stops: "The people of the South are friends and anxious to be received as such. . . . A plain fact like this one which a single, unarmed soldier of the Union has brought prominently forward, should silence the angry epithets with which northern radicals expect to go through the coming canvass in triumph.

The country requires only clear evidence of the willingness of the Southern people to return to their place in the Union, and here it is."[32]

Bates had an encounter with a member or representative of Union League South. He reminisced, "An agent of the League called on me and requested a private interview, which I granted. His object in calling was to induce me to become a member of the League. His arguments and the inducements offered by him I will pass over for the present.[33]

Gilbert Bates made his last significant stop in Alabama at the city of Tuskegee. Located about forty miles east of Montgomery, Tuskegee was founded in 1833. However, the land where the town was to be laid out had been settled in the aftermath of the French and Indian War. A Creek chief named Taskigi served as the town's namesake. Tuskegee, along with other towns in Macon County, of which Tuskegee served as the county seat, became an active trading center as the years passed. As the Civil War approached, Tuskegee and the area around it had served as a cotton plantation that depended on slave labor.[34] Unlike many of the locations Bates visited during his march, Tuskegee was largely untouched during the war years of 1861 through 1865.

Gilbert Bates arrived in Tuskegee February 23, 1868. He attended church in the town that morning. His afternoon was filled with visits as "many ladies and gentlemen called on me."[35]

The following day, Bates witnessed young ladies trimming his flag "with laurel, gave me bouquets, etc. . . . One young lady presented me with a handsome cigar case." Bates glowed in reading the attached card upon which a man penned, "Accept this 'cigar case,' Sergeant Bates, from a true Southerner, but one who respects your noble mission and the banner you carry."[36]

A truly heartwarming incident took place in Tuskegee; a girl, eight years of age, carried a doll and approached Bates. He said that she had received the doll "as a New Year's gift, which she valued only as little girls can." When the young girl found out that Bates was the father of a little girl, the maiden "came to me with the doll and asked the name of my little girl." Bates answered that Hattie was the name of his daughter. The Southern miss "at once handed me the doll, and told me to give it to Hattie . . . she would not have given it to anyone else." Bates was overcome with emotion and "kissed the little child again and again."[37]

Bates Enters Georgia

WITH GEORGIA BEING THE THIRD CONFEDERATE STATE WITH A CAPI-
tal city he planned to visit, Bates was certainly aware of the siege of
Atlanta, as well as conflicts such as Chickamauga and Resaca. Governor
Joseph Brown had surrendered at the end of the war and later served
a prison term in the District of Columbia. Of the 100,000 Georgians
who served in the ranks of the Confederate States of America, some
40,000 men had been lost to the effects of the Civil War. In addition,
approximately 460,000 freedmen were striving to gain equality in its
aftermath. Like Mississippi and Alabama, the citizens of Georgia were
living through the hardships of Federal Reconstruction. Unlike the other
Southern states that were involved in the turmoil of Reconstruction,
Georgia had not created a set of Black Codes.[1]

That was the state Gilbert Bates entered on February 25, 1868. As
experienced in Mississippi and Alabama, Bates was gladly received in
Georgia. He recalled, "At Columbus, another fine reception awaited . . .
during my sojourn . . . I was the constant recipient of attentions."[2]

Bates expounded upon his impressions of Columbus: "My course
thus far had been strewn with flowers, and here the same compliments
were paid me. The places in the South which, during the war, were most
zealous in the rebel cause, were the larger towns and the cities. Newspapers, telegraphs, and railroads gave them greater facilities for obtaining
information. Thus far . . . the larger places had given . . . the most enthusiastic receptions . . . the same sentiments of regard actuated the country
people . . . they had no facilities for making demonstrations."[3]

An early-March article appeared in the *Daily Phoenix* saying, "This ex-Federal soldier . . . has bet a large amount that he could make a trip on foot through the South . . . reached Columbus, Ga., on Tuesday, the 25th, and was received with demonstrations of kindness."[4]

A brief description of Bates followed: "He . . . is about thirty . . . of medium height, slimly built, and has a thin, frank, open and intelligent face. His dress is of silk velvet, and around his waist he wore . . . a red sash . . . His baggage goes by rail, under charge of his servant."[5]

Columbus, located on the Chattahoochee River and eighty miles east of Montgomery, Alabama, was once known as the Coweta Reserve. In 1828, the city was founded as a trading post on the site of a former Creek Village. A relatively unique aspect of its origin lies in the fact that it is "one of the few cities in the United States to be planned in advance of its founding." It is also known as "the last frontier town of the original Thirteen Colonies."[6]

Approximately sixty years after the American Civil War, George J. Burnes compiled his memories of wartime Columbus. In "Columbus as it was during the war 1861–65," Burnes focused on the manufacturing facilities, but also noted the large number of hospitals that were located in the city. In addition to thousands of bales of cotton, Burnes remarked that factories for drums and fifes, watches, wool jeans, cannons, and oil-cloth were among the locations that produced items largely intended to benefit the Confederate cause.[7] Some of those buildings, or the remains of them, were present at the time Bates visited Columbus.

Some four decades after it was founded, Columbus was the location of what has been debated as "the last battle of the Civil War." On April 16, 1865, a week after Lee surrendered to Grant at Appomattox, Confederates and Federals struggled to gain control of "the second largest industrial city in the Confederacy." Although Union General James Wilson was unaware of the surrender, he victoriously led his troops against the inexperienced Confederate forces of Major General Howell Cobb. With the victory in hand, Wilson gained control of a large naval facility and factories that produced military materials and goods.[8]

Having had a well-experienced visit in Columbus, Bates was recorded as leaving for Macon after only one day and night spent visiting the citizens of Columbus.[9]

Bates reached Macon, Georgia, where he was "entertained in regal style, received by authorities, cheered by the people, called upon by the prominent citizens of the place, supplied with a beautiful carriage and with any quantities of bouquets."[10]

The city of Macon, located on the Ocmulgee River, originated as Fort Hawkins, on the orders of Thomas Jefferson, in 1806. It was named Macon seventeen years later. The settlement's namesake was North Carolina statesman Nathaniel Macon. During the American Civil War, a prisoner of war camp, hospitals, and factories, notably a rifle manufacturing facility, were located in and around Macon. The town was able to escape the damage inflicted upon many other communities during the war, but Macon became the home of the state government when its leaders fled Milledgeville as the Federals approached. Later, following the capture of Confederate president Jefferson Davis, Macon served as his initial location of detention.[11]

Full of confidence related to his visit in Macon, Bates proclaimed, "I was indeed a favorite. I venture to say that no man in the United States, either North or South, would have received from the citizens of Macon a heartier reception." Bates stayed in Macon for two days; and, as he said, "I enjoyed every moment of the time."[12]

Somewhat distraught to have left Macon, Bates soon reached the outskirts of Milledgeville, Georgia. The history of the city of Milledgeville began in 1803 when the state of Georgia sought a site for a new state capital. Named for one-time Georgia Governor John Milledge, the settlement was located on the Oconee River. The city shares a relationship with Washington, D.C., in that those two communities are reportedly the only two U.S. cities that were designed to become capitals. A history of the city says, "Many area homes and structures survived the periodic fires and willful destruction of the War Between the States." Interestingly, Milledgeville would lose the honor of being the state capital the year after Bates visited.[13]

Just west of Milledgeville, Bates had what he called "the only conflict which attended my whole journey through the South. It was entirely unexpected and startling." Bates elaborated upon the skirmish, "If it had not been for my glorious flagstaff, I might not have survived to tell the tale. Five curdogs, of a disagreeable size, set upon me furiously, and seemed determined to punish my intrusion. The battle was hot and heavy for about fifteen minutes."[14]

Continuing his discussion of the canine encounter, Bates wrote, "I plied the flagstaff with vigor and dexterity, and, at last, the victory was mine. I can account for the hostility of the dogs only on the ground that they are 'rebels yet,' and have not yet been reconstructed, nor taken the test-oath. It seems to me that such a display of the red-handed spirit of rebellion will necessitate a military government over that country, until fruits . . . for repentance have been brought forth."[15]

Bates concluded his recollection of his struggle with the pack of dogs, "Perhaps negro suffrage would teach better sentiments to the canine tribe, so that, after time, a Northern man can go through that country peacefully, in no danger of being attacked by hounds, who then would have learned humbly to lick the dust at his feet. That would be complete Reconstruction. The only disrespect shown the United States flag during my whole march came from these dogs near Milledgeville. No white man offered me it the slightest insult."[16]

On March 5, 1868, Bates reached Milledgeville, Georgia. As noted, at the time, Milledgeville was the capital of Georgia. The city had an 1860 population of 2,480; it had slightly increased to 2,750 by the 1870 census.[17]

Bates made few comments about his time in Milledgeville aside from, "At this place I was received in the same enthusiastic manner as in the other cities. . . . Here, the officer of the army called upon me, and many Confederate soldiers did the same."[18]

Bates Travels through Georgia

BETWEEN HIS VISITS IN MILLEDGEVILLE AND AUGUSTA, BATES MADE A couple of peace-keeping stops. One of the sojourns was a largely undocumented trip to Sparta. A comment Bates made about his time in that community was, "March 9th, I left Sparta and resumed my tramp through long stretches of pine forest, and over a road which was very sandy."[1]

Sparta, Georgia, was founded in 1795 and had once been the site of a cotton plantation and a trading post. It is located approximately halfway between Macon and Augusta, and would have been situated about twenty-three miles east of Milledgeville. A noted historian bragged about Sparta's history by proclaiming that people who are "curious about Georgia's cultural roots might find answers in that remarkable small town of Sparta where both races have seen such travail but where they have somehow survived and contributed to Georgia's culture, via writing, education, and an extraordinary architectural legacy that cannot be equaled elsewhere in the state."[2]

Sparta supposedly gained its name from the fighting ferocity of its residents during the Creek Indian Wars of the early 1800s. It was noted that the men fought like Spartans, and the name stuck. The town grew into a major cotton producer, and wealthy individuals of the area produced homes visible at the time Bates visited. The salvation of many of those homes was a status owed to troops serving under Confederate captain Harry Culver, who were able to cause the retreat of Federals at nearby Sandersville; that allowed Sparta to remain unmolested.[3]

Bates made one other mention of Sparta: "About five miles from Sparta, at a place called Culverton, I met a large crowd of people waiting for my arrival." According to information about the incident, a school at Culverton, located fourteen miles east of Sparta, had dismissed for the arrival of Bates, and schoolchildren gathered around him to shake his hand and see the flag.[4]

The exhibitions of kindness toward Bates continued at Culverton: "I was cordially invited to remain there for some time and take dinner with them, but I could not accept. So, bidding them good-bye, I set out again. I had proceeded only about a mile, when a boy came riding after me, at full speed, on horseback.[5]

Bates remarked, "He reined in his horse, as he came up to me, and cried out, 'Sergeant, wait a minute, if you please. I missed seeing you at Culverton, and I want to shake hands with you. . . . I love that flag, and always shall love it.' Saying this, almost out of breath, he took my hand. In a little while, he turned his horse's head and rode back."[6]

Bates made several comments about Southerners. He stated, "An earnest, impulsive people are the Southerners, and the boy represents their character pretty well." As Bates continued his trek from Culverton, he "met about twenty ladies on the roadside. . . . There was no house in sight, and I wondered how they came there, and what they were doing."[7]

His questions were answered with the following observation: "I soon found that they had brought dinner to me, intending to intercept me on my way. I enjoyed the entertainment very much, particularly on account of the manner in which it was given."[8]

Bates did not fail to mention his feelings toward females: "The Southern ladies are loyal enough now. What harm will it do if they deck their brothers' graves with flowers? I, as a Northern soldier, can take no offense at such a natural mark of affection."[9]

Continuing his march, Bates added, "After taking my departure from the ladies, I proceeded for several miles without seeing anyone . . . far from any house, I met a man who had served in the rebel army. He had been engaged in chopping wood . . . he had been watching for me several days . . . and asked me to accompany him to his home."[10]

Bates encountered a sad side: "He told me that the grave of his brother, who had fallen in the rebel cause, was not far from the road-side. I went with him to the spot. He stood upon one side of the grave and I upon the other. Unconsciously, we bared our heads. A plain wooden headboard marked the place. As I read the inscription, he asked why such a bad state of feeling should continue to prevail, why should there still be enmity between the North and South?"[11]

As the visit concluded, the grief-stricken brother, "reached me his hand over the grave of his brother. I clasped it in the deepest emotion. Will anyone say that I did wrong in taking the hand of one against whom I had fought, but who was willing to stand by the old flag and bury the difference of the past?"[12] Once again, if even on a small scale, the outcome Bates had strived to attain by conducting his march had been attained.

Bates walked from the graveside and moved toward Augusta, reaching that town on March 14, but a Columbus, Ohio, newspaper recorded the date as March 11. In part, the paper said, "Sergeant Bates . . . was received here this afternoon . . . and welcomed to the hospitality of the city by Lieutenant Ells. Sergeant Bates will remain at the Planter's Hotel for a few days."[13]

The Planter's Hotel had been built in the eighteenth century and hosted such dignitaries as the Marquis de Lafayette. In 1863, the hotel had sold for $109,000. A major rise in the level of the Savannah River flooded the hotel in 1865, and an article from that year noted, "At the Planters Hotel . . . water was . . . three to five feet deep . . . that popular caravansary was for the day approachable only by navigators." Despite hardships that befell the hotel, it continued as an Augusta landmark, with businesses such as machine shops noting their proximity to the establishment. Likewise, when Screven House in Savannah, Georgia, changed proprietorship in 1868, a local newspaper proclaimed that T. S. Nickerson, the new manager, was also associated with the Planter's Hotel.[14]

Augusta, Georgia, had an 1860 population of 12,493, and there was an increase to 15,389 in 1870. Augusta, formed in 1736, was the second town of Georgia, the thirteenth and final British colony. Located 160 miles east of Atlanta, Augusta is situated on the Savannah River and was "a pivotal site in the Revolutionary War." It also served as the capital of Georgia from 1785 until 1795. It was in Augusta where Georgia ratified the U.S. Constitution and became the fourth state in the nation. The 1847 completion of the Augusta Canal led to it growing into the "second largest inland cotton market in the world during the cotton boom."[15]

The state of Georgia's official site proclaims, "Augusta enjoyed prestige as the principal market of the expanding Georgia backcountry during the Antebellum period." The Georgia Railroad also placed its headquarters in Augusta in 1840. Boats traversing the Savannah River used the wharfs at Augusta. A variety of science and religion publications, such as the *Southern Medical and Surgical Journal* and the *Southern Cultivator* were published in Augusta.[16]

During the Civil War, Augusta provided cotton goods, guns, munitions, shoes, food, and other items to the Confederate States of America. A major contribution of Augusta to the Confederate effort was the Confederate States Powder Works. That institution produced 2.75 million pounds of gunpowder in its twenty-six buildings located on the Augusta Canal. The city also served as a major medical facility during the war, with homes and churches, including Augusta Presbyterian, serving as hospitals after the Battle of Chickamauga. In the latter house of worship, pews were removed to make room for beds for the wounded. Magnolia Cemetery, located in Augusta, was used as the burial location of many of the deceased soldiers.[17]

Bates exclaimed of his arrival in Augusta, "The same ovation awaited me there. I remained several days, and twice attended the theater. One evening, as I was sitting in the theater, a negro sent word to me that my life was in danger. I knew no attempt would be made in the building, and therefore told a friend of mine to step out and see the state of affairs."[18]

Bates made additional remarks that detailed a serious situation, "He came back after a little while, and told me that quite a number of negroes in and about the building were waiting for me to come out of the theater, when they intended to set on me and shoot me. My friend had armed himself with two revolvers, and resolved to see me safely home."[19]

As the details emerged, the situation became more life-threatening. Bates explained, "When the play was over, we waited until nearly all the audience had passed out, when we moved out of the building. My companion did not attempt to conceal the fact he was armed. As we passed out, the negroes were looking savage enough, and an occasional whisper passed between them, but no violence was shown."[20]

With the peaceful outcome of the situation, Bates expounded upon the cruel intentions of local citizens, "We reached home in safety. But, after the occurrences of that night, I was always more cautious about the negroes. They would not of themselves do me any harm, but unscrupulous white men, who infest the country, are constantly putting them up to all sorts of mischief. They pretend to be the negros' friend, and say to them that such and such men intend to make slaves of the blacks again, and thus madden them to the commission of deeds of outrage. The presence of such men in a community is worse than the murrain among cattle."[21]

In an article written for a Nevada periodical, Bates also bragged about his companion in noting, "At . . . Augusta, Georgia, he saved me from serious harm and perhaps death from the skulking blood hounds of the League." Bates was certain that members of the Union League South were determined to commit bodily injury to or kill Bates. The incident at Augusta marked the second time, Vicksburg being the first, in which Bates was convinced that an accomplice, or perhaps a member, of the Union League South had planned to perform an evil act upon him.[22]

Bates Enters South Carolina

GILBERT HENDERSON BATES RECORDED THE DATE OF HIS ENTRY INTO South Carolina as March 16, 1868. However, if his earlier recollection was that he arrived in Augusta, Georgia, on March 15 and stayed there several days, the accuracy of the Bates memoirs has to be questioned. Despite this minor discrepancy, his claim that he was "heartily received in Hamburg [South Carolina]" gives some additional credibility to his recollections of what took place on the trip.[1]

The situation Bates encountered in South Carolina was less than half a decade removed from the conclusion of the American Civil War. An estimated 69,000 men, or 23 percent of the total white population of North Carolina, fought for the Confederate States of America, the nation against which Gilbert Bates fought. Confederate generals with South Carolina connections encompassed Wade Hampton, James Longstreet, Johnson Hagood, States Rights Gist, and Arthur Manigault. Multiple battles or engagements also occurred within the borders of the state. Those included Fort Sumter, the location where the opening shots of the war were fired, Fort Wagner, and Honey Hill.

Bates was able to cross into South Carolina by traversing a bridge that spanned the Savannah River, the primary obstacle between Augusta and the South Carolina line. He evidently spent a short time in Hamburg; he wrote, "after shaking hands and exchanging salutations, I resumed my tramp."[2]

The town of Hamburg, South Carolina sits on the Savannah River, a 313-mile-long waterway. The town's founder was Henry Shultz, a

German immigrant who had made a fortune in Augusta, Georgia before losing his wealth. Shultz became determined that he would establish a trade-oriented city opposite of Augusta. Hamburg drew quickly during the 1820s and 1830s, but floods struck the community during the two following decades. By the late 1850s merchants abandoned Hamburg, and in the postwar era it became "a haven for emancipated slaves." By 1876, approximately a decade after Bates passed through Hamburg, the city's charter was revoked, and the town "faded out of existence."[3]

A March 18, 1868, edition of the *Daily Phoenix*, based in Columbia, predicted his historic arrival in that city by stating, "Sergeant Bates is expected to arrive here this afternoon, at 4 o'clock. He will likely reach the ferry about 3. Give him a hearty reception."[4]

The route Bates followed placed him in Columbia, South Carolina, the state capital, on March 18, by his recollection. His quest in reaching Columbia was a difficult one to fulfill; Bates penned, "The march had been severe. The weather was rainy, the roads bad, and the streams were swollen enormously, and had no bridges over them. I was compelled to ford the streams on foot, and of course was frequently wet with cold water."[5]

In 1786, the South Carolina Legislature created Columbia; the name, approved via a vote, outpaced Washington for the designated state capital. As for growth, the 1860 census revealed a population of 8,052. That number increased to 9,298 by 1870.[6]

The arrival of Bates in Columbia was met with skepticism from a writer in an Anderson Court House, South Carolina paper. The article proposed, "The avowed object of this singular journey . . . is to disprove the assertions . . . that the South is yet disloyal. . . . With the sincerity and manliness of this action, we are more than pleased, and are willing to accord the just . . . praise to the honest, patriotic soldier. Further than this, we are disposed to agree with: 'The adventure proves nothing, the event will prove nothing, and we can't but doubt Southern enthusiasm over the stars and stripes.'"[7]

A Columbia newspaper more favorably recorded Bates's arrival, "As was . . . expected, considerable interest has been excited among our citizens . . . this interest was manifested . . . by the large number of persons who appeared on the banks of the river. Punctual to the hour, the soldier pedestrian, with his flag over his shoulder, appeared on the opposite bank of the Congaree."[8]

"After a short delay," the article continued, "he was ferried over, and upon reaching the Columbia side was cordially taken by the hand, and at once made to feel that, notwithstanding the assertions of prejudiced or unthinking individuals to the contrary, there are to be found in the State of South Carolina those who will 'render unto Cesar' whenever they are fully satisfied as is the present instant, that Cesar has a just claim on them."[9]

A less than favorable recollection of the entrance of Bates appeared in a Yorkville, South Carolina, newspaper: "A crowd of two or three hundred, most of them negroes, had collected to welcome, or to gaze at him. . . . 'Three cheers for Sergeant Bates and his Flag' was offered and given in a somewhat feeble voice."[10]

The Yorkville commentary continued, "The reception was not exactly enthusiastic as we understand the term. It was kind, merely. The crowd followed the Distinguished Arrival up something like a hundred yards, when they halted."[11]

Bates remarked about the reception he obtained upon his arrival in Columbia, "I crossed the Congaree River in a ferry boat, and found hundreds of the people of Columbia waiting to receive me. The Mayor [Theodore Stark] made the speech of welcome. I was then placed in a carriage and driven to a hotel. A large procession followed in carriages, on foot, and on horseback, led by young ladies on horseback."[12]

A record remarked, "Col. Samuel W. Melton delivered a speech at the Sergeant; and in handsome style complimented him on his present undertaking to relieve the South of an aspersion upon her good name and good faith. He told the Sergeant that he was welcome to Columbia, the place where secession commenced, and the place where Sherman had been."[13]

It was noted, "The speech was well-received, and was greeted with some applause. It seemed to strike Sergeant Bates dumb, for he said nothing. Some say he ejaculated, 'Thanks!' but we didn't hear it. Perhaps he was too full for utterance, or . . . not full enough. . . . Like Grant, he doesn't want to speak. . . . Or . . . he has no story to tell."[14]

Riding in the carriage that "had been placed at his disposal," Bates arrived at the Nickerson Hotel. While T. S. Nickerson owned the hotel, sometimes called Nickerson's Congaree House Hotel, the manager was a Mr. Wright. The original establishment had been a location where Mary Chesnut composed many entries in her famous diary, later published as *Mary Chesnut's Civil War*. The hotel also served as Confederate general Pierre Gustave Toutant Beauregard's headquarters until Federal officers took control of Columbia. Fire destroyed the structure, and Nickerson reopened his hotel in vacant buildings of Columbia College.[15] The latter was the location where Bates slept while in Columbia.

Bates had his recollections reinforced; a Columbia publication stated, "S. W. Melton . . . on behalf of those present, delivered a short address of welcome . . . he said that the right feeling people at the South fully appreciated his efforts in their behalf in this self- imposed pilgrimage . . . no radicals were present to welcome him, their earnest desire was that he should be insulted and his flag made to trail in the dust. Neither was . . . any extreme Southern men present, they also were opposed to him . . . those who stood before him were the great mass, who earnestly desired a settlement of the present troubles and . . . readmission to Congress and the Union."[16]

The day after he arrived in Columbia, Gilbert Bates recalled that he was "shown about the city." He also received a serenade from a large gathering of citizens.[17] The places and sites Bates came upon during his tour were to have a lasting impact upon his impressions of the South Carolina capital. It is unknown how much Bates knew about the condition of Columbia prior to his visit, but his words show that he gained some knowledge.

A short article in the March 20, 1868, issue of the *Daily Phoenix* proclaimed, "Sergeant Bates will remain in Columbia until Monday next. . . . He went on a tour of observation around the city . . . and was pleasantly received wherever he made his appearance. Owing to a slight strain of the leaders in one leg, he was prevailed upon to remain here longer than he intended."[18]

While in Columbia, Bates seized the opportunity, and he succeeded in securing Richard Wearn and William Preston Hix, a Confederate veteran, for a photograph. The two men were in a photography business for approximately fifteen years and are likely most famous for their post-war images of the destruction dealt upon Columbia. When the image of Gilbert Bates was made, copies were sent to President Andrew Johnson and to Wisconsin Senator Doolittle.[19]

Bates detailed what he encountered: "Columbia was burned during the war, either by rebel soldiers or by Sherman's; some doubt seems to exist about that. As the city now stands, it is only a forest of blackened chimneys, surrounded by ashes and desolation."[20]

Interestingly, the Yorkville, South Carolina, paper predicted, "If [Bates] could pass these old chimneys and staring ruins in safety, he might expect to go on unmolested until the little flag he bore should kiss the father of the flags now waving over the Capitol in Washington."[21]

In early 1865, federal troops of General William Sherman marched toward South Carolina and reportedly "took particular delight . . . carrying the war to South Carolina." There is debate to this day as to which side's soldiers were responsible for the conflagration. A federal general said, "A drunken soldier with a musket in one hand and a match in the other is not a pleasant visitor to have about the house on a dark, windy night." Sherman avoided taking blame and wrote, "Though I never ordered it and never wished it, I have never shed any tears over the event, because I believe that it hastened what we all fought for, the end of the War."[22]

Despite destruction dealt upon their city, Columbia's citizens put aside the terror of war to welcome Bates. He wrote, "My reception . . . was just as cordial as in any of the others; but it seemed more so, from the fact that the city was in ruins as a consequence of the war. . . . There is a newspaper in town called the *Phoenix*. The name is most appropriate, for if there is one city on earth that needs a Phoenix to raise her once again from her ashes, it is Columbia."[23]

His comments regarding the *Columbia Phoenix* indicate his cultural awareness of Columbia, South Carolina. The *Phoenix*'s first issue was printed March 21, 1865, weeks after fires destroyed about one-third of the city. It proclaimed, "Our city shall spring, from her ashes, and our *Phoenix*, we hope and trust, shall announce the glorious rising! God save the state!"[24]

The month after the paper was founded, it divided into a daily paper called *Columbia Phoenix* and *Columbia Tri-weekly Phoenix* that was printed Tuesday, Thursday, and Saturday. In the ensuing months, the daily paper altered its name twice, settling on the *Daily Phoenix* in July 1865.[25]

Bates stayed in Columbia for four days, and contended that he, "verily believe I shook hands with every man in town."[26]

With his strained leg recovering to the point where he was able to continue his march, Bates decided upon March 23, 1868 as his departure date. The *Daily Phoenix* recorded, "Sergeant Bates resumes his walk tomorrow morning. We commend him to the people of the different towns through which he will pass."[27]

An Ohio publication printed a notice from Columbia saying, "Sergeant Bates left here this morning for Charlotte. He expected to arrive in Richmond on the ninth of April, and the capital on the 14th."[28]

A South Carolina journal offered, "Our people sincerely wish, as we ourselves do, that Sergeant Bates may succeed in showing a crazy North that the South are not, as they believe, savage Indians and graceless dogs. But our people seem to have the idea that there is no use in making a fuss about this matter. They wish Sergeant Bates well, and bid him welcome and God-speed on his way; but are slightly opposed to [making] him into a hero."[29]

Lastly, the Yorkville article added, "Suppose he . . . succeed? What then? Then, the madness of the North will still go on. If he fail? Then, the madness of the North will still go on."[30]

Bates Travels through South Carolina

GILBERT BATES LEFT COLUMBIA'S CONFINES AT 8:30 ON THE MORNING of March 23, according to Columbia's news source, the *Daily Phoenix*. He then made his way toward Winnsboro, South Carolina. He had marched down Main Street in Columbia and arrived at his destination of Winnsboro "about 6 o'clock in the afternoon." It was duly recorded that Bates was hampered as, "his ankle was somewhat swollen, and his progress materially impeded in consequence."[1]

The formation of Winnsboro took place when Richard Winn moved from Virginia to the location that would eventually become the settlement of Winnsboro. Located in the upper Piedmont Region of the state, Winnsboro is referred to as the "Charleston of the Upcountry." The village was chartered in 1785, and it gained a post office as Winnsborough in 1795. In 1829 the U.S. Post Office Department changed the municipality's name to Winnsboro. However, it would be 1832 before the town was incorporated. The town clock in Winnsboro is modeled after Philadelphia, Pennsylvania's Independence Hall and is considered to be the "longest continuously running town clock in America." An interesting perspective of Bates's visit to Winnsboro rests in the fact that Catherine Ladd, a contributor to the design of the Confederate flag, was a resident of the town.[2]

When Gilbert Bates arrived in Winnsboro, the *Daily Phoenix* announced the plans of the event. "Sergeant Bates will leave Nickerson's Hotel, on Monday next, the 23rd instant, at 10 o'clock and arrive in Winnsboro the same evening."[3]

Bates wrote about arriving in Winnsboro. He recalled, "The whole town were out to receive me. A delegation of Confederate soldiers met me a mile from the town and escorted me in. About seventy-five soldiers altogether entertained me in a most hospitable manner."[4]

A Confederate veteran sent for Bates. It was said that the former Confederate "was suffering from the effects of injuries received during the war, and was very near his end. He had sent for me, a Northern man, to express thoughts which lay nearest his heart. He spoke of the war, and the desolation which it had wrought, of the passion and hatred which it had engendered, and expressed the belief that the Northern people could not be aware of the true feelings of the South, otherwise they could not pursue their present policy of resentment and distrust."[5]

Bates felt kindness toward the man whose "whole existence seemed embittered by the sad condition of the country. He thanked me for my efforts to dispel the false impressions prevailing ill in the minds of the Northern people, and hoped that I would be successful." Bates expressed compassion: "The gratitude of that dying man more than repaid me for all the trouble I had undergone, for the separation from my family, for the long weary marches which I had made through rain and mud; it repaid me for all the dangers which I was constantly passing through, and for the scenes of suffering and distress which presented themselves daily before my eyes."[6]

Resolution to the tragedy of the ex-Confederate came soon. Bates remarked, "I left him, knowing that he must soon go to another world. But I felt sure that he was an honest, upright man, and had the best interest of the country at heart. I bade him goodbye in sadness. The news of his passing reached me soon after, and . . . was not unexpected. He has gone to a better world."[7]

Bates stated, "I do not believe that in the presence of the Father of the Universe, in Heaven above, the Northern hero and the Southern hero are still warring with each other . . . their spirits are as peaceful and calm as their bones which lie side by side on the battlefield. As the grass grows green over their graves . . . so their souls in the realms above pour forth harmonious praise, without discord, without hatred, in the perpetual concord of Heaven."[8]

On the morning of March 24, Bates left Winnsboro. When he reached a point some seven miles from the city limits, Bates noticed a man running toward him. The man caught Bates and spoke, "Sergeant, my name is John Vincent. You see I am an old man, but I served four years in the Confederate Army. I can assure you . . . all the Confederate soldiers are your friends. They are the friends of all the Northern soldiers who are true men and have magnanimity."[9]

The elderly Confederate veteran continued, "A great many of the Northern people, I fear, don't understand us. We are willing today to fight for the stars and stripes and the Constitution against any nation in the world. Just tell your friends that . . . and they won't think so badly of us. We are all Americans, and love the old flag, every one of us."[10]

Gilbert Bates received more positive comments as he approached the town of Chester, South Carolina. The town of Chester had gained a touch of notoriety following the arrest of Aaron Burr. As Burr was being transported to be tried for treason, he jumped from his horse at Chester and attempted, unsuccessfully, to escape.[11]

Bates had grown tremendously thirsty as he reached a point thirteen miles from Chester, and he soon noticed a man watering his mule. Bates asked the man for a drink; the man stared at Bates and then exclaimed, "By all the blessed saints, if here isn't Sergeant Bates . . . a drink of water . . . ye shall have it an' welcome." The man called his wife and explained to the lady what he knew about Bates. The couple, surnamed Duffy, not only fulfilled the request for water, but also insisted that Bates sit at their table for a meal. The visit included Bates and the Duffy couple sharing family information about each other. Bates remarked, "I partook of it with a relish and soon . . . left my friends who asked God's blessing on me, my wife, and family. There is nothing more hearty than Irish hospitality the world over."[12]

The progress Bates had made since leaving Columbia was recorded in the March 27, 1868, issue of the town's paper, the *Daily Phoenix*. The publication noted, "The Winnsboro and Chester papers state that Sergeant Bates was kindly received by the citizens of those places. In Winnsboro, he stopped with Mr. Marcus Brown, and in Chester at the Nicholson House."[13]

A short distance from the Duffy home, Bates ran into a group of young boys who were near a creek. The boys informed Bates that he was about six miles from Rock Hill, South Carolina. They also told Bates that, if he desired, he would be able to find employment in Rock Hill. Bates reached Rock Hill at five o'clock that afternoon.[14]

Rock Hill had been formed in 1852 as a watering station and depot on the Charlotte and South Carolina Railroad. When the construction supervisor made notations on his map, he noted a spot where a small, flinty knoll intercepted a road leading to the community. Rock Hill is the largest city in York County and rests south of the North Carolina border.[15]

As he had done several times previously, Bates obtained a welcome from a large crowd. Bates was also given a serenade the evening of his arrival. The following morning, he met an elderly gentleman named Mathews. Aside from losing two children in the American Civil War, Mathews had served with his children in the Confederate army. Mr. Mathews insisted that he walk with Bates the following morning, at which time Bates planned to depart from Rock Hill.[16]

Mathews informed Bates of a bridge spanning the Catawba River. Mathews felt that the structural soundness of the bridge, largely destroyed during the War Between the States, had been compromised and could possibly lead to Bates being injured. Bates wrote of Mathews, "He took me by the hand and led me across the bridge as if I were blind. This is but one of the many instances in which I was shown such parental tenderness."[17]

Once Mathews led Bates across the bridge, he left Bates to continue the march alone. According to Bates, a short time after he had resumed his march, he arrived in Fort Mill, South Carolina. Twenty-five Confederate soldiers met Bates at Fort Mill, and they "informed me that they had assembled to give the flag an escort out of South Carolina into North Carolina."[18]

Fort Mill, South Carolina, which Bates called Fort Mills, was founded in the mid-1700s through the efforts of Thomas Spratt. The Catawba Indian territory, some 4,535 acres, was given to Spratt in appreciation for his part in pushing the Shawnee Indians from their land. The town went through names such as Little York, Fort Hill, and then Fort Mill. In 1811, a post office was established, and twenty-two years later the latter name appeared. Reportedly, a colonial-era British fort and a grist mill provided the eventual name. Historically, Fort Mill was the location of the last meeting of the Confederate presidential cabinet on April 27, 1865.[19]

Bates continued his recollections regarding his exodus from South Carolina, "I gave my consent very readily. The procession was formed, and we started for the boundary line ... about six miles distant. A strong breeze was blowing at the time, and I entered the state of North Carolina with colors flying. As I crossed the line, the escort gave me three cheers."[20]

In a defiant tone, Bates concluded, "My friends in Wisconsin used to say that if I ever set foot in South Carolina, I would never come out again, unless it was in a coffin. If they could have heard those cheers, they would have given up all ideas about coffins."[21]

CHAPTER THIRTEEN

Bates Moves into North Carolina

GILBERT BATES'S FIRST SCHEDULED STOP IN NORTH CAROLINA WAS the city of Charlotte. In 1768, the area's early settlers had named the location after King George III's wife, Charlotte. Therefore, Charlotte was regularly referred to as the Queen City. Thirty-one years later, a boy named Conrad Reed found a seventeen-pound glittering rock, the first gold discovered in North America. Despite this event, railroads had a more significant impact upon the city's growth. A crossroads created with the junction of a rail line that ran from Charlotte to Columbia, South Carolina and another from Raleigh, North Carolina to Charlotte made the location "a hot spot . . . from 1861 to 1865." Ironwork and cannon manufacturing were dominant industries of the period, and Confederate president Jefferson Davis held his last full cabinet meeting in the town.[1]

As for North Carolina, it held several sites of military engagements from the Civil War. Bentonville, Fort Fisher, Albemarle, Roanoke Island, and Fort Anderson were among the locations of varied numbers of battle casualties. Additionally, from a non-slave population of approximately 662,000, North Carolina had supplied 155,000 troops to the Confederate States of America; some 40,000 of those were killed during the war. By contrast, an estimated 49,000 North Carolinians served the various branches of the military of the United States during the conflict.[2] Those facts greeted Bates as he entered the state some three years after the war.

Gilbert Bates arrived in the Queen City at three o'clock in the afternoon. The mayor and city council members met Bates on the outskirts of the city; the mayor then made remarks about Bates and "tendered me the hospitalities of the city." Bates took a carriage to the Mansion House, where a dry goods store occupied the lower floor. Buxbaum and Lang, a merchant partnership, carried clothing articles that were advertised as having prices "as low as any merchant in this city." Interestingly, Buxbaum and Lang also advertised that their business, a corner store, was located "under Mansion House."[3]

Bates wrote about the experience, "Several hundred people had assembled in front of the hotel, and, as I sprang out of the carriage, before entering, Mr. James Gleason, a war-worn veteran of the Confederate Army, who is still suffering from his wounds, proposed three cheers." The cheers Gleason solicited were for Bates, the U.S. flag, and "the white man's government." Bates recalled the cheers as "rousing."[4]

Needing a new pair of shoes, Bates remained in town for those to be made. As he waited, Bates estimated that "everybody called to see me, and among the number several prominent Confederate officers."[5] Once again, the mission Bates had set while making his sojourn across the South had yielded positive results.

He also added, "Late in the afternoon of March 27th, a young man, James Orr, called to see me, with a small bundle in his hand. He said he had been a soldier in Lee's Army . . . he held in his hand a United States flag, belonging to the headquarters of a corps . . . captured by . . . the Southern army." The Confederate veteran informed Bates that hard fighting and many lost lives had been spent in acquiring the flag, but that he felt that Bates had now "recaptured it."[6]

James Orr said, "Sergeant, without firing a gun, it is yours, sir; take it." Bates recalled, "He then explained . . . that the flag had been placed among the archives of the rebel government as a trophy. But when those archives were scattered, after the fall of Richmond, he obtained possession of the flag. [He] now presented it to me as a trophy of my peaceful triumph."[7]

Following his visit with the Confederate in Charlotte, Bates walked to his next destination, Concord, North Carolina. The history of Concord contains an interesting aspect from the late 1700s. German and Scots-Irish area settlements had disagreed as to where the seat for a recently formed county should be located. In 1796, the resulting compromise created a twenty-six-acre site that became known as Concord. The name, indicating the spirit of the settlement, can be defined as "harmony."[8] This name in itself epitomizes the efforts of Gilbert Bates.

Gilbert Bates reached Concord on March 28, 1868. Bates was again welcomed into a city with a group of citizens and the mayor outside of town. He noted, "As I approached the city limits . . . bells commenced ringing, and rang a joyous peal as I walked up to the Court House. . . . The mayor made a little speech. . . . I was shown my room at the hotel, and received numerous calls."[9]

Bates added, "At night, they gave me a serenade, and called me out for a speech. I responded to the best of my ability; several of the party followed, and our meeting was prolonged an hour and a half. The next day being Sunday, I was very reluctant to set out, and should not have done so, but for the reason that the newspapers had announced me at certain places on the route."[10]

In attempting to keep his media image positive, Bates concluded, "Moreover, if I had not kept the appointments, some paper would have accused me of trying to elude someone who wanted a shot at me."[11]

Bates left Concord, and recalled, "Within three miles of Salisbury, I was met by a large crowd of persons. . . . From that point all the way in the city, the road was lined on both sides by people . . . assembled . . . to witness my approach. About a mile from the city, the Mayor met me."[12]

Bates remarked, "The city had surrendered to my banner without terms . . . preparations had been made . . . [for] my arrival, and that I would find everything in readiness for me at the Boyden House." Bates entered his room and found a bouquet of flowers, a present from a local lady. He remarked, "Nothing could have been more cordial than my reception in this place."[13]

A colonial assembly established Salisbury in 1753. From its beginning as Rowan Court House, the settlement was the county seat of Rowan County, and in 1755 the name was changed to Salisbury. The original town layout was much like that of Philadelphia, Pennsylvania, with a gridiron street system, open spaces, and setbacks for buildings. A boost in growth occurred with the North Carolina Railroad's arrival in 1855, and industry and commercial enterprises appeared along the rails.

Salisbury gained a reputation as the "economic and political center of western North Carolina" during the 1800s. The arrival of the American Civil War created the establishment of a federal prisoner-of-war camp in Salisbury, the only such location in the state. Overcrowding and "poor sanitation of the prison led to a death rate of over 25%."[14]

Salisbury had fallen under federal occupation by early 1865. Near that timeframe, Thomas Howerton, the proprietor of the Boyden House for fifteen years, decided to retire. A January 8, 1866, issue of *Carolina Watchman*, a Salisbury newspaper, published an ad notifying the public that Calvin Scott Brown had leased the late Boyden House and planned to reopen it as Brown's Hotel. Calvin Scott Brown said, "I am now having it thoroughly repaired, determined that it shall be second to no Hotel in North Carolina. . . . My table will be supplied with the best provisions that this market will afford, besides oysters, fish and game." The Boyden House, or Brown's Hotel, often entertained the most influential Salisbury visitors such as former Confederate major general Robert Hoke, general D. H. Hill, and Robert Edward Lee.[15]

Bates did not write any comments about the remainder of his stay or his departure from Salisbury. He left the Boyden House, determined to reach Thomasville, North Carolina. His primary comment about Thomasville was that it "is not a large place."[16]

A brief history of Thomasville was written in 1921 by Mrs. John T. Cramer, the daughter of the town's founder, John Thomas. Mrs. Cramer wrote that her father left the state senate after offering his strong support of the surveying of the North Carolina Railroad, and founded the settlement with four hundred acres. Thomas built the town's first store in 1852, and he established a college in 1856. Mrs. Cramer wrote, "In 1861, the great Civil War began, demoralizing everybody. . . . Thomasville furnished a company, and the ladies made the uniforms. . . . Times were hard . . . but thanks to my mother we escaped much."[17]

Wounded warriors from the Battle of Bentonville were taken to Thomasville in large numbers, and soon a group of federal soldiers, as well as a band under the leadership of Jack Leland, from Cleveland, Ohio, camped in and around the Thomas yard. The effects of war were numerous; among the most noticeable was the decreased population. In 1860,

Thomasville had a population of 308. When the war ended, the number had declined to 217.[18]

The postwar population certainly coincides with the comment Bates made regarding the size of Thomasville. However, he went on to say, "When I was about two miles distant from it, quite a crowd of people . . . with a brass band, met me. They gave three hearty cheers for the Sergeant and the United States flag, and at once formed in procession to act as an escort."[19]

Bates added, "The band struck up a . . . tune, and we marched into the town. Quarters had been provided for me at the house of Mrs. Taylor. That night I was serenaded again. I dare say it was the same band which discoursed the music. The next morning, I set out, accompanied for a mile or more by numbers of people, and the brass band once again supplied the music."[20]

For his final comments on the unity exhibited in Thomasville, Bates uttered, "In passing the Female Institute, any quantity of flowers was offered me, many more than I could hold in my hands with comfort. The ladies waved their handkerchiefs and wished me God speed."[21]

The school for girls that Bates mentioned was Thomasville Female College. The college began in 1856, when John W. Thomas purchased the Glen Anna Female Seminary and moved it into a new building north of the railroad on the eastern edge of his land. Thomas also served as president of the school. The 1857 graduating class consisted of five women, but the American Civil War negatively affected the ability of the institution to stay afloat.[22]

An informative aspect of the life of Thomasville Female College, which closed in the late 1800s, comes from an 1861 letter Thomas wrote to a prospective student's father. The cost of the institute was described as "Board and washing, $25 for session; Tuition in English, $7.50 for session; Music, $8 for session; French, $4 for session; Latin, $4 for session."[23] It is reasonable to assume that the students Bates witnessed paid similar costs to those Mr. Thomas detailed.

Sergeant Gilbert Henderson Bates.

Bates displaying a flag such as
he carried across the South.

SERGEANT BATES.

Published by E. & H. T. Anthony & Co., 591 Broadway, N. Y.

Entered according to Act of Congress, in the year 1872, by E. & H. T. Anthony & Co., in the
office of the Librarian of Congress at Washington.

SERGEANT BATES.

Entered according to Act of Congress, June, 1868.

SERGEANT BATES.

Published by E. & H. T. Anthony & Co., 591 Broadway, N.Y.

Entered according to Act of Congress, in the year 1872, by
E. & H. T. Anthony & Co., in the office of the Librarian of
Congress at Washington.

Bates, four years after his Southern walk, was photographed in New York.

This 1868 image shows Bates as he appeared at the time of his Southern trek.

Vicksburg, circa 1860. This is one of the earliest known views of the Hill City.

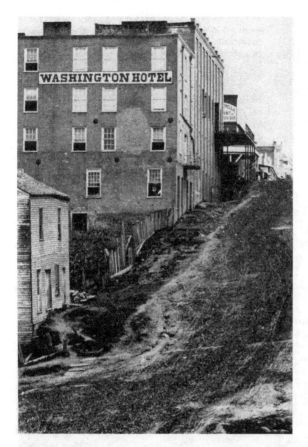

This view of Vicksburg's China Street displays the Washington Hotel, a location where Bates stayed while visiting the city, circa 1876.

The Grant/Pemberton Monument at Vicksburg National Military Park.

Mark Twain, the famous humorist, wrote negatively of Bates and his proposed march for unity.

This June 20, 1863, *Harper's Weekly* print shows the raising of the Stars and Stripes over the state capitol in Jackson, Mississippi, during the Civil War.

Andrew Barry Moore was Alabama's governor at the onset of the American Civil War.

Lewis Eliphalet Parsons served as the governor of Alabama during the final stages of the war.

The Alabama capitol building, located in Montgomery.

General James Holt Clanton visited with Bates. The former Confederate officer died an untimely death in Tennessee in the early 1870s.

[CITY OF COLUMBUS, GEORGIA.—Sketched by Theodore R. Davis.—[See Page 597.]

Columbus, Georgia, as shown in this sketch from the September 19, 1868, issue of *Harper's Weekly.*

Planters Hotel in Augusta, Georgia, circa 1875.

The ruins of Columbia, South Carolina.

BOYDEN HOUSE,

Mrs. Dr. REEVES, Proprietress.

Salisbury, N. C.

Bates visited the Boyden House in Salisbury, North Carolina.

William Woods Holden was a counterpart of Bates.

The state capitol in Raleigh, North Carolina.

North Carolina governor Jonathan Worth.

The Exchange Hotel in Richmond, Virginia, offered Bates a brief respite from his travels.

Bates visited Libby Prison, one of the most notorious such locations of the War Between the States.

Bates was shown Tredegar Ironworks, the site of Confederate armaments production.

The state capitol in Richmond, Virginia.

Bates paid homage to Confederate General Thomas J. "Stonewall" Jackson by visiting this Guinea Station house where the officer died.

The Mansion House was another location Bates visited.

SERGEANT BATES WITH THE FLAG PASSING THROUGH RICHMOND.—[SKETCHED BY W. L. SHEPPARD.]

This 1868 *Harper's Weekly* drawing indicates the pomp and circumstance surrounding Bates arriving in Richmond.

Bates Visits Greensboro
and Raleigh, North Carolina

As Bates progressed from Thomasville, his next destination was Greensboro, North Carolina. He noted that as he approached the city limits of Greensboro, "a great crowd of people, male and female, black and white, with the Mayor at their head, welcomed me as a guest of the city. The band played a march, and we moved on through the streets to the hotel, where rooms had been provided for me."[1]

Ironically, while Bates was in Greensboro, he met and visited with a group who had a distinct characteristic from the vast majority of people with whom he had recently visited. Bates elaborated, "I met quite a number of Wisconsin men: Col. John Crane of the 18th Wisconsin Infantry; Col. Thos. B. Keogh, of Milwaukee; P. F. Duffy, of Lafayette County, Wisconsin, and several other men who had been soldiers in the Union army.... Our meeting was very pleasant."[2]

Although the city of Greensboro was named in honor of General Nathaniel Greene, it never had the third *e* in its name. Originally spelled Greensborough, the settlement owes its existence to a $98.00 purchase of forty-two acres from Saura Indians. The town grew slowly after its 1808 founding; only 369 people lived there by 1821. Rail lines and textile mills provided livelihoods for many of its residents, but the population reached only 497 in the 1870 census.[3]

There are several sites that Bates may have seen during his time in Greensboro. Some of those related to the war in which he served include the Ralph Gorrell home, which served as General Joseph Johnston's headquarters while his Confederates were in Greensboro. Another historic location is related to Johnston; he stood near the railroad overpass near East McGee and South Elm Streets while delivering his farewell address to his troops. A residence that was once located in the 300 block of South Elm Street was where Johnston and General P. G. T. Beauregard met with Jefferson Davis on April 13, 1865. In that home, Johnston informed Davis that there was no hope for the Confederate military, and Davis ordered Johnston to meet with Federal General William Tecumseh Sherman to seek peace. The Britton Hotel, at 116 West Market, served as the parole issuance site for the Confederates after their surrender. In addition, 300 unknown soldiers, casualties from the Battle of Bentonville, are buried in Green Hill Cemetery.[4]

Lastly, in relation to Greensboro sites Bates likely witnessed, J&F Garrett & Company, manufacturers of the Tarpley breech-loading carbine, had a factory at 322 East Washington Street. The facility only produced a few hundred of the weapons because a gap between the barrel and the breech lock grew wider with each shot, causing safety and performance issues with the gun.[5]

At Greensboro, Bates once again ran into pressure from the Union League South. He recalled, "At Greensboro . . . I was offered $10,000 which I was to receive, provided I would stop the march and go home, I was to do it apparently in disgust, and in the interests of the Republican Party. The offer came from W. W. Holden, of [North Carolina]."[6]

Bates went on to say, "Although a poor man, nevertheless neither myself nor the flag I carried was for sale. On my way through North Carolina, I was informed by members of the League that the organization in the state was already powerful and was growing more so at a rapid rate; that Governor Holden was at the head of the League, and that they were guided in all political matters by him."[7]

William Woods Holden was born an illegitimate child in Hillsborough, North Carolina, in 1818. He had little education but managed to hone his reading and writing skills while serving as apprentice to a newspaper editor. He later earned a law degree, yet Holden left that profession to enter the newspaper vocation full-time. Holden later entered politics and served two terms as North Carolina governor. At the time Bates visited North Carolina, Holden was between terms.[8]

A June 1865 article from *Western Democrat* hailed Holden's ability to serve as governor shortly before his provisional term, as an appointee of President Andrew Johnson, began. A portion of the write-up said, "We know that Mr. Holden has the ability to discharge the duties of Governor creditably, and we believe he has the influence with the national Administration which will enable him to do much toward ameliorating the condition of the people of North Carolina."[9]

By late June 1865, Holden had issued the following, "Whereas, by the Proclamation of Andrew Johnson . . . I have been appointed Provisional Governor of the State of North Carolina . . . to prescribe, at the earliest practicable period, such rules and regulations . . . for convening a Convention . . . for the purpose of altering or amending the Constitution . . . to restore said State to its Constitutional relations to the Federal government."[10]

The allegations against Holden were reinforced in an article written a couple of weeks after Bates visited. The commentary offered, "The President of the Union League for North Carolina has organized a league of the negro women. . . . The manner in which the heads of the league accomplished their purposes . . . is fitfully characteristic of W.W. Holden. It is done by lying and gross deception."[11]

Bates found a desire to break away from his itinerary while in Greensboro. He detailed, "I determined to take a ride to Raleigh, although that city lay outside my line of march. My plan was to take the cars for Raleigh, make my visit there, return to Greensboro, and resume my journey on foot . . . on the first day of April, I took the train for Raleigh."[12]

The history of Raleigh, North Carolina, can be traced to the "Lost Colony," where Virginia Dare was born and the colony's settlers disappeared with only the word "Croatoan" as evidence. The city that Bates would visit approximately three hundred years later is located some two hundred miles from the colonial tragedy. In 1792, after years of discussion and debate, the modern-day Raleigh was named and selected as the new state capital. By 1800, the population approached 700 people, and, in

1820, that number had increased to 2,674, making Raleigh North Carolina's third largest city. In 1860, Raleigh fell one spot in rank of citizens among North Carolina cities with a population of 4,780.[13]

The North Carolina Secession Convention was held in the state Capitol in May 1861. It was noted that Raleigh "served as the center of Confederate power" in the state, while the daughters of two future Confederate generals, Robert Edward Lee and Leonidas Polk, were educated at St. Mary's School in the city. During the war, Raleigh was a Confederate supply center, and three Confederate hospitals were located in the confines of the urban area. In addition, Camp Mangum sat in the city and served as the training site for thousands of men in gray.[14]

From the standpoint of devastation, Raleigh was able to avoid any major conflict throughout most of the war. Skirmishes took place when General William Tecumseh Sherman's troops reached the area in 1865. On April 12, 1865, Governor Zebulon Baird Vance sent a commission that included two former North Carolina governors to meet with Sherman to offer the surrender of Raleigh. The surrender took place the next day, as did the promise that the town would be spared the destruction Columbia, South Carolina and other areas had suffered.[15]

Following the assassination of President Abraham Lincoln, Federal troops in Raleigh planned retaliation by storming through the city. General John Logan threatened his own troops by having gun emplacements pointed at them. That movement negated the threat upon Raleigh. Two weeks after the surrender of the city of Raleigh, General Sherman met Confederate general Joseph Johnston at the Federal headquarters in Raleigh. The Bennett Place, a small farmhouse in nearby Durham, a settlement located between Raleigh and Greensboro, served as the site of their meeting to sign the agreement to officially end the war.[16]

Bates recalled that at every station along the route he used to reach Raleigh, "crowds were gathered to catch a glimpse of me and my little flag; and when we reached Raleigh, I found an immense assemblage about the depot."[17]

The *Daily Phoenix* of Charleston, South Carolina, also reported the reception of Gilbert Bates in noting, "Sergeant Bates . . . seems to have nearly finished his task, having arrived safely in Raleigh, North Carolina

... the old soldier had received marked demonstrations of respect, courtesy and hospitality from the Southern people all along the line of his extended march."[18]

The article also proposed, "It is not surprising ... to find a radical journal endeavoring to injure the military record of Sergeant Bates when in the United States Army, and to represent that he was rather an indifferent soldier. If it were true, it in no wise diminishes the significance of the fact that the flag has traveled through the whole South and been respected."[19]

Bates ate at a Raleigh hotel before being given a tour of the city. In addition to visiting public buildings, Bates was the guest of a Mr. Betts, who took him to the state house. One of the individuals with whom Bates was able to speak was Governor Jonathan Worth. The thirty-ninth governor of North Carolina, Worth was born in Guilford County, North Carolina in 1802. A Quaker, Worth was the oldest of twelve children. He served in various government posts from 1830 until removed as governor by military decree three months after Bates visited.[20]

Concerning his dialog with Governor Worth and the remainder of his day, Bates penned, "After half an hour's conversation, we took our leave of him, and visited the other public buildings in the city. At five o'clock p.m., I took the train for Greensboro. At every station there were more people collected about the depots than in the morning."[21]

At one point during his return trip, Bates was able to converse with a crowd of fifty schoolboys who had gathered to see him and his flag. When Bates had the flag brought from the railcar, "They cheered. . . . One of the boys said, 'I have seen that flag before.' Some of the boys had served in the army during the war, and one of them, only fifteen . . . years of age, had lost a leg."[22]

Bates was uplifted when one boy said, "Sergeant, we would fight for that flag as quick as you would, but you folks up North don't believe it, do you? . . . Now come right out and say what you think, do the Northern people believe we would fight for the flag?"[23]

In an attempt to satisfactorily answer the boys, Bates said, "there are many people in the North who still . . . believe that you hate the flag, and would do nothing to defend it . . . they do not know your true sentiments. They have been misled by bad men and bad newspapers."[24]

Bates held the opinion that he "never saw a finer set of boys." His feelings were reinforced when the boys waved their hats and cheered as the train moved toward Greensboro.[25]

April 2, 1868, was the date Bates had planned to leave Greensboro. He explained the change: "Several Confederate soldiers insisted on my remaining and spending the day with them. All the unpleasant memories of the war were dropped; the verdict of battle was recognized by all; no one suggested that any attempt ought ever to be made to reverse that verdict."[26]

The Confederates collectively claimed, "We all felt that we were citizens of one country, that the future which lay before us always find us citizens of one country, inseparably united. Each one felt that it was his duty to become reconciled and bury forever the angry passions of the past, and the sectional antagonism which had become almost hereditary."[27]

One Confederate veteran added additional support to Bates: "Those men, whose manhood has been tested on the battlefield, have no desire to renew bloody conflict. . . . If the settlement of the reconstruction question had been left to the soldier on the battlefield, in the hour of triumph, it would have been arranged amicably, justly, and magnanimously."[28]

Exhibiting his disgust of bureaucracy, the Confederate veteran added, "The petty spite of some politicians, the inveterate hatred of others, and the wild utopian schemes of others, have kept the country divided, and have prevented a reunion of the people, which was spontaneous and almost irrepressible at the close of the war. Against them let the evils of the past three years be directed, for they lie to their charge."[29]

Having had insightful conversations with numerous individuals and groups of the Greensboro and Raleigh areas in recent days, Gilbert Bates restarted his march on April 3, 1868.

The dichotomy of the conditions and mindset of those around him was duly recorded: "I resumed . . . marching through mud and rain. The bad weather made no difference in the warmth of the reception extended me by the people. In every village, town, and hamlet on my route, a crowd of persons were always assembled to welcome me and my flag."[30]

Bates met Governor Holden at Reedsville, North Carolina. During this final act of association with anyone from North Carolina, Bates noted, "Our interview lasted half an hour."[31]

Although highly motivated and having primarily been shown an overwhelming level of support, the meeting with Governor Holden, noted earlier as having included a push for Bates to end his march, partially altered the positive mindset Bates had held. Bates wrote, "I soon took my departure, and walked towards the Virginia State line. Virginia, the 'Mother of Presidents' and the 'Mother of States.' I crossed the line. Only one state lay between me and my journey's end. With renewed vigor I pressed forward."[32]

Chapter Fifteen

Bates Reaches Virginia

Gilbert Henderson Bates arrived in Danville, Virginia, at 4:00 p.m. on April 4, 1868. He mentioned a great crowd of people, as well as a band, gave him a reception that was largely identical to those he "had met with at all other cities, and need not be described more minutely."[1]

Before Danville was settled, the area served as the home for various Native Americans for hundreds of years. A twenty-man expedition explored the area in 1728 and, for an unknown reason, named a nearby river "Dan." In 1793, Virginia's General Assembly formed a tobacco inspection station at the site, known by then as Wynne's Falls. Later that year, the village that had evolved was renamed Danville. A post office was established in the town in 1800, and the area received a charter in 1830. Six years later, the population had increased to almost one thousand. In addition, after some six years of construction, the Richmond and Danville Railroad was completed in 1856. The 140-mile line drastically affected the future of Danville.[2]

Tobacco continued to be a major aspect of Danville's existence, and the reputation of the town led to its designation as the "World's Best Tobacco Market." That product, along with the Richmond and Danville Railroad, contributed to Danville serving as an important location during the American Civil War. In the 1860 census, at the eve of the Civil War, Danville was recorded as having approximately 3,500 citizens.[3]

Many sons of Danville, Virginia served in the War Between the States, and the town became a major supply "connection to Richmond." A local church donated its bell to be melted down to make a cannon for the Confederate artillery. Food, clothing, armaments, and medicines were sent through Danville to the Army of Northern Virginia. An armory and hospitals, housed within buildings that had served as tobacco facilities before the war, also occupied the community's landscape during the conflict. When the wounded from engagements such as Seven Days' Battles and the Peninsula Campaign burdened Richmond's hospitals, Danville became a standby site. At the suggestion of General Robert Edward Lee, Danville also obliged the need for prisoner-of-war facilities.[4]

Danville also served as a significant site in the final days of the Confederate States of America. In early April 1865, General Lee informed Jefferson Davis that he was unable to hold Petersburg, a fact that clearly endangered Richmond, the Confederate capital. Following a hurried move, Danville served as the Confederacy's last capital for one week, April 4–10, 1865.[5]

Leaving Danville, Bates expressed a level of disgust regarding the attention his march had caused. He transcribed, "Continual marching, in all sorts of weather, was beginning to wear on me. My foot and ankle became swollen and painful, and caused me no little trouble in walking. Knowing that I was announced at all the cities for certain days, it became necessary for me to keep up."[6]

While Bates did not mention marching through Pittsville, Virginia, a poorly spelled article titled "Sergeant Bates at Pettusville, Va.—Mr. Nasby Is Present When He Arrives" seems to indicate just such an event. Pittsville is located in the Danville metropolitan area and has the potential of being the community of which the article's author, Petroleum V. Nasby, spoke. In 1860, Pittsylvania County, of which the aforementioned village was a part, had a population of 32,104. That number had decreased to 31,343 with the 1870 census.[7] However, if the name of the Virginia town of which Nasby wrote was conjured in his mind, there is little need to adhere to the content of his article.

Petroleum Vesuvius Nasby, often noted as Petroleum V. Nasby, was the pseudonym for David Ross Locke, a New York–born editor who held a strong pro-Union stance and was said to have been a favorite war columnist of Abraham Lincoln. Locke gained fame while writing for his Ohio newspaper. He often wrote his stories from the viewpoint of a highly illiterate Southerner.[8] This practice was the case in Locke/Nasby's article related to Bates.

The satirist, in non-standard English, noted, "It okkured to me that it would be a payin invest ment ef I shood go out to Pettusville, wich is a beautiful village containin one dry goods store and 13 fooid groseries, sitooated about sixty miles from [Richmond] and witness the reception that shood be given him. Wat transpired thrilled me; in fact I never felt sich a thrill uv joy in my life ez I did when I saw this battle-scared veteran."[9]

Nasby added,

> *The devosiun to the old flag, wich a site uv it stirred up in the breasts uv the people uv Pettusville, reely surprised me. Never shel I forget the site that met my eyes. The Sergeant wuz met three miles out uv town, by a perceshun wich accompanied him in, marchin in the following order: Band, playin "The Bonny Bloo Flag"; Detachment of the Pettusville Avengers made up uv soljers wich formely served in the 13th Virginia . . . Detachment uv the Pettusville Cadets, made up of sons uv Confedrit soljers who wuz killed in the servis, with black banners, onto wich wuz inscribed, "We will avenge our slain sires."[10]*

Telling more about the parade formation, Nasby mentioned "Four survivors uv the late unpleasantnis, carryin each a flag capcheered from Wisconsin regiments. Ban playing Dixie. Citizens on foot and hossback and in carts."[11]

The reception for Bates, according to Nasby, the humorist, included,

> *The Mayor . . . and the town clerk . . . and the procession stopped, while the formalities wuz gone through with. The Mayor received the Seargeant in these words: "Understanding that ez we do, that yoo chivalrously made a wager . . . with a Wisconsin ablishnist that yoo cood walk from Vicksburg to Washinton . . . is entirely satisfactory to us, that yoo are not in no sense, nor never wuz at any time, in sympathy with the Ablishen or ez they falsely style theirselves, the Republican party, we extend too yoo the hospitalities uv Pettusville."[12]*

The mayor expressed more:

Yoor exyeaience hez showd how falsely we hev bin judged by the crooel persekooters uv the Northern States. You hev bin met on evry hand with nuthin but kindness. Southern hospitality uv the broadest kind hez bin extended to yoo. Yoo hev hed a chaw off uv evry plug . . . yoor nose shows that sense yoo entered the Sunny South you have not bin aliowed to taste water, wich is our idee uv hospitable treatment. Wat does it prove? . . . 'taint the fla we object to so much ez it is the men who hev bin in the habit uv carrying it.[13]

Additional words from the Mayor toward Bates included,

In yoor hands, and the hands uv sich ez you, the flag is to as the old flag it wuz then, and its sacred to us becoz under it we cood do all these things. . . . Hed it remained sich we never wood hev raised our hands agin it. . . . It meant freedom for us . . . But when the North dispooted our control uv it and put it in the hands uv A. Linkin, an Ablishunist, it wuz our flag no more. Then we felt it must come down . . . its mission wuz ended and that to us it wuz nothin.[14]

The mayor added that he had not only raised his hand against the U.S. flag, but he also said that he fired onto it. The ceremony was briefly interrupted at that time as a shot fired from a nearby funeral procession led to a quick investigation.[15]

Bates, or so Nasby claimed, briefly replied to all of the comments, adding that he had, indeed, been treated kindly throughout most of his journey. The procession resumed its walk, and the group made its way to the town hall, where, according to Petroleum Nasby, "Sergeant wuz interdoost to the principal citizens, including the officer uv the Ku Klux Klan." Those in attendance were willing to express their affection for the U.S. flag.[16] Nasby noted, "I notist soljers in the service uv the late Confederacy, who kist it in the fervor of their devoshun. One man, who had served four years in Forrest's command, wept, ez his eyes lit onto it, and he remarkt that it wuz the happiest moment uv his life; and a lady, the wife of an ex-kernel uv Lee's, whose buzzum wuz decorated with a pin made from a Federal soljer's skull, kist the corner uv it, persistin that it wuz deerer to her than life."[17] With that, the event Bates had encountered during his departure from Danville concluded.

A Richmond newspaper exclaimed that Bates was traveling the Danville Road and had made a short appearance at the Clover Depot. In turn, according to the report, "he expected to reach Amelia Courthouse .. . at 5:40 o'clock he passed through Burkville, stopping for dinner. He was then in good spirits, and started off at a good pace, although still suffering from a swollen leg, injured by a fall through a bridge."[18]

On April 7, 1868, Bates, after what he termed "a forced march," reached Amelia Court House. His journal reads, "I arrived at 11 o'clock at night, in the rain. I found Mrs. Joseph Cance awaiting my arrival. Her house was illuminated, and every one of the family was up. Mrs. Cance had stationed a 'lookout' on the road to watch for me and conduct me to the house. On entering, I learned to my surprise that a sumptuous supper was prepared for me."[19]

Joseph Cance's name appeared in a July 17, 1861, issue of the *Daily Dispatch* in Richmond, Virginia. It was announced that Cance would be entering a bakery partnership with George Hundley and that the business would regularly stock green and black teas, spices, tobacco, and candles. An October 24, 1864, edition of the same publication noted that Cance was seeking an exemption to serve in the Confederate military, as his "plea is based upon the fact of his being an undomiciled foreigner." A postwar article noted that Cance's bakery was the scene of an assault, and Cance was willing to "become the surety" of one of the involved parties.[20]

Joseph Cance joined four other bakers in providing goods for a July 4, 1866, celebration that was touted in a Richmond daily newspaper. Sadly, misfortune appears to have beset Cance; three consecutive issues of a local publication contained a notice from Davis and Moise, Attorneys at Law. They noted that Cance's books, notes, and accounts had been placed in their care, and individuals with any debts to Cance should report to the legal firm immediately. On July 26, 1867, at the request of Cance, his bakery was to be auctioned. By February 1868, Cance was being notified in his local paper that he had failed to retrieve his mail from the post office.[21]

The next mention of the Cance name was far more positive, as the *Daily Dispatch* remarked, "On his [Bates's] arrival at Amelia Court House . . . Mrs. Joseph Cance gave him a fine supper, and had a hot breakfast prepared the next morning before his departure.[22]

As for his report of the hospitality of the Cance couple, Bates commented that he enjoyed a "sumptuous supper" that was provided for him. He went to bed after his meal, and Bates requested that he be awakened at 4:00 the next morning; that early departure was needed in order for him to make it to Richmond by the time he was expected. It is thought-provoking that Bates discovered the next morning that Mrs. Cance's servant "might not wake me at the right time;" in order to eliminate the issue, she stayed up all night "in order that there should be no mistake."[23]

Mrs. Joseph Cance had not only sat up all night to make certain that Bates was able to make his scheduled departure, but she also managed to prepare "an inviting breakfast" for him. Bates remarked he was unable to eat a single bite, as it was "so early in the morning." He then "bade my kind friends good-bye," and he set out for Richmond, Virginia.[24]

Amelia Court House, the town that Bates was leaving, had a great deal of history in relation to the war in which Bates had fought. Named for Amelia, the daughter of Great Britain's King George II, the village was settled in 1735. General Robert E. Lee, after leading his Confederates from Petersburg, spent April 4 and 5, 1865, in Amelia Court House waiting for supplies from Richmond. Those supplies never arrived. The last major engagement of Lee's army with Union forces, Sayler's or Sailor's Creek, occurred on April 6, 1865, on the border of Amelia County.[25]

Richmond and Beyond

THERE WAS AN ITINERARY PUBLISHED FOR THE BATES TRIP AS HE approached Richmond, and it said, "At 4 o'clock p.m., he will enter the city by the Danville Railroad, and those who wish to see him . . . had better be punctually on the ground, as he has reached all of his stopping places punctually at the hour announced. Whether he will go right on toward Washington, or spend the night here, he has not yet decided."[1]

Regarding Bates arriving in Richmond, "There seems to be . . . an entire misapprehension of the antecedents and purpose of Sergeant Bates. He is no money-making Yankee, or sportsman walking for a wager. So far as he is concerned, not one cent of money is at stake. . . . Without unnecessary parade, let us give Sergeant Bates a cordial welcome to the capital of Virginia."[2]

Despite encountering a menacing group who possessed shotguns and were "shooting . . . and lazily moving around from one place to another," and enduring a "foot [that] was paining me somewhat," Bates managed to cross the Richmond and Danville Railroad to enter Richmond at 4:00 p.m.[3]

A newspaper noted, "Sergeant Gilbert H. Bates . . . reached Richmond . . . at half-past 4 o'clock. There was a large crowd waiting both in Manchester and on this side [of] the river to welcome him, but owing to the uncertainty as to his route of entry, the people were divided between the three bridges which span the James."[4]

Unfortunately, Bates had entered Richmond on a route other than what was expected. Therefore, "they . . . assembled at a bridge further down to receive me. It . . . became known where I was, and the people crowded . . . me by the hundreds . . . constantly . . . increasing in numbers."[5]

A reporter wrote, "the crowd was composed almost entirely of white persons . . . a number of ladies were present. After crossing the bridge, the pressure was so great about the Sergeant that his walk was greatly impeded . . . he struck out at a double-quick . . . flag unfurled."[6]

Bates added, "I pressed forward through them towards the Exchange Hotel. The further I advanced, the greater the crowd. It was no easy matter to work my way through the thousands who thronged the streets . . . finally, I succeeded in reaching the hotel. . . . I was shown my room."[7]

A write-up of Bates's arrival at the hotel mentioned, "He came to a halt at the Exchange Hotel, where Colonel Carrington and his courteous sons were prepared to give him an Old Virginia welcome. The crowd pressed in the hotel to such an extent that he was obliged to seek immediate refuge in his room."[8]

Prior to the Civil War, the Exchange Hotel, noted for its grand veranda and high-ceilinged parlors, was a suitable destination for those traveling on the Alexandria Railroad or the Virginia Central Railroad. In March 1862, the hotel treated its first of an estimated 70,000 patients who sought care during the war. An estimated seven hundred soldiers succumbed to their wounds and are buried on the grounds of the hotel.[9]

Richmond, Virginia, had served as the capital of the Confederate States of America after the brief tenure of Montgomery, Alabama as the same. Libby Prison and Belle Isle were two of the prisoner-of-war facilities of Richmond, a city that held an economy that was multifaceted. Tredegar Ironworks, a major facility that supplied ordnance and railroad iron, was a catalyst for the local economy. Other means of employment included grain milling and tobacco. The city had initially opposed secession, but Lincoln's call for 75,000 volunteers and his persistent push to resupply Fort Sumter led to Virginia leaving the United States.[10]

It was recorded that "Word of Virginia's secession produced jubilation in Richmond." In the view of many modern historians, Virginia seceding held significance for military, economic, and symbolic reasons. Richmond was located in close proximity to Washington, D.C., it was the "South's leading industrial city, an important transportation hub," and it held the largest population of any Southern state. However, as the war raged on, the rallying cry of "On to Richmond" became a motivating factor for the opposing Federal forces.[11]

Richmond's population exploded during the war. Groups of Confederate soldiers, laborers, politicians and their families, refugees, and journeymen made their ways into the confines of the Confederate capital. Sadly, "less savory sorts" such as spies, gamblers, and prostitutes flooded the city's establishments. Some 38,000 people were counted in the 1860 census for Richmond; 11,739 of those were slaves. Although no accurate citizenry count was conducted during the war, estimates ranging from 100,000 to 150,000 have been given for the number of people claiming Richmond residence by the end of the war.[12]

Fresh in the minds of those who had survived the influx of people and continued to call Richmond home were the facts that a major crime wave overwhelmed the small police force present in wartime Richmond, smallpox and other diseases ravaged the populace in 1862 and 1863, while the scarcity of food and fuel added to the misery level. Additionally, in 1863, the second full year of the war, prices were 700 percent higher than at the onset of the conflict. Sick and wounded soldiers and civilians flooded the hospitals of Richmond as well. Chimborazo Hospital, the largest in the Confederacy, treated an estimated 78,000 patients between 1861 and 1865.[13] As he had encountered in numerous locations in his previous layovers, Bates would be meeting people who held those mixed memories from a war not so distant in the past.

In Richmond, Gilbert Bates, fatigued and hungry, spent a short time in his Exchange Hotel room, unready for fellowship until he had rested and "taken my dinner." After eating, Bates "rode through the principal parts of the town," flag in hand.[14]

The fact that Bates sought respite from the crowd drew notice in a newspaper: "After an hour's rest . . . found it necessary to close the room door in order to keep back the host who were anxious to 'shake hands,' he entered a hack, in company with Major Vaughan of Montgomery, Ala., and Mr. Carrington of the Exchange Hotel, and drove to the Capitol Square."[15]

A major event of his Virginia visit occurred at this point: "I alighted at the eastern entrance of the Capitol grounds and marched through . . . ascended to the dome, and waved my flag over the city which was once the stronghold of the rebellion. Thousands of persons had gathered in the grounds and in the building."[16]

As Bates descended into the rotunda, he met hundreds of those who had gathered to show their support for the flag and him. The lack of cohesion and impartiality was shown in the words of Bates: "The Conservative members of the Convention, at that time in session, came into the rotunda and shook hands with me. The negroes and carpetbaggers were cross and sullen."[17]

It was added, "A crowd of nearly a thousand persons had assembled . . . many persons pressed up to grasp his hand; but . . . the Radical members of the Convention stood aloof."[18]

The *Daily Phoenix* noted, "In the Convention, a speaker refused to give way to allow Sergeant Bates to be invited on the floor, saying he did not wish to see the flag brought in under Copperhead auspices."[19]

The relatively short article in the April 9, 1868, issue of the *Daily Phoenix* reported the events from the early stages of time Bates spent in Richmond. It noted, "Sergeant Bates arrived this afternoon. . . . About 500 persons were at the bridge, awaiting his arrival. He went off in a brisk trot to the hotel, and at 6 o'clock appeared on the top of the Capitol and waved his flag to a large crowd."[20]

Bates left the rotunda and boarded his carriage for a short ride to his hotel. No other public activities were noted for that day, but Bates spent the following day visiting camps in the area and having his photograph taken. Meeting "the prominent men of the city on local and national affairs," Bates found a common thought pattern. He noted, "They all bore the same testimony. They were willing and anxious to return to the Union, but they hated military rule, and they detested Negro suffrage."[21]

The periodical proclaimed, "Many prominent citizens at once called and congratulated him . . . and expressed in kind terms their appreciation of the object of his tramp through the South."[22]

On April 10, 1868, Bates left Richmond, Virginia, "with reluctance, there of two days had been unusually pleasant. Everyone was kind to me."

An Alexandria, Virginia, newspaper, the *Alexandria Gazette*, abruptly noted, "He was to have left Richmond this morning, on his way to this city." Another explained that Bates had fallen through a bridge, and the resulting injury "lamed him, he will not leave for Washington till Friday morning."[23]

An update on the progress of Bates, as well as his time traveling from Richmond, included, "Sergeant Bates was to leave Richmond . . . but the inclement weather may have interrupted his program . . . via the track of the Richmond and Fredericksburg Railroad . . . to Alexandria, passing through Stafford C.H. Dumfries, and Occoquan. He will stop a short time at Mount Vernon."[24]

Bates arrived at Hanover Junction at 6:00 p.m. In the late 1600s, the area that had once been hunting grounds for Native Americans such as the Chickahominy and Pamunkey began serving as tobacco fields. In 1720, Hanover was officially formed and named for England's King George I, the Elector of Hannover, Germany, at the time of his ascension to the throne. The resulting settlement was eventually the location of the intersection of the Richmond, Fredericksburg, and Potomac and Virginia Central Railroads. Those lines played an integral role in supplying General Robert E. Lee's Confederates. Significant battlefields in the area include Gaines Mill, North Anna, Old Church, and Cold Harbor.[25]

In Hanover Junction, an invitation from Mr. Thomas W. Gill secured Gilbert Bates a room for the night of April 10, 1868. Bates made no comments about the accommodations, food, fellowship, or additional aspects of the visit with Mr. Gill. Bates left the following morning and "pressed forward through that terrible country, woods and undergrowth, and mud abounding in every direction." He also recalled that, on an infrequent basis, he met "some solitary man."[26]

At 5:00 p.m. on April 11, Bates reached Fredericksburg, Virginia. He recorded that when he arrived, he was "drenched with rain, bespattered with mud, and thoroughly fatigued."[27]

Fredericksburg, Virginia was formed in 1728, and was named for Frederick, Prince of Wales, King George II's son. Fredericksburg grew steadily and served as a port city on the Rappahannock River. Flour and grist mills combined to aid the economy of the town that had come to rely heavily upon canals rather than the railroads. The 1860 population of Fredericksburg was 5,022, but it had decreased to 4,046 by the 1870 census. Sadly, the city made its mark in history through a duo of battles, one in 1862 and another the following year. The former engagement resulted in total casualties of more than 18,000. In fact, with a majority of the Federal wounds and deaths sustained in the vicinity of Marye's Heights, Fredericksburg became one of the bloodiest conflicts of the American Civil War and "a crushing defeat for the Union." Makeshift hospitals filled Fredericksburg in the aftermath of the 1862 conflict, with homes and churches being utilized.[28]

While in the Fredericksburg area, Bates also managed to visit the house where Confederate general Thomas J. "Stonewall" Jackson died. Bates wrote about the admiration Jackson held among the people of the South: "The Southern people have a giant affection for the memory of this man. He was known to be a thoroughly honest and upright man, a good General, and as fearless as the bravest."[29]

Having suffered multiple wounds from friendly fire during the Chancellorsville Campaign, General Jackson had been carried to Guinea Station, Virginia. The effects of the amputation of his arm and pneumonia proved too much for the thirty-nine-year-old officer. An extremely religious man, Jackson died Sunday, May 10, 1863, after uttering, "Let us cross over the river and rest under the shade of the trees."[30]

Completing his visit at Guinea Station, Bates marched forward. The roads Bates encountered as he moved from Fredericksburg on April 12, 1868, hampered him in his planned progress. Bates wrote, "the mud deeper, the rain heavier, the streams had fewer bridges, and the weather much colder."[31]

Bates managed to devour a "cold dinner on the road and trudged on towards Dumfries." His arrival in Dumfries was mentioned in an article, "Sergeant Bates left Fredericksburg . . . and was to have reached this city at 4 o'clock this evening." In fact, Bates arrived in Dumfries at 6:00 p.m., following a day that had been "cheerless and cold." Bates was quick to point out, "Here again, I was heartily welcomed, and spent the night."[32]

The town of Dumfries, Virginia, began as a gristmill on Quantico Creek. Some sixty acres of land, located on the creek and named after

Dumfriesshire, Scotland, would serve as the foundation for the community. For approximately fifteen years, beginning in 1763, Dumfries
became a thriving port, but a shift from shipping tobacco from the area
lessened its importance. In 1837, Dumfries was described as "one of the
oldest towns in the United States . . . could boast of much commerce, but
. . . a variety of circumstances, like many old settlements, is now in a great
measure abandoned, and many of its excellent dwellings are in a state of
rapid decay."[33]

Leaving Dumfries on the morning of April 13, Bates marched
toward Alexandria. He remarked, "From the top of Johnson's Hill, I
looked across the country and across the broad Potomac towards Washington, and saw the grand, white, beautiful dome of the Capitol rising
upon my sight, reposing so majestically like a snowy mountain peak in
the distance."[34]

His elation at viewing the Capitol caused Bates to inscribe, "A thrill
of ecstasy shot through my veins and arteries. The end of my journey was
near. From yonder distant dome I should wave my flag for which I had
acquired so much love, and my labor would be done."[35]

Bates continued, "The capital [city] seemed to welcome me, my
friends seemed to welcome me, my home, my wife and children welcomed me . . . more than all, I was successful in my enterprise, and had
proved the truth of assertions regarding the people of the South. No rebel
fiend had 'cut my heart out before I got ten miles from Vicksburg.'"[36]
Bates obviously felt that his intended goal of promoting unity among
Northerners and Southerners was largely met.

The additional insight into his trip to this point led Bates to scribe,
"No one had trampled my banner in the dust. No one had called upon
me to renounce my Northern opinion or to accept Southern opinions.
I had proved all such allegations to be false, and had [freed] millions of
my fellow countrymen from the lies which demagogues had circulated
against them. No one was near me. I was alone with my flag amidst the
desolation which war had wrought, but my soul was filled with a joy
which no words can describe."[37]

Gilbert Bates knew the distance he had to travel to reach Washington, D.C., was far beyond what he could physically endure in order to

successfully enter the nation's capital. Accordingly, he determined to end his day's march in Alexandria.[38]

The *Daily Clarion* of Jackson, Mississippi, made a simple announcement of the arrival of Bates the following day. The article said, "Sergeant Bates reached Alexandria, Virginia, yesterday with 'the flag.' He will arrive in Washington [April 15]."[39]

Alexandria, Virginia lay directly across the Potomac River from Washington, D.C. It had been noted that the citizens of the town fully realized that their location, in addition to the significance their town's designation "as a transport center, would make them an inevitable target." The truth of that belief came to light on May 24, 1861, the day after Virginia voted to join the Confederacy. On that day, federal troops entered the city and began a four-year occupation, which holds the distinction as the longest occupation of any Confederate city. The city of Alexandria avoided the commonplace destruction of numerous cities across the South, but, by the end of the war, its economy was said to be "in shambles." Another aspect of Alexandria rests in the fact that, as a federally occupied city, it became a haven for escaped slaves. Physically weakened and often sick or malnourished, large numbers of these downtrodden individuals passed away in Alexandria and were buried in a cemetery created from confiscated Confederate sympathizer's land holdings.[40]

Alexandria was also the location of the Marshall House, a hotel from which the Confederate flag flew defiantly after the onset of Federal occupation. On May 24, 1861, Federal colonel Elmer Ellsworth, a twenty-four-year-old New Yorker, led seven men to the roof of the Marshall House in order to remove the Confederate flag. As Colonel Ellsworth carried the flag down the stairs that led to the roof, he was killed when James Jackson, the hotel's proprietor, fired at him with a shotgun. Ellsworth's death was avenged moments later when one of his men bayoneted Jackson. Both men were labeled martyrs, and their deaths were used as recruiting tools for their respective nations. "Remember Ellsworth!" and "Remember Jackson!" were often heard as rallying cries. Interestingly, their names were regularly used for newborns of the North and South.[41] In addition, it was said that Abraham Lincoln wept when he heard of Ellsworth's untimely death.

The report of Bates arriving in Alexandria was announced in the April 14, 1868, issue of the *Alexandria Gazette*. It recorded, "Sergeant Bates entered this city yesterday evening by the Hunting Creek Bridge Road, and striking King Street at the corner of Alfred, marched down it and up Fairfax to the Mansion House, at a rapid gait, with the United States flag flying over his head. He was entertained at the Mansion House, and last night was waited upon by and received the attentions of many citizens."[42]

The decision of Bates to remain in Alexandria overnight took on a calming culmination. Bates remarked, "Here, I spent the night. In the evening the ladies and gentlemen of the city gave me a surprise in the shape of a masquerade. They came to the hotel in all describable forms and figures, with costumes as quaint and droll as the fashions of fairy land. The evening passed away very pleasantly."[43]

CHAPTER SEVENTEEN

Washington, D.C.

THE *ALEXANDRIA GAZETTE* PUBLISHED AN ARTICLE ANNOUNCING THE upcoming D.C. arrival of Bates. The write-up noted, "Sergeant Bates' servant man, with the Sergeant's baggage, arrived here this morning. The Sergeant left Fredericksburg yesterday morning, and was to have reached this city at 4 o'clock this evening."[1]

The article from the *Alexandria Gazette* also made mention of a business card: "The following is the Sergeant's card: SERG'T GILBERT H. BATES. Edgerton, Wisconsin. From Vicksburg to Washington, on foot and alone, with the United States Flag."[2]

The ultimate goal for Gilbert Henderson Bates was reached on April 14, 1868. Bates recorded his movements: "The 14th day of April was to be the last day of my march. I arose in the morning with alacrity, and, after taking quite an early breakfast, left Alexandria for Washington. The morning was clear, and as I walked along, I occasionally met persons on the road. Everyone knew who I was, for my arrival had been announced. I spoke with nearly everyone whom I passed."[3]

The anticipation for Bates arriving in D.C. was high, and a newspaper in West Virginia covered the excitement: "By nine o'clock this morning there had assembled at Long Bridge, a numerous concourse of citizens, and when it was announced a few minutes after ten o'clock, that Sergeant Bates was at the Virginia end of the Long Bridge, the crowd was quite large, many ladies and distinguished personages being among the number."[4]

"After reaching Arlington Heights, I descended to the Long Bridge and commenced crossing the Potomac. This was about nine o'clock in the morning. I had got about half-way across, when I saw a gentleman on horseback coming from the Washington end of the bridge."[5]

In 1808, President Thomas Jefferson authorized the Long Bridge; construction was completed the following year. Fires, ice storms, and high waters caused damage to the structure at various times, but by the onset of the American Civil War the construction of rails across the mile-long crossing was under way. The Long Bridge served as an important source of troop and supply movements during the early phase of the war. In 1863, a more substantial railroad bridge enabled locomotives, rather than horses, to pull loads of freight over the Potomac River.[6]

The April 21, 1868, issue of the *Western Democrat* of Charlotte, North Carolina recorded, "Sergeant Bates crossed the Long Bridge . . . the weather was unfavorable, but the crowd was very large. Bates wore the jacket and pants presented to him in South Carolina and sash presented to him in Montgomery, Ala. He carried a horn cup, presented to him by the ladies of Vicksburg, Miss., and his flag."[7]

A different period paper remarked that Bates was a small, well-built man who "wore a suit of black velveteen with a red sash, high cavalry boots and a slouch hat and feather."[8]

Another publication of the era elaborated, "Sergeant Bates . . . health is excellent." An edition of a South Carolina paper simply referred to Bates as "the man with the flag."[9]

The man Bates encountered on the Long Bridge asked, "Is this Sergeant Bates?" Bates replied positively, and the man added, "We are from the same state, Sergeant. . . . My name is Mr. Doolittle. I wish to thank you, sir, for having done a glorious act."[10]

Bates addressed Doolittle: "Senator, I have heard your name spoken a thousand times at the South. They look upon you as an unselfish, noble-hearted man all through that country."[11]

James Rood Doolittle, born in New York in 1815, was trained as an attorney. Locations of his practice included New York and Wisconsin, and he held the posts of district attorney and judge throughout his career.

In 1857 he was elected, on the Republican ticket, to the U.S. Senate and was known as a strong supporter of Lincoln during the American Civil War. A January 1863 article in a Wisconsin newspaper reported his reelection: "At 2 ½ o'clock, James R. Doolittle was elected United States Senator by a vote of 73, to 57 for E. G. Ryan, 1 for M. H. Carpenter, and 1 for Jas. S. Brown."[12]

Doolittle rode to the end of the bridge, conversing with Bates about the journey across the South. Doolittle then invited Bates to call on him while in Washington. Bates recalled, "He was the first man who welcomed me at Washington, whether by design or accident on his part, I am not able to say. I had never seen him to speak with him before, but I learned to like him well before I left the city."[13]

Senator Doolittle's diminishing popularity was not noted in a Bates journal entry, but a periodical printed soon after Bates left D.C. was clear in its content. It said, "For the office of U.S. Senator, we want a man of ability, a man of integrity, of experience, of undisputed political soundness, and a man on whom they can place implicit confidence. . . . We were badly sold when we reposed our confidence in James R. Doolittle, and have lived to repent of that false step. It should . . . teach us a lesson, and admonish us to examine well the past record, and carefully weigh the political integrity of our representatives in the future. . . . We have repented of that act, but don't know that we shall ever be forgiven, therefore let us not be "Doolittled" again.[14]

Bates reached the end of the Long Bridge and was the recipient of a welcome from a group comprised of "hundreds of people," and when Bates "stepped upon the soil of Washington, they cheered me again and again."[15]

A Columbia, South Carolina–based publication, the *Daily Phoenix*, announced the arrival of Bates in Washington, D.C. by briefly noting, "Sergeant Bates arrived at 1 o'clock today and met with an enthusiastic reception."[16]

Yet another paper said Bates, "who had undertaken to carry the . . . flag from Vicksburg to Washington to show there is no trace of the rebellion left in the South . . . arrived today and made a commotion among the boot blacks, the newsboys, and the Ohio Democratic delegation."[17]

The Conservative Army and Navy Union sent a committee that escorted Bates to the home of Colonel Founts. Bates remained at the Founts home, located at the "corner of Maryland Avenue and Fourteenth Street," until he marched "up Fourteenth Street to Pennsylvania." By 1:00 p.m. Bates was in a meeting with a committee from the Citizens of Washington. The latter group was in the accompaniment of a band. Bates recalled that the groups not only welcomed him to the capital city, but also stood "in readiness to accompany me to the President's House and then to the Capitol."[18]

One source recorded the series of events: "Sergeant Bates and the Conservative Union men embraced one another, to the intense delight of the boot-blacks. Bates was then escorted to a lager beer saloon."[19]

A crowd of people formed a procession that included the band; the group progressed "up Fourteenth Street to Pennsylvania Avenue." Bates walked in front of everyone, "with my flag unfurled. In spite of the heavy rain which had commenced to fall, the streets were thronged with people, and occasionally they almost obstructed the way."[20]

An article from the day recorded, "Sergeant Bates reached here today about noon, and was met at the Long Bridge by a deputation of the Conservative Army and Navy Union, and escorted to the President's House, where he will be welcomed." Formed in 1841, the Army and Navy Union is the oldest veterans' organization in the United States, and its name allows members of all service branches to join the organization.[21]

"It is expected that he will unfurl his flag from the dome of the Capitol this evening. Notwithstanding the rain, a large crowd greeted the Sergeant, and followed the procession up the avenue."[22]

Bates continued, "The balcony and steps of the Treasury Department, as well as the windows and offices of the buildings on the opposite side of the street were crowded with people who cheered lustily as the procession passed by." A period paper added, "As he passed Willard's and the Treasury Building, he was enthusiastically cheered, always returning the compliment by raising his cap."[23]

An article in the *Staunton Spectator* expounded, "The Convention met at 4 o'clock . . . a noise was heard and a rush made towards the door. Some one exclaimed, 'Fight outside;' but it was found out that the excitement was caused by the arrival of Sergeant Bates with his flag."[24]

Regarding the interruption, it was noted, "Mr. J. C. Gibson moved that he be invited to a privileged seat on the floor. Mr. E. Gibson seconded the motion as an honor to the flag. Mr. Porter, Radical, who had the floor, refused to yield it for this motion. He did not want the flag introduced under Copperhead auspices."[25]

Mr. Gibson made the statement, "Whereas, Sergeant Bates, an officer of the Federal army in the late war, has reached this city on his tour through the South for the promotion of harmony between the sections, and for the advancement of reconstruction; therefore, Resolved, that a committee of three be appointed to a privileged seat on this floor."[26]

The outcome of the resolution was detailed, "Mr. Clements, Radical, moved to postpone indefinitely. Bland, negro, seconded the motion. The motion carried: ayes, 48; noes, 25. Not a Conservative voted in the affirmative, and Captain Parr and Mr. Winston were the only Radicals voting in the negative."[27]

A major highlight for Bates took place when he reached the Executive Mansion. He wrote, "I was met by the President in the portico, who shook my hand cordially, and remarked, 'All I want to do is simply to welcome you and your flag.'" The President then invited Bates into the White House and led him to the East Room; the men "entered arm-in-arm."[28]

Andrew Johnson had become president with Lincoln's assassination. A Tennessean, Johnson had remained in the Senate despite his home state's secession, a fact that made him a Northern hero and labeled him a traitor in the South. Johnson became Lincoln's vice president in the 1864 election, and was seen as a man who could help unify the nation. In March 1867, Johnson offended the Radicals in the Senate by dismissing Secretary of War Edwin Stanton, disobeying the Tenure of Office Act, a ruling that stated the president was unable to dismiss a congressionally approved cabinet post without approval from the same. That led to an impeachment of Johnson. His spring 1868 trial, concluded just before Bates arrived in D.C., ended in an acquittal by one vote.[29] As Bates had witnessed in the Southern states through which he marched, he was subjected to the effects of division and animosity in the nation's capital.

A periodical titled *Spirit of Jefferson* noted that President Johnson remarked, "Sergeant Bates, I again welcome you to the National Capital and to the Executive Mansion. I heartily welcome your flag, our flag; may it always be as glorious and victorious as in the past."[30]

George Washington had selected the site of the Executive Mansion, and the cornerstone was laid in 1792. In 1800, President John Adams and his wife moved into the unfinished residence. During the War of 1812, the British burned the structure. After white paint was required to cover the soot that remained after its renovation, the mansion became known more commonly as the White House.[31]

Speaking to Bates and a portion of the procession that had entered into the East Room, President Andrew Johnson said, "I merely desire to sincerely and cordially welcome you and your flag with which you have travelled so many miles. I have no address or speech to make, but wish to testify my gratification at seeing you in Washington."[32]

Fully completed in 1826, the East Room measures approximately eighty feet by thirty-seven feet, and it is typically the location of large gatherings in the White House. Federal soldiers sometimes stayed in the room during the Civil War, and a journalist remarked that the room had "suffered considerably . . . from the hands of relic-hunting vandals." The largest room in the president's home, the East Room had been filled with mourners who surrounded Abraham Lincoln's body. Andrew Johnson's daughter had pursued the task of renovating the East Room as well as the entire mansion.[33]

President Johnson's meeting with Bates was recorded: "Bates called upon the President today to perform what he considered a very agreeable duty. The duty he had was to deliver to the President the kind messages for the Chief Magistrate of the nation which he had received in the swamps and woods, along the stretches of pine forests through which his route now and then lay, at the lonely farm house and in the villages, cities and towns."[34]

It was said, "At the request of the President, the Sergeant explained the circumstances under which he had taken the long journey which he has just completed . . . he said that the journey was undertaken to disprove certain foolish and unfounded expressions made."[35]

Bates relayed messages requested of him earlier in his march: "A gray-haired man . . . 'we are praying for him;' and, 'Say to him, said hundreds, God bless him.'" Bates informed President Johnson, "Many, very many, begged the Sergeant to tell the President that their hope was that Heaven would bless Andrew Johnson in his efforts to secure their rights in the old Union."[36]

Bates added more recollected remarks to President Johnson: "At Richmond, Virginia . . . a fine looking old lady, working a passage through the crowd, came to me as I was making my way out of the city, and with tears . . . said, taking my hand, 'Tell Andrew Johnson that he has the warmest prayers of the matrons of Virginia for his welfare and happiness.'"[37]

Making other comments to President Johnson, Bates noted that gray-haired men who trembled with old age had also urged Bates to express Heaven's blessing to Johnson. Bates reminisced, "Just beyond Montgomery . . . my flag was decorated with flowers and a laurel wreath, by a young lady, who said to her mother, as she returned to me my colors, 'I wish I could send by Sergeant Bates a bouquet to President Johnson.'"[38]

Bates continued, "They would dismiss schools to meet me . . . many of the little girls would want to kiss me and wave my flag. My rooms have been decorated with evergreens, and in North Carolina girls strewed my way with flowers and pitched bouquets upon my breast. In passing through North Carolina and Virginia I had a bouquet in my hand every hour of the day."[39]

An additional story from Bates was,

Between Selma and Montgomery . . . I went to an elegant residence occupied by a gentleman named White . . . Whitehall. . . . My flag was unfurled, but he did not know me, nor had he heard of my singular journey. He, however, warmly welcomed me, and I explained to him how I had come to seek shelter under his roof. . . . He told me Wilson had passed through that country and destroyed all he had. During a talk of two hours, there was hardly a moment that his eyes were not moistened with tears. In the morning, I found my flag all decorated with wreaths of laurel and flowers. . . . The old man tried to bid me goodbye, but he broke down and for a few minutes wept like a child.[40]

The final recorded comments Bates made to President Johnson included, "I honestly believe, sir, that in every State through which I passed in my journey I could raise a thousand men for the defense of the flag as quickly as I could anywhere in the entire Union. I have taken by the hand dozens of ex-Confederate soldiers whose warm grasp, quivering lips, and moistened eyes could not lie."[41]

The president conversed with Bates a short time longer, and Bates was invited to call on the president again. It was also stated that Johnson "expressed his gratitude at seeing him after his long journey." At that point, the president excused himself from the room, and Bates reportedly "bowed [and] thanked the President in a low tone." Another point made was, "At the President's request, the band played 'The Star-Spangled Banner.'" Bates reminisced, "His daughter, Mrs. Patterson, presented me with a beautiful bouquet of flowers. Subsequently, I was subjected to the ordeal of shaking hands, but I soon made my way out of the White House."[42]

Martha Johnson Patterson was one of five children born to Andrew Johnson and his wife. Patterson took on the social role of first lady, filling in for her mother Eliza, who was prone to avoid such tasks. In her-mid thirties, Martha managed the White House duties and attempted to calm a mourning and confused staff. A longtime member of the staff wrote, "No woman could have acted with greater sense or discretion. . . . She made no pretenses of any sort, but was always honest and direct." Although her father's administration was one of turmoil and controversy, Martha Patterson strove to take the White House to its former level of grandeur.[43]

A unique perspective of President Johnson's visit with Bates was reported in a Vermont paper: "The President, on Saturday, gave Sergeant Bates fifty dollars in gold." A weekly publication incorrectly predicted, "The whole thing was concocted to make democratic capital, and will end with the appointment of Bates to some little office in the gift of the President."[44]

The Capitol and Washington Monument

Upon the conclusion of his visit with President Johnson, Bates wrote, "The procession was reformed, and we marched to the Metropolitan Hotel." That establishment was the result of the modification and combination of "a row of Federal-style townhouses." In 1820, Alexandria resident Jesse Brown bought the Davis Hotel and, after enlargement and remodeling, established the business as Brown's Indian Queen Hotel. The hotel was controversial due to a "lurid picture of Pocahontas" that graced a sign on the front of the building. Brown died in 1847, and his two sons enlarged the hotel, adding a facade of white marble from the same quarry as that which supplied the Capitol. Four years later the business reopened as Brown's Marble Hotel. The Brown family sold the hotel in 1865, and the new owners christened it the Metropolitan Hotel. It would maintain that name until it closed in 1932, at which time the *Washington Post* proclaimed it as having "been in continuous operation longer than any other hotel in America."[1]

At the Metropolitan Hotel, Bates was introduced to several people, the first of whom was "Mr. C. A. Eldridge, Representative from Wisconsin." Eldridge made a speech, the contents of which were duly recorded. Eldridge voiced, "Fellow Citizens: it is owing to the fact that I am a citizen of Wisconsin that I am allowed on this occasion a brief moment to present . . . to you the guest of the citizens of Washington a worthy son of the State of Wisconsin, Sergeant Bates."[2]

Charles Augustus Eldridge was born in 1820 and joined his family in a move from Vermont to New York, where he studied law. In 1848, he moved to Wisconsin and pursued his law practice before entering politics. Elected to Congress in 1862, Eldridge voted against the impeachment of President Andrew Johnson in 1868.[3]

Following a round of heavy applause, Mr. Eldridge maintained, "He finding a popular, or existing, [belief] in the State of Wisconsin, like that, perhaps, in every Northern State, that the people of the Southern States, whom our conquering arms subdued, were hostile to the flag and Government of the Republic, undertook to carry that flag from Vicksburg to Washington . . . for the purpose of planting it on the dome of the Capitol, and showing the actual feelings toward it."[4]

Bragging about Bates, Eldridge proclaimed, "He has demonstrated to the people of the country and the world that no such hostility exists, and that the people of the South submit to the flag of the Union in good faith, and are determined to maintain their allegiance to it, as they expect the people of the North to maintain theirs." Another riotous round of applause began.[5]

As the rain fell in torrents, Mr. Eldridge continued, "I will not detain you in this pelting storm. I understand Sergeant Bates will now proceed to the dome of the Capitol with the flag which he has borne in honor and triumph from Vicksburg to Washington."[6]

For his final remarks, Eldridge uttered, "But my friends, I cannot forget the fact that it is just seven years this day since the flag of the Republic was lowered in humility and sorrow from the battlements of Sumter. . . . And this young man, who without money and alone, and on foot, has earned it for more than fourteen hundred miles, will now plant it in glory and triumph upon the dome of the National Capitol." A major interruption of comments occurred at that point as applause grew to an even louder level than previously expressed that day.[7]

Following Eldridge's speech, remarks came from William Mungen, an Ohioan who had been an officer during the Civil War and was serving as a senator in April 1868. Upon Mungen's finale, Bates was given three more cheers. A similar act was pronounced and directed toward his flag. At that point, according to Bates, "I left the balcony, descended to the street, resumed my place at the head of the procession, and walked to the east front of the Capitol for the purpose of unfurling the flag from the dome."[8]

A small group accompanied Bates as he ascended the steps leading to the Capitol rotunda. Perhaps the most humiliating act of the trip took place at that juncture. Bates lamented, "The Chief of the Capitol Police halted us, and said that he had positive orders not to permit Sergeant Bates to carry his flag into the Capitol, or to make any demonstrations."[9]

The lack of cooperation on the part of the Capitol Police warranted coverage in newspapers as far away as Louisiana. A Shreveport periodical proclaimed, "Sergeant Bates ... approached the western gates of the Capitol grounds, where to his surprise, he was met by a police force, who said they were instructed not to allow him to enter." The statement slightly varied in another publication: "he was halted by the Capitol police, who said they had orders not to permit any demonstration whatever in the building."[10]

As quickly as the restriction had been given, an option was announced. Bates related, "An order was then produced from General Michler, Superintendent of Public Buildings, giving me permission to ascend to the dome. The policeman gruffly remarked that he did not get his orders from General Michler, but if the order was endorsed by the Sergeant-at-Arms of the Senate, he would allow me to pass in."[11]

Nathaniel Michler was born in Pennsylvania in 1820 and graduated seventh in the West Point class of 1848. Specializing in engineering, Michler served in Texas, Maryland, Virginia, and Panama prior to the Civil War. During the War Between the States, he saw various levels of service at the Wilderness, Spotsylvania, Cold Harbor, and Petersburg. He was breveted Brigadier General, and from 1866 until 1871 he served as superintendent of public buildings in D.C.[12] He held that post at the time Bates visited the nation's capital.

The situation served as fodder for an article in a period paper: "The Sergeant, bearing aloft the little flag, sought admittance at the eastern door, but was again stopped by the Capitol police, two of whom seized him by the collar, and informed him he could not enter the building unless be would throw down the flag."[13]

The article added, "Where was General Dix, and 'any man who directs the American flag to be thrown down, shoot him at once!' What a difference in the exclamation . . . the Rump Congress assumed to order . . . Bates not to enter the Capitol . . . unless he threw down the flag."[14]

In an act of intervention on behalf of Bates, "Someone went to Mr. Brown, and after twenty minutes' delay, obtained his signature." Sergeant-at-Arms George Brown had left Scotland as a child, and a political connection with an Illinois lawyer enabled him to become mayor of Alton, Illinois. He established a newspaper, the *Daily Morning Courier*, which was labeled as the state's best daily paper outside of Chicago. Brown eventually served in the Illinois legislature and introduced a resolution that condemned Stephen Douglas. Assuming the role of Sergeant-at-Arms in 1861, Brown disclosed that his most difficult day in the post took place "when he arranged for Lincoln's body to lie in state . . . in the Capitol Rotunda." In March 1868 he was given the task of presenting "President Andrew Johnson with a summons to his Senate impeachment trial." Brown appeared on the cover of the March 28, 1868, issue of *Harper's Weekly*, providing the only known likeness of him.[15]

The confusion continued as Bates claimed, "The policeman then said I could not go in unless I had also the endorsement of the Sergeant-at-Arms of the House of Representatives. Someone set about finding him, but he was not to be found."[16]

A periodical summarized the events: "After some delay, Sergeant-at-Arms Brown endorsed upon the order to admit Bates, but when this was presented to the Chief of the Capitol Police, he still refused unless Sergeant-at-Arms Ordway's endorsement was also obtained."[17]

Nehemiah George Ordway was born in New Hampshire in 1828 and served as a sheriff and a postal agent in his younger years. He was elected Sergeant-at-Arms for the U.S. House of Representatives in 1863 and would hold that post for ten years. He also later served as a New Hampshire state senator and then governor of the Dakota Territory.[18]

A slightly different account of securing permission for Bates appeared in an article published the following week. It said, "An application was made to the Sergeant-at-Arms . . . in order to fix the responsibility for the outrage, whereon this official passed into the Senate . . . to consult . . .

as to what should be done, and ascertain who would take the responsibility. The sequel is consistent with the program. The Sergeant-at-Arms returned to this office."[19]

A local newspaper noted, "Mr. J. Corson, U.S. Capitol police, writes that Sergeant Bates wanted to go on the dome with his party and fling his calico to the breeze, we quote his own words, and that after parleying he consented to let Sergeant Bates and ten or twelve of his men in, but refused the crowd. The admirers of the flag will no doubt note especially the calico. There is something very rebellious and treasonable in such an expression, isn't there?"[20]

It was recorded, "This . . . policeman, who soon disappeared . . . necessarily closed the doors of the building against the gallant Sergeant and his banner."[21]

Bates recorded his actions of the ensuing minutes: "I waited, cold and wet, outside the rotunda, while scores of people, white and black, were allowed free entrance, and no questions were asked. I held in my hand a little flag about five feet long and three feet wide. I had carried it over fourteen hundred miles through the heart of the Southern country, and it had been cheered by a million voices on the way."[22]

Additional remarks from the situation included, "Was it for this that I must be debarred from the Capitol of my country, which I fought to defend? Was it for this little flag, the emblem of our nation, which could not possibly be in any one's way, whether I carried it to the dome or not, was it for this that I must be kept in the rain and cold at the bidding of an insolent policeman?"[23]

The disgust Bates held at this point of his journey overflowed into his recollections of the march: "That flag, the stars and stripes, was insulted by the policemen of Congress. I had waved it from the capitol of every Southern State from Mississippi to Virginia, and no one raised the slightest objection. But, in Washington, the officers of Congress refused to allow me to wave the flag from the dome of the Capitol, when it was known that such was my wish and purpose."[24]

Bates continued, "No one ever claimed that any harm could be done by granting my wish. Mr. Ordway could not be found. Even if his endorsement had been obtained, the police would have demanded some other endorsement."[25]

A revelation revealed, "Several prominent Radicals of the Senate and the House, spoke to the Chief of Police, and cautioned him about allowing Sergeant Bates to enter the Capitol with his flag. They did not like my way of doing things, and intended to put a stop to it. One thing is certain, whatever may be the reason, I was kept out of the Capitol because I bore the American flag in my hand, by the power which controls the Houses of Congress."[26]

Putting the situation into perspective, Bates bellowed, "My flag and myself were only once before insulted during the march, and that was not far from Milledgeville, in Georgia. The insult was given by several mongrel cur-dogs, which I cudgeled thoroughly with my flagstaff."[27]

Bates summarized his mindset in regard to the rejection his flag and he received at the Capitol, "Ashamed of the spirit which controlled Congress, outraged by the persistent insolence of the police, enraged at the insult which had been offered to me and my flag, I turned from the steps of the Capitol, resolving to finish my march under more favorable circumstances, when my flag would be received at least as cordially as it was in the so-called rebel States. Congress may have become so powerful that they did not respect that banner, but let the future decide that."[28]

Sadly, the failure of Bates to fly the U.S. flag over the Capitol gained a sentence of a rather lengthy article by exclaiming, "Thence, he proceeded to the Capitol, where he failed to gain admission."[29]

A glimmer of hope appeared during this time of deep despair. Bates wrote, "I was about to return to the hotel when a friend suggested to me that I should go to Washington's Monument and unfurl the flag there."[30]

Minimal insight about the event was provided in a period newspaper, which stated, "The whole party turned from the Capitol in loathing, and sought the Washington Monument, where he unfurled the flag amid congratulations."[31]

Another articled added, "The crowd . . . proceeded thither, and in a few moments the door to the unfinished structure was opened by the patriotic janitor, without inquiring whether Sergeants-at-Arms Brown and Ordway had endorsed any official paper or permit to enter . . . and the flag which the Sergeant has so successfully carried, was displayed at this place."[32]

The cornerstone for the Washington Monument, an intended memorial to the nation's first president, was laid July 4, 1848. Among the thousands of people who attended the event was a young Illinois congressman named Abraham Lincoln. Controversy over the procurement of stone for the monument halted the construction in 1854 when the structure was approximately one hundred fifty feet tall.[33] That was the structure's condition when Bates unfurled his flag.

Gilbert Bates proudly elaborated upon his actions involving the unfurling of his flag at Washington Monument. He exclaimed, "I did so, over that unfinished and neglected column of marble which is proposed as a monument to the 'Father of his Country.' I unfurled my weather-worn flag, which for nearly three months had been carried by me, alone, through the Southern States, over hills and through valleys, plains, forests, hamlets, villages, town, and cities."[34]

When Bates reached Washington Monument, "Hon. E. O. Perrin, of New York, recently-appointed Chief Justice of the Supreme Court of Utah, was called upon." Edwin Oscar Perrin, born in Ohio, had moved to Memphis to practice law. He also served as Navy Agent and Purser of the Memphis Navy Yard from 1845 to 1849. He later opened a law firm in New York and held various positions at a number of locations. The Senate rejected President Andrew Johnson's nomination of Perrin for Chief Justice of the Supreme Court of the Utah Territory. The year Bates visited D.C., Perrin was elected to serve as Clerk of the New York Court of Appeals. Perrin would remain in that post until his 1889 death.[35]

As a preview to what was to occur, a view of a paragraph from a period newspaper proves beneficial. The periodical proclaimed, "a speech was made by Mr. Perrin . . . who referred to the fact that Bates had marched all through the Southern States, and had not been stopped in his progress until he reached the doors of the Capitol of the nation."[36]

Mr. Perrin took the opportunity to speak: "Sergeant Bates, as unexpectedly to myself as to you, the Reception Committee have this moment requested me to welcome you and your flag, after having been driven from the portals of the Capitol. After such a repulse from such a source, no place could be more appropriate than here, at the base of this unfinished monument, erected to commemorate the virtues of George Washington, the Father of his Country."[37]

Perrin added,

> *Could the spirit of that great patriot look down upon this melancholy scene today, he might deliver another farewell address to all the hopes and prospects of a distracted country. Look but a moment on the picture. That silken banner, wrought by hands upon the banks of the Mississippi, and placed in your keeping by the citizens of Vicksburg on the 28th . . . January, has been borne by you, over mountain and valley, 'mid sunshine and rain, by night and by day, for nearly three weary months, through the States of Mississippi, Alabama, Georgia, North Carolina, South Carolina, and Virginia, and everywhere throughout these once rebellious States it has been hailed with joy and gladness.*[38]

A period article added, "E. O. Perrin, of Tennessee, spoke, and said that had Bates carried a negro on his shoulders from Vicksburg, they would have allowed him to place the negro on the Goddess of Liberty."[39]

Mr. Perrin continued, "Every city, village, and town joining in the glad shout, old men and young men, soldiers and citizens, matrons and maidens, all, all welcoming it as the harbinger of better days. Even at Montgomery and Richmond, the boasted capitals of the late Confederacy, you were escorted to the dome of each Capitol, and the stripes and stars kissed again the balmy breeze of the once rebellious South, amid the loud plaudits of a conquered people."[40]

Additional words from Perrin were, "I learn, from good authority, that but one paper in all the South cast any imputation upon you or your banner, Pollard's *Southern Opinion*, a rebel sheet, which echoes only the opinion of Pollard, and hardly that."[41]

Perrin was likely referring to Edward Pollard's 1866 book *The Lost Cause: A New Southern History of the War of the Confederates*. It has been noted that Pollard's book celebrated, interpreted, and recalled "the fallen Confederacy to those who were part of the four-year experiment and to their children and grandchildren."[42]

Perrin stated the contents of Pollard's article were that "He called upon the 'people of Carolina to meet you on the border, welcome your insolent approach, and seat you on some tall, solitary chimney, left by Sherman as a bleak monument of his vandal raid, and there let you wave your rag of oppression amid the hootings and curses of an insulted people.'"[43]

It was stated that no one responded to Pollard's "unjust call." Perrin went on to say that he felt safe in making a prediction that "the whole revolutionary Northern press, down to 'my two papers, both daily,' will catch this inspiration, join the vile strain, and echo back some fiendish chorus. Indignant rebuke followed the appeal down there; and, believe me, that here the reddest thunder-bolt in God's fiery wrath is reserved to come down upon the heads of those who fatten on spoils, revel in plunder, and prostitute their patronage, all in the name of 'liberty' and the flag of their country."[44]

Perrin made a point that he had heard Bates stand firm that at all points along his journey he was the recipient of "warm, joyous, patriotic greeting, and all without the expenditure of one dollar" from Vicksburg, Mississippi to the nation's capital.[45]

The ensuing words from Perrin were directed toward the opponents of Bates: "Yet here, in the capital of the nation, by men full of professions and boasting of loyalty, you have met your first, your only rebuff. At the moment you expected to crown your triumphal march by planting that flag upon the dome of the Capitol, the massive doors of that temple of liberty are slammed in your face by the very men who have bolted and barred out infinitely more loyal Representatives than themselves, and you are driven to Washington's Monument; and there, with bowed head, you have unfurled your banner."[46]

Perrin added, "Had the so-called rebels torn from it twenty-seven bright stars, a Radical Congress would have welcomed the dismantled ensign with shouts of joy, as being evidence of an unrepentant people. But it was a standing rebuke to them to find it pass safely and triumphantly throughout your entire journey, without an insult, and requiring no reconstruction at their hands."[47]

Additional statements from Perrin included, "It matters not, therefore, if you did defend that flag during the war, and love and revere it in time of peace, you are guilty of a 'high crime and misdemeanor,' and serve impeachment for presuming to float it from yonder dome, with thirty-seven stars upon it, representing as many states, while the hump below have sworn that ten of those stars represent only 'conquered provinces,' joined to the Union by loyal bayonets, and governed by five military dictators."[48]

"Your mistake, Mr. Sergeant, is an innocent and a natural one. You believed in the professions of these men. You thought their loud boasting of love for the Union was sincere. The people once thought like you, but like yourself, they too have been undeceived, and find that, while they kept the word of promise to the ear, they break it to the hope."[49] Those words from Perrin added more insight into the animosity Bates experienced in Washington, D.C.

Perrin added more information in relation to the rationale behind those who held little respect for Bates, "Had you taken some dusky son of Ham, and borne him . . . upon your back through the sunny South, and landed him safely here, a Radical Congress would have opened wide those bolted doors, and when you thrust your sable brother, the American citizen of African descent, into the outstretched arms of the Goddess of Liberty which crowns the dome of yonder Capitol, one loud, long shout of joy would have gone up from those gilded halls below, and you would have been hailed as a hero and crowned with the laurel."[50]

Continuing his discussion of the treatment Bates had received, Perrin articulated, "Seated in the same Capitol from which you are driven, they strike down the Supreme Court, trample upon the Constitution of our fathers, ride over the sacredness of law, and, in madness of their wrath, drunken with power, they are this moment enacting the solemn farce of impeaching a President for the high crime and misdemeanor of refusing to bow down to their party lash, and daring to stand between them and an outraged Constitution."[51]

Speaking of Andrew Johnson, Perrin uttered, "This 'traitor President' gave you and the flag a warm welcome today, and the loyal Senate, that bars you out of the Capitol, may, for that high crime, frame another charge in their bill of indictment."[52]

Adding to his feelings of disenchantment for the treatment of President Johnson, Perrin stated,

The President stood beneath the flag in the time of war, and such men love it in time of peace. When the rebellion raged, he did not continue to dwell in those marble halls, but resigned his cushioned seat in the Senate, gave up his five thousand a year, and bearing a commission from President Lincoln, he went back to his own Tennessee, then surrounded by rebel armies, and beneath just such a banner he "fought out the good fight" till he brought back the land of Jackson to the Union of our Fathers; the only State yet restored since the Confederacy of Jeff Davis crumbled to the ground. Yet he is a "traitor," and the men who did not insult and repulse your flag are "rebels."[53]

Continuing to express his disgust, Perrin added, "Compare his record with the military career of that radical body that has just repulsed you, and are now sitting in solemn mockery as a High Court of Impeachment on him. Call the roll of 'High Court,' and then call the roll of all the armies of the Nation, and show me the name of a single Senatorial Impeacher that ever followed that flag into battle, or fought beneath its stripes and stars."[54]

Perrin elaborated, "From what source, then, do they obtain their warrant to condemn better and braver men? On what bloody fields did they win their laurels? During four years of sanguinary war, and almost four of unreconstructed peace, what arms did they ever face except the ebony, and alabaster arms in the ladies' gallery?"[55]

More comments from Perrin included, "I well remember, in the compromise days of 1850, Daniel Webster, the great expounder of the Constitution, after voting for those measures that spread the bow of promise in the political heavens, returned to Boston and asked the poor privilege of defending his course, and the same Radical fanatics that drove you and your flag from the Capitol today barred the doors . . . against Daniel Webster. Like yourself, he was driven into the inclement . . . and gave them that rebuke."[56]

Perrin addressed Bates and noted the pain Bates felt at the rejection from those in various Washington posts: "Sir, after receiving such an ovation through the entire South, I can well imagine your feelings of sadness, mortification, and disgust, when thus rudely repulsed by those false pretenders who claim such exalted patriotism, and are forever prating of their devotion to the National flag . . . people must soon see their shameless hypocrisy . . . empty boasting; and, in the face of such an insult, you might, while driven from the Capitol, look back contemptuously."[57]

Perrin added, "Despair not, you will find yourself in good company, and plenty of it, and will have received the same measure of reward meted out to every Union soldier, high or low, from George B. McClellan to the humblest private, who, having served his country on the field of battle, refuses to serve the 'Radicals' at the ballot box."[58]

Offering hope for the future, Perrin exclaimed, "the day will soon come when your bright banner can and will float from yonder Dome, every star having a State, and every State having a star. God grant that it may come quickly; for on that proud day . . . an outraged Constitution will be vindicated, a fettered judiciary made free, and last . . . the Nation's Executive will be rescued from an outrage. . . . Then, sir, will your late triumphant march live fresh and green in the memory of a grateful nation."[59]

Perrin also noted his personal feelings toward those who refused Bates the opportunity to fly his flag from the Capitol dome: "while the very names of the men who drove you from the Capitol will be forgotten, or remembered only with the scorn and contempt which will ever follow the betrayers of a confiding people."[60]

Extending an invitation to Bates, Perrin said, "I have finished; unfurl your banner to the breeze. . . . Let it float from this neglected, unfinished shaft, a standing reproach to that reckless Congress that squanders millions of the people's money on Freedmen's Bureaus . . . but cannot spare a dollar to the memory of George Washington, whose sacred ashes slumber today 'in a conquered province' outside of the Union he created and loved so well, and in the sight of the very Capitol that bears his honored name."[61]

Beginning to wrap up his remarks, Perrin exclaimed, "They have disgraced themselves, humiliated you, and outraged the people, yet your banner . . . bear it on proudly to your far western home. It will be welcomed everywhere by the people who went forth to defend it, with even greater gladness that by those who seek once more its protecting folds, and yearn for the happy days that are no more."[62]

Perrin concluded, "In the name of all the people, North, South, East and West, we bid you 'God speed.' Long may you live to enjoy the pleasant memories of the past, and share with us all the blessings of the future. For as sure as yonder sun now shines upon us, our Union will be restored, Congress rebuked, and the nation saved." As Perrin finished, the flag Bates had carried across the Southern states and to the doorstep of the Capitol was taken to the top of the Washington Monument "amid tremendous applause and nine rousing cheers."[63]

Besides Perrin, other individuals held disgust at the treatment Bates had received. One expressed,

The treatment of Sergeant Bates exhibits radical partisanship in its true colors. The President of the United States welcomed him; Democratic members of Congress welcomed him; the Soldiers and Sailors of Washington welcomed him, but the radical Congress refused to recognize him. He was more than their standard of loyalty called for. The flag he bore was, in their eyes, "a polluted rag" and a "flaunting lie." It was the flag of the whole Union, with uniform stripes and undimmed stars. But this was not unexpected from the same men who have in a manner stricken down the courts, erased the Constitution, and who now are prosecuting their attempts to overthrow an independent branch of the government.[64]

On April 24, 1868, the *Aegis and Intelligencer* of Bel Air, Maryland, mentioned Bates and summarized the offensive reception he was given at the Capitol. In part, it stated, "Bates arrived in Washington last week, and proceeded at once to the National Capitol with the intention of displaying his flag from the dome, but was denied admission."[65]

The Maryland manuscript added, "The cause for this step is difficult to imagine. During the debate in the Senate, on the bill making appropriations for miscellaneous and impeachment expenses, the following discussion took place in reference to Sergeant Bates and his flag."[66]

It was said that Bates had an order from General Michler allowing Bates to go to the dome to display his flag. The Capitol police stopped him and would not allow Bates to proceed unless he had an order "endorsed by the Sergeant-at-Arms of the Senate." As noted earlier, that signature was secured, but the inability to obtain that of the Sergeant-at-Arms of the House, a hurriedly made request, eventually led to the flag-raising being relocated to the Washington Monument.[67]

Bates Reminisces

Gilbert Henderson Bates had finished his trek from Vicksburg to Washington, and he made the declaration in writing: "I left the Monument and returned to the hotel. My journey was finished. My work was done. Whether it was well or poorly done, let others decide."[1]

Although no additional explanation or information was provided, a North Carolina reporter offered, "The authorities at the Capitol are shifting the responsibility of having denied admission to Bates."[2]

Bates made four distinct remarks about the march he had undergone. He said, "It has clearly fixed upon my mind these truths: First, the Southern people revere the flag, and are willing to fight for it against any foe."[3]

As for the second point Bates felt he had learned from his experience, he remarked, "They have a strong desire to live in the Union and under the Constitution, but they hate military domination, and detest Negro suffrage. They cannot endure the idea of being governed by negroes."[4]

A third lesson was, according to Bates, "Any Northern man will be well received at the South, provided he does not seek to degrade their society by placing the negroes in power to govern them."[5]

Lastly, Bates recalled learning that Southerners "dislike and oppose the Radicals, not because they fought each other in the war, for they fought the Democrats as well, but because Radical Reconstruction seeks, by bayonet, to force the intelligent white man down to the earth and elevate the ignorant and incompetent negro over him."[6]

Bates wrote his evaluation of the effects of his unique walk: "I set out upon my march convinced that the Southern people had resumed their affection for the flag and the Union. I was equally convinced that thousands of the Northern people believed the contrary, and for that reason were sustaining a policy which ground the people of the South to the earth."[7]

Bates added, "Men said that my heart would be cut out, before I could go ten miles from Vicksburg, by that terrible rebellious people. I have walked over fourteen hundred miles in their country without an escort, without any weapon but a pen-knife, without any money, with only the American flag for a defense, and I received nothing but blessings and thanks and kindness at every step of the way."[8]

For his additional perceptions of Southerners, Bates stated, "The people of the South are not rebellious. Heaven knows it. They feel as the people of the North feel. We should not like to be governed by the bayonet. . . . We should not like to have political power given to a great mass of ignorant negroes . . . in our own State against our will and by force, and have hundreds of thousands of our intelligent fellow citizens disfranchised and driven from the polls."[9]

Bates made a comparison of the nation's people, "The Southern people are no more rebellious today than the people of Illinois, Ohio, and New York would be if Congress should govern those States by the bayonet and attempt to fasten upon them detested negro suffrage. I set out in an enterprise to demonstrate that fact."[10]

Offering his final journal entry as an analysis of his march, Gilbert Bates penned, "If I have succeeded in placing before the minds of my countrymen of the North, even in a modest degree, a truthful juncture of the sentiments of the South; if by any word or deed of mine men shall be disabused of their erroneous and cruel opinions, and shall thereby treat the South, as part of our common country, with generosity and magnanimity; if any act of mine has tended to restore peace and harmony and confidence once more between the two sections, Heaven be praised, I shall not have lived in vain."[11]

Bates explained his planned departure from D.C.: "I hope on Monday next to leave for my home near Edgerton, Wisconsin, where I have a wife and two children. The last work I did before I left home was the cutting of two cords of wood. I left a tree partially cut, and I want to get home to finish it."[12]

Captain Mayne Reid offered a tribute to Bates, and the by-then famous soldier included it in his recollection of the march. Born in Ireland, Reid went to America in 1840, and he moved from New Orleans, to Nashville, Pittsburg, Philadelphia, and then New York before serving in the Mexican-American War. Reid wrote approximately seventy-five novels as well as short stories, poems, and romances. Known for his outlandish appearance, Reid was especially fond of lemon-yellow gloves, clothes of unusual patterns and loud checks, and he wore a monocle.[13]

Titled "From Vicksburg to the Sea," Reid's poem for Bates said:

> Bear on the banner, soldier bold!
> How Southern hearts must thrill
> To see the flag, so loved of old,
> Waving above them still!
> What cords 'twill touch, what echoes wake,
> Of that far truer time!
> Who knows but it the spell may break,
> That madden'd them to crime.
> Bear on the banner! Hold it up!
> But not by way of taunt;
> They've drunk too deep the bitter cup
> To need such idle vaunt.
> No; be it like a brother's hand,
> To soothe a brother's pain,
> From hasty blow of quarrelsome brand
> Ne'er to be given again.
> Bear on the banner! Spread it out,
> O'er all Secessia's land.
> Sure, they will hail it with a shout,
> And take the proffered hand?
> I cannot think their hearts are dead,
> Southrons! 'twould grieve me sore
> Recall your ancient spirit fled,
> And patriots be once more!
> Bear on the banner! Hold it high,

And once more let them see.
The white star on its azure sky,
Those symbols of the free!
Oh! May they think of that strange star,
Once seen in Eastern night;
And like the "wise men" from afar,
Bow down before its light.
Bear on the banner, soldier, bold!
It is a thought of worth;
And often will the tale be told
Around the winter hearth,
Ten thousand, thousand eyes are bent,
Upon thy daring deed,
A nation, now no longer rent.
Is wishing thee "God speed!"

An 1871 poem titled "The Ballad of Sergeant Bates" appeared in Howard Miller's book *The Student's Dream and Other Poems*. Immortalizing the march and Bates, the verses progressed:[14]

The cruel Civil War was o'er,
In peaceful relaxation.
For three long years had now reposed,
The soldiers of the Nation.
When in Wisconsin, round a fire,
Some neighbors talked of state,
And one condemned with manly zeal
As waxed the warm debate
The slow-paced plan of Reconstruction
That Congress had imposed,
Asserting that the Southern mind
True loyalty disclosed.
Another said with heat, "Not so,
The rebels hate us still;
Nor will I think them free of it
Until on any hill.
In all the South the stars and stripes,

Without the sense of fear,
May float aloft its ample folds
Without a soldier near."
Then Sergeant Bates, 'twas he, replied:
"This I'll engage to show;
I'll take that banner that we love,
And through the South I'll go.
From Vicksburg unto Washington,
In open light of day,
Alone, unarmed, and moneyless,
I'll walk the beaten way.
I want not wager or reward;
One long request I ask,
While I am gone from home and friends
To do this pleasant task,
That you who wish it done agree,
My family to pay
A workman's wages, less nor more
Than just one dollar a day."
'Twas done as soon as said, and he
Who loved the South set out
To take his chance for good or ill
That ambushed all the route.
And men looked on with fear the while
This strangest test was made;
And some looked on with love and hope,
And some their hate betrayed.
For many wished him harm who thought
He might get safely through,
And with his honored banner prove
The Southern States were true.
For well they knew their lease of life
In base-born politics
Was only due to knavery,
And bolstered up by tricks.
So, they made prayer to evil gods
To look with anger down,
And in some rebel haunt to blast

Him with their vengeful frown.
But Heaven holds but one alone
Their heathen gods are dead,
And this One looked in love on him,
And evil angels fled.
And where he thought to move alone,
There thousands came to meet him;
And where he thought to hear no songs,
The Nation's anthems greet him.
The old men wept to see once more,
In love and not in hate,
The olden banner borne aloft
Through all the tranquil state.
And children ran to catch the glow
Of friendly love upon it;
Nor did one rebel finger raise,
Or eye avert to shun it.
And he who came in poverty
Lacked nothing on his way;
For food and shelter rich and poor
Gave freely every day.
That banner proved his talisman
On every route he bore it,
And barred gates and bolted doors
Flew open wide before it.
Unarmed a single soldier bore
It through the Southern Land,
Where once a hundred thousand men
Were all too small a band.
But when he came to Washington,
Where government hath home,
To fling unto the breeze his flag
From out the central dome,
A tyrant Congress, sitting there,
The stately portals closed,
And bade that flag, on which in love
A Nation's eyes reposed
Be gone, unfurl itself elsewhere.

"Then, throw it to the sun,"
Said one, "from that unfinished shaft
To godlike Washington;
For he was Nature's Noble, born,
And to his country true;
But these are little men and base,
And know not what they do."

CHAPTER TWENTY

Pundits of Bates

THE IMPACT AND EFFECTS OF THE MARCH GILBERT HENDERSON BATES initiated were argued for decades. The severity and origin of undue insults ranged from those people questioning the motives and sincerity of the endeavor to individuals who called for killing Bates. Many of the comments that follow were written after Bates made a visit to a particular city. Other remarks sought to point out or create a single or set of negative aspects of Bates, his supporters, or the event. In addition, many of the more ambiguous aspects of Bates's post-march life are referred to in these snippets, providing insight into his activities and movements in later life.

On April 25, 1868, an article in a Rock Island, Illinois, paper noted a Chicago publication's comment that cast a negative view of Bates. The *Evening Argus* said, "*The Chicago Journal* shows its hate for the national flag, and a brave Union soldier by the following mean notice: 'On Monday, three thousand persons marched in Baltimore after Sergeant Bates, the copperhead pedestrian who has been perambulating the South, bearing the United States flag, and receiving ovations from rebels.'"[1]

The May 2, 1868, edition of the *Weekly Echo* in Lake Charles, Louisiana noted that a paper based in the North "insults all the Union soldiers of the land by denouncing the brave and gallant Sergeant Bates as 'a crack-brained fellow anxious for some cheap notoriety,' and adds the falsehood that 'he always managed to keep a safe place in the rear when his comrades were carrying the national flag through the south.'" The Louisiana report also announced, "It calls the march of Sergeant Bates 'a miserable farce' and otherwise insults the gallant Union soldier and the flag he bore."[2]

An 1868 convention in New York somehow managed to garner another animosity-filled sentence subjecting Bates to an analogy. Noting the convention, the author offered, "Soldiers there are, unfortunately, who held places in the Union army, who are willing, like Sergeant Bates, to turn Union victories into rebel triumphs and exchange the blood bought preservation of the nation for a mocking surrender of the government into the hands of its virulent foes."[3]

As Bates traveled to various locations and made speeches about his march across the South, he was immediately met with nay-sayers. From Wisconsin, Bates's home state, one offered, "Poor Sergt. Bates is evidently but a novice in the diplomatic art. He has not learned the great secret of seasonable subsiding. Instead of biding his time, he wants to be head man on all occasions, and so makes himself too commonplace."[4]

Another paper based in Wisconsin provided an adversarial notation by printing, "appeals . . . in behalf of Sergeant Bates . . . now destitute . . . would it be impertinent to suggest that he ought to go to work?"[5]

A similar mindset was indicated in a post from a New Orleans reporter, "The Sergeant, being a lusty, handsome fellow, is there any radical objection to his going to work at some honest calling? If he were a young man of spirit, he would advise the charitable citizens of New Orleans to invest their superfluous money in buying artificial legs for Confederate cripples instead of bestowing on an idle, able-bodied young man."[6]

Three years after Bates made his march across the South, a Maine newspaper commented, "Sergeant Bates was allowed to travel, after the war, from the Gulf of Mexico to Washington . . . but what did this prove? Only that the fell spirit of discord and ruin is not open and above board, and stalking in the bright sunlight of day."[7]

As time progressed, the name-calling became more direct and the reporting locales more distant from location of the offending individual. For example, an article from Tucson, before Arizona attained statehood, noted, "The *Springfield Republican* calls the great American standard-bearer, Sergeant Bates, 'the champion jackass of the world.'"[8]

In January 1873, a harsh comment appeared in a Wilmington, North Carolina, newspaper: "Sergeant Bates proposes to travel all around this country with an English flag. What an unflagging nuisance Sergeant Bates is getting to be."[9]

Another cruel write-up was provided in a Pennsylvania paper proclaiming, "*The Titusville Herald* published an obituary notice of Queen Victoria on Saturday last. Will it please kill Sergeant Bates next?"[10]

Another adverse Pennsylvania comment came from a farmer who "bet Sergeant Bates one hundred dollars that he cannot carry a red flag through a flock of turkeys . . . or . . . one hundred to ten that he cannot carry the flag through a certain field . . . if [Bates] allows him to turn in his Durham bull."[11]

A derogatory display of regard for Bates's work ethic was given in a Columbia, South Carolina, tabloid, which voiced, only five years after his visit, "An almost incredible paragraph is circulating . . . that Sergeant Bates is actually . . . reduced to the humiliating necessity of working for a living, just like any ordinary private citizen."[12]

Attempting to follow a similar example to that Bates established, a young Virginia man was recorded as having a desire to carry a Confederate flag as he marched across a series of Northern states. The *New York Herald* reported, "A misguided youth in Alexandria, Va., in imitation of Sergeant Bates, proposes to proceed to Boston for the purpose of starting from Bunker Hill on a tour through the Northern States, carrying with him the rebel flag unfurled. We are inclined to regard this as a foolish as well as a hazardous undertaking."[13]

The New York articled continued, "It is calculated to arouse memories of such places as Andersonville, that might as well be smothered. Moreover, this Alexandria adventurer should remember that his case and that of Sergeant Bates are slightly different. While he is carrying a flag that constitutes no national emblem, and travels through a region that claims to be the conqueror, Bates carried the victorious American standard, the emblem of a powerful nation, through a defeated section of the country and among a subdued, if not a subjugated, people."[14]

As a final insult to Bates, the New York paper remarked, "Besides, it was the only flag that could be recognized even by these unfortunate people, and hence not likely to be insulted . . . the whole affair is a humbug of the first water."[15]

A short and negative reference to Bates appeared in an article from a Jasper, Indiana periodical that said, "Sergeant Bates . . . earns a frugal living by carrying the American flag in the most daring manner through peaceful rural neighborhoods."[16]

A Memphis periodical denounced the significance of Bates in saying, "Sergeant Bates wants to have a war with Spain. . . . As a pedestrian and flag bearer, Sergeant Bates has displayed very fair qualities, and would probably make an efficient bill poster if he could be prevailed upon to advertise anybody else but himself. The voice of Sergeant Bates for war, however, amounts to about as much as a penny whistle in a thunder storm."[17]

From Bates's one-time home state of Wisconsin, write-ups included, "It seems as though Sergeant Bates, the great American flag idiot, is striving for no other end than to get his name into some forthcoming biographical dictionary. He has abandoned his idea of nailing the American flag to the North Pole, and now turns his attention to the introduction of prairie chickens into the island of Madagascar."[18]

The *Bolivar Bulletin*, based in Bolivar, Tennessee, told that an unidentified Western paper "introduces Sergeant Bates as 'the flag-toting fiend.'"[19]

Referring to Bates, an article admonished, "Don't swear; we only wish to mention the fact that he is alive, and that he proposes to start from Windsor, Ontario . . . to carry the stars and stripes unfurled to Toronto."[20]

Some eight years after his march through the South, Bates had a plan to perform a venture of the same nature while in the accompaniment of others. A Hillsborough, North Carolina, bulletin alleged,

The South has escaped the grasshopper and the army worm, but she cannot escape the national nuisance, Sergeant Bates. During the approaching fall he proposes to wrap himself and thirteen companions in American flags and proceed from Bunker Hill to every town and city in the Southern States, assessing the inhabitants as he passes through to pay the expenses. We don't see why the South is to be afflicted by this fellow . . . we cannot endear Sergeant Bates. If he comes . . .

we hope that he and his thirteen banner-bearers will be put upon the chain-gang as vagrants, even if such a proceeding should involve the country in civil war. So says the Augusta Chronicle and Sentinel.[21]

Cruel intentions were expressed in the words, "Wicked men are trying to persuade Sergeant Bates to carry the Pope's flag through Germany before he dies. In that way, he might bring joy to his country and secure an early grave."[22]

In 1875, Gilbert Bates made a trip to Canada. One of the earliest attempts at casting a negative perspective on this event appeared in a Nevada newspaper: "The great American jackass, otherwise known as Sergeant Bates, is marching through Canada. [A] $7.25 reward is offered for his head on a charger."[23]

During Bates's Canadian adventure, a column cried, "Crops are big, money is easier . . . fall trade is good . . . Bates is in Canada, and why can't we all be happy this winter!"[24]

More unfounded negative remarks regarding Bates included, "Sergeant Bates is in Canada. We are very much afraid that they will not bury him on consecrated ground; and occasionally the harrowing thought comes over us that they may possibly not bury him at all."[25]

Another record of Bates in Canada said, "Sergeant Bates dares to carry the American flag through Canada, but he has no money to pay traveling expenses, and his friends are afraid to send him funds to move, for fear he will come home."[26]

It was noted of Bates during his tenure in Canada, "Sergeant Bates has been hindered at London, Canada. They will not allow him to walk; at least they will not allow him to walk out of town until he pays his hotel bill."[27]

During Bates's Canadian adventure, a mishap on the trek was unfavorably covered in an Albany, Oregon, newspaper: "A mule has kicked Sergeant Bates in Canada. Bless that mule. Bates is now freezing there on the fires of patriotism."[28]

From New Orleans, in April 1876, came, "Sergeant Bates can now tote the American flag in all countries but his own. He has worn himself threadbare in the United States."[29]

In the summer of 1876, a harsh passage prevailed in a Watertown, Wisconsin paper, "It is said that one Johnson, of Gloucester, Mass., will attempt to cross the Atlantic in a dory soon. He might take Sergeant Bates along, and bob for whales . . . on the way. The country can afford to spare some of its cheap sensationalists."[30]

Bates served as fodder for an undesirable international comment in a November 1876 statement: "It will be a matter of disappointment to many to learn that Sergeant Bates has decided not to carry the Russian flag through Turkey."[31]

A Dallas daily stated, "Dallas has had a good many trying experiences . . . but amidst all of her afflictions she has been spared the affliction of Sergeant Bates, the champion peripatetic fraud and national tramp."[32]

The critics of Bates and the rumors surrounding him became even more vile as the ten-year anniversary of the march approached. A Delaware daily described, "Sergeant Bates, the renowned flag-carrier attempted to commit suicide last night. His family have been utterly destitute for nearly a year."[33]

A Cincinnati publication similarly remarked, "A special today . . . says that Sergeant Bates, the flag carrier, attempted to destroy his life by taking an overdose of laudanum. Sergeant Bates has been residing at Saybrook for some time past, and it is known that his family have been in utter destitution for nearly a year, being objects of public charity."[34]

Laudanum was a mixture of alcohol and opium, and it was used to relieve headaches, insomnia, and a variety of other issues. Due to its highly addictive nature, an undetermined high percentage of its users became dependent upon it.[35]

Approximately two weeks later, a South Carolina news outlet offered, "Sergeant Bates . . . attempted to commit suicide the other day. His family are living at Saybrook, Illinois, in perfect destitution, the objects of public outcry."[36]

Seemingly unsympathetic to the demoralizing comments regarding Bates, "We don't like to see Americans making fools of themselves . . . that remark doesn't apply to Sergeant Bates. He was a fool from the beginning."[37]

Some eight years after his march across the South, Bates was the subject of an article in a South Carolina newspaper. The reporter who penned the notice began with a positive stance, but quickly devolved into a demeaning dissertation of him: "The irrepressible Sergeant Bates has turned up in Philadelphia. He proposes to establish a camp near the centennial grounds next summer, where poor, crippled soldiers of either army may find a soldier's fare and a soldier's welcome. To raise funds for this purpose, Sergeant Bates is about starting on a lecturing tour, which will extend through the Southern States. We will trust his tour will not be extended into the State of Newberry. We have no use for tramps down here."[38]

On April 4, 1878, Bates gave a speech in the small town of Gibson City, Illinois. After his presentation, Bates stood outside the lecture hall and visited with a gentleman surnamed Swimford. At that point, "two desperate looking characters came up to the place where Bates and Swimford were standing." When Swimford left the scene, "Bates was knocked down and terribly beaten, and robbed of a diamond and $37 in money, besides a watch and chain."[39]

Another precise cutdown of Bates indicated, "The fools are not all dead yet. Sergeant Bates is alive . . . and is in destitute circumstances."[40]

The *Alpena Weekly Argus* argued, "A remarkable book had appeared in Germany titled 'Of the Rare Act of Prolonging Life till 115 Years.' Great efforts are being made to keep this book out of the hands of . . . Sergeant Bates."[41]

A year after the suicide attempt articles began circulating, a Nevada newspaper noted, "The pleasant, but, we fear, groundless, report is in circulation that Sergeant Bates, the flag bearer, is dying. Ring out the wild bells, and let him die."[42]

In 1879, a man named Potter grew determined to push a cart from Albany, New York to San Francisco. In belittling this planned effort, a Louisiana publication proclaimed, "Sergeant Bates limped from one end of the Union to the other, carrying the American flag over his shoulder, the derision which greeted his absurd and wholly unnecessary test of loyalty should have been enough to discourage any further demonstrations of that character. But it was not." The editorial went on to say, "The sergeant, whose skull was stuffed with patriotic zeal to the exclusion of brains, was followed by the Albany numb-skull."[43]

Rumors about Bates's poor health continued to circulate; this is shown in an 1881 Chicago article that was written in Saybrook, Illinois: "Sergeant Bates . . . is lying at his home in a very low condition, and it is thought that his recovery is very doubtful."[44]

Approximately thirteen years from the time Bates made his march, Russian Czar Alexander II was the victim of an assassin's bomb. Insensitive to that, a periodical proclaimed, "A communist . . . in New York told a . . . reporter that Gould and Vanderbilt would soon follow the czar. The people of America had much rather see Sergeant Bates . . . cut off by the assassin's bomb."[45]

One month after the remarks about the bomb, another article erroneously exclaimed, "Sergeant Bates . . . is dead, leaving his wife and six children in extreme poverty."[46]

A week later, a Minnesota weekly backed off the claims of Bates passing but remarked, "Sergeant Bates . . . is reported as dying in extreme poverty in Saybrook, Illinois. He has a wife and six children who will be left destitute."[47]

Additional information included, "Sergeant Bates . . . was visited a few days ago by a reporter who found him in a dilapidated cottage, without carpets or curtains, or furniture worth mentioning. The man whose strange freak has made his name known to all the country, looked pale, haggard and emaciated. . . . For years Bates . . . has not been known to do any kind of work except to write queer things about his flag-carrying schemes, or to run to some neighboring town and deliver a lecture on the same subject."[48]

The criticism of Bates and his frugality, or lack thereof, proceeded: "he was made the recipient of a large number of presents, including jewelry, books, paintings, etc. All these, one by one, have been disposed of to furnish the means of subsistence for the deluded creature."[49]

"Poor Sergeant Bates" was the title of an 1883 article that boasted that he "is living in a retired village in Illinois, poor and helpless." The reporter referred to Bates as "a retired crank" with "crank" being equated to "the latest slang for semi-lunatic." It was also noted that Bates was "dilapidated and torn down to the last degree." Other negative remarks about Bates included that he "continually dwells on the flag business" and that "in a few short months he sank into obscurity, at the same time coming to the conclusion that the flag-carrying business financially could not be called a great success."[50]

Publications across the nation used Bates as an unfavorable comparison. In referring to the early stages of the temperance movement and one of its most prominent leaders, the *Daily Astorian* acknowledged, "Miss Frances E. Willard, president of Woman's Christian Temperance Union, has declared her intention to carry the white ribbon from Florida to Oregon. We hear Miss Frances would weaken before she crossed the Rockies." Adding Bates to the conversation, the reporter held, "Sergeant Bates . . . has all the pedestrian business pre-empted, anyhow."[51]

When Bates planned to make an 1883 tour with his son, the press had a fit over the idea. A Savannah, Georgia, paper imparted, "Sergeant Bates with his flag is abroad again. This time his fourteen-year-old boy is with him carrying the flag, while the Sergeant does the talking and distributes conciliatory literature." The planned date for departure was October 1, 1883. While Bates held the idea of promoting "a better feeling" between the two former enemies, the North and the South, it was said of him that he "is probably a crank, and if he lives to be a hundred . . . will keep up his whine about a better feeling." The write-up went on to defame Bates: "He doesn't seem to know, and probably doesn't want to know, that the feeling . . . is just about as good as . . . between Wisconsin, the state in which he formerly resided, and Illinois, in which he now resides . . . his craze is of a kind that is harmless."[52]

Fifteen years after Bates left his home and family in an effort to promote unity and peace, his family also became targets of less-than-favorable comments in the press. A Minnesota man proposed, "It was bad enough when the country had one Sergeant Bates, but there was hope that the old man would die sometime and the walking American flag nuisance would thus terminate. But now comes the discouraging news that Sergeant Bates has a son, and father and son are about undertaking a joint flag marching expedition."[53]

The ridicule of the Bates family continued, "This thing having started from generation to generation the hope for relief is indefinitely postponed. Supposing . . . Sergeant Bates is gathered to his fathers or his grandfathers, that his son should have a son, and so on. . . . If there was any portion of the country where the American flag was in danger, the valor of the Bates family might be commended, but it is simply a prostitution of the national colors for bread and beer."[54]

Bates arrived in Chicago in early October 1883, planning to march to Atlanta, and the reception at the Chicago City Council meeting was far from positive. In an article titled "Sergeant Bates Not Appreciated," it was told, "The Council kindly allowed . . . Bates to use the Council chamber last evening for the purpose of delivering a lecture. He did not lecture. When the hour arrived, the only persons present were the Sergeant, his son . . . and one reporter . . . said . . . he would get the ear" of the citizens of Chicago and would not be kept from doing so even "if he had to stand on the curbstone and gather a crowd by sheer force of lungs."[55]

Soon after the proposed trip of Bates and his son was discouraged and demeaned, the animosity toward Bates was voiced in a Nevada newspaper. "Sergeant Bates is a bummer. He wants to live without work, because he carries an American flag, but he is no worse than hundreds of others who would be dreadfully offended if they were called anything but United States officials, and yet they think they ought to live without working because they once followed an American flag, mostly at a good safe distance."[56]

The insults continued during the fifteen-year anniversary of the Bates march: "It is suggested that Sergeant Bates should get on a railroad track and defy a train to run over the American flag, or even shake it in a bull's face, he can get up a difficulty in either case."[57]

Speaking engagement dates for Bates appeared in a November 1883 Hopkinsville, Kentucky, issue. For example, Bates planned to speak at Petersburg on November 23, Hopkinsville on November 24, Pembroke the following day, and Trenton on Monday, November 26. The high level of presentations Bates made were recorded, "He has delivered over 1,800 free lectures in the Northern states within the last seven years."[58]

A Paris, Kentucky newspaper reported in December 1883, "Sergeant Bates . . . is now lecturing in Southern Kentucky . . . the fool-killer can't attend to his business promptly without more assistance."[59]

By late December 1883, Bates and his son were in Chattanooga, Tennessee, as they traveled from Chicago to Atlanta. From the time the duo departed Chicago, Bates had given eighty-five free lectures. A Memphis reporter remarked, "How he pays expenses we are not advised. Carrying the flag has not been attended with any risk more than of a cold or the rheumatism since 1865."[60]

The animosity and accusations toward and against Bates continued as an 1884 Tennessee newspaper noted, "It seems that the great chronic tramp, Sergeant Bates, has proven to be nothing but a Republican spy after all. . . . The Sergeant believes that a Solid South still exists, and a Solid North will be a national necessity for some years yet. He is merely carrying out his orders from the party bosses, no doubt, in his false and slanderous statements. Because the dirty tramp was not made a hero of, he says that the South hates the old flag."[61]

Another degrading set of statements regarding Bates said, "The miserable deadbeat . . . the Sergeant has been treated like any other tramp who tries to get a living at the expense of people who have to work for others."[62]

Bates appears to have traveled the nation in the years after his march; an 1884 article admonished,

> *Sergeant Bates is in Washington, having finished a trip from Chicago to Savannah, Georgia. This is the crank who roams through the country on foot carrying the American flag to prove the friendliness with which the stars and stripes are observed throughout the Union. In the present instance, the friendly spirit does not seem to have been exhibited to the usual extent, for Sergeant Bates complains of ill treatment on his journey. It would be unfair . . . to interpret the coolness of the South towards . . . Bates as indicating a lack of respect for the flag. It was the bearer, not the flag, that brought forth the gibes and sneers of the people. . . . Let Sergeant Bates attempt to beat his way*

through the North with the flag as his only excuse, and he will find no
heartier welcome than in the present case. Sergeant Bates has become
a nuisance.[63]

During the Christmas season of 1884, a disheartening rumor regarding Bates appeared in an Idaho paper. It offered, "Sergeant Bates . . . is in poor health and at the point of starvation at his home in Saybrook. Today his army saber, which clanked at his heels in his travels, was levied on and sold for debt."[64]

An 1885 article provided possibilities that Bates was the recipient of a major inheritance. The write-up pronounced, "Benevolently patriotic persons, who, having heard that Sergeant Bates was in a state of destitution, have thought of diverting their proposed . . . contributions to the flag-carrier's benefit, may now adhere to their original purpose of patronizing Liberty. A wealthy citizen of Philadelphia has died and left the Sergeant $13,000, which, if he does not spend it for flags, should be sufficient to keep him from the alms house."[65]

Also hinting at newfound financial stability, a South Dakota reporter stated, "Sergeant Bates has found a friend in need in the shape of an admirer who has just left him a legacy of $13,000. The sergeant did not find 'showing the flag' a paying business, and has lately been in extreme want, so that this streak of fortune comes in good time."[66]

While Bates was said to have become financially destitute, had attempted suicide, and had passed away, an 1885 passage in a Montana news source, and reinforced in several other papers across the nation, continued the negative aspects of his alleged job-seeking: "An amusing letter was received at the Post Office Department recently from Sergeant Bates. He wants a place in the department. The letter relates that [he] has walked 48,000 miles, made 2,600 lectures . . . all the while carried the United States flag and advanced the notion that sectional hatreds . . . should be forgotten."[67]

CHAPTER TWENTY-ONE

Praises for Bates

BATES'S MARCH THROUGH THE SOUTH, AS WELL AS HIS EVENTUAL TREK through England, produced positive comments all around the world. As with the comments that were less than favorable, many of the positive remarks record the only references to a variety of activities in which Bates participated after his American sojourn.

Bates noted in a manuscript published in 1873 that he "had to run the gauntlet of criticism common to all whose conception of duty had led them into a prominent position before the world; and I have also shared, and to a much greater extent . . . the sometimes fulsome flattery which are equally the lot of such men. I have been called at once a hare-brained visionary, a patriot, a fool, a man of courage . . . and a remarkably shrewd, thoughtful individual."[1]

One of the earliest examples of positive views appeared in March 1868, while Bates was still engaged in his march. The article said, "The condition of the South and the feelings of the Southern people cannot be successfully misrepresented long in the face of such facts as the journey of Sergeant Bates across the Southern States with only the stars and stripes for his scrip and purse."[2]

After Bates visited Columbia, South Carolina, the *Daily Phoenix*, a publication in that city, claimed, "This patriotic Union soldier who has taken upon himself the praiseworthy task of [ending] . . . the unfounded assertions of the enemies of the Constitution and the Union . . . that Northern men were not safe in the South. . . . The Sergeant is a good walker and stands the fatigues of his journey very well. . . . He deserves well of the Southern people . . . he is really the champion in this task . . . we earnestly commend him to their good graces and kind attentions along the rest of his route."[3]

It is well documented that Bates was offered $10,000 to make a premature end to his march. If the accusations that Bates was financially destitute were true, his refusal to accept the bribe shows a great deal about his character and morals. Those facets are also recorded in an article that told, "He said he had been offered $10,000 to work for the Radical party, but the interest and perhaps the life of the country depends upon the result of the next Presidential election, and that is more valuable to him than gold."[4]

A Pennsylvania paper proclaimed, "The popular Northern sentiment, that no man was safe in the South, who supported the American flag, was rife in Wisconsin, and led to the boast by Sergeant Bates of that state. . . . There is no fear of insult to the American flag in the South."[5]

A mixed review of Bates's success was offered in a June 1868 issue of an Ohio tabloid. The puzzling scenario was, "At present time, a Union man is not sure of his life one day . . . rebels will enter his . . . house and murder him in cold blood, without any cause, except for being a Union man. While Sergeant Bates was carrying a Union flag through the South unmolested, Union men were being shot down in cold blood, in different parts of the same region. How do the Democracy explain this?"[6]

Within weeks of completing his historic march across Dixie, Bates was approached about making a similar trek through New England. A Virginia paper proclaimed, "he promptly denied on grounds of being extremely hazardous to life and property." The proposed New England venture was explained, "The proposition is that the Sergeant shall undertake a trip through all the New England States, except Connecticut, carrying the flag . . . and in all other respects the same as he did in his late tour through the South." However, Bates rationalized that the trip was too risky because, "To undertake a journey through the New England States without money is equivalent to starvation . . . [and] to travel through that region with money he ran a great risk of being robbed on the way."[7]

Bates visited New York City in July 1868, and he was met with wonderous rounds of applause and appreciation. Appearing at the Soldiers and

Sailors Convention, "a great stir and boisterous cheering announced an unlooked-for sensation. This was no less a distinguished personage than Sergeant Bates with his inevitable flag and suit of black velvet. Amid round after round of applause, and with springy step, he marched down the aisle and ascended the platform, where he was introduced to the Convention."[8]

The ovation for Bates continued at the New York Convention, "His reception was most enthusiastic, and the cheering was louder than on any previous occasion. The Sergeant was honored with a seat among the dignitaries on the platform. The Committee of Soldiers and Sailors then entered the room. . . . This delegation was cheered, but with far less enthusiasm than was manifested at the appearance of the Sergeant."[9]

In August 1868, just months after Bates reached Washington, D.C., a South Carolina daily declared, "Sergeant Bates has published a volume entitled 'Sergeant Bates' Triumphal March,' containing an account of his unmolested trip from Vicksburg to Washington, alone and unarmed, bearing the United States flag."[10] While this announcement largely appears to be positive, it is noteworthy that it was located on the third page of a publication produced in one of the primary cities that Bates visited for the intention of instilling peace and forgiveness.

In what could be contrived as a nineteenth-century book review, it was noted, "We have received from the Sergeant a copy of his pamphlet describing his solitary journey from Vicksburg . . . to Washington, D.C. It is very short, but, we suppose, is merely the forerunner of a more extended work. . . . The pamphlet is a very readable one."[11]

A September 1868 article acknowledged,

The celebrated soldier, who carried the American flag, on foot, from Vicksburg to Washington, starts . . . on a grand horseback march from the capital of New York to St. Paul, the capital of Minnesota . . . clad as when he made the trip from Vicksburg, carrying the same flag . . . and also wearing the elegant sash presented him by the ladies of Montgomery, Alabama. . . . Sergeant Bates is a young man, a gentleman, a tolerably good soldier, a lover of his country, and we recommend him to the public as entitled to their heart-felt esteem. His trip is a long one, but he will make it and do good by it.[12]

Bates appeared in Columbus, Ohio, in October 1868. His reception was recalled, "This patriotic soldier . . . was a perfect ovation. . . . Last night, he delivered a stirring speech before the White Boys in Blue at Thurman Hall. He will march at the head of the procession . . . this afternoon, carrying the flag presented to him at Vicksburg and which he carried through the Southern States."[13]

A crime involving Bates as the victim was reported in a New Orleans publication in December 1868. Titled "Sergeant Bates Is in Grief," the contents were, "Sergeant Bates . . . came to New Orleans lately and was entertained or was on exhibition at the display of Democratic banners at Masonic Hall . . . the Sergeant found himself among thieves last night, who at Irvin's lodging house, corner of St. Charles and Gravier Streets, robbed him of ninety-five dollars in greenbacks and the pocketbook presented to him by President Johnson. The Mobile people to which he goes to lecture will make up the Sergeant's losses in the Crescent City."[14]

Three days after he was robbed, Bates was given some sense of justice when a young boy hired to sweep a store discovered miscellaneous items. The report stated, "The papers stolen from Sergeant Bates . . . were found . . . later stowed away between the show window casing and wall of a neighboring store on St. Charles Street, where the thief, finding them useless to him, had probably placed them in passing as being likely to be thence recovered and returned."[15]

Bates sought the return of the gift from President Johnson, and his plea was published a short time after the robbery. Bates's request read, "The sergeant says he is willing to let the ninety dollars in money go, provided the thief will but return him the pocketbook, a memento from President Johnson."[16]

While Bates's critics claimed his financial struggles were due to character flaws or a lack of motivation, his supporters felt far more compassion for the situation Bates faced. It remarked, "Bates is now without a penny. He is a gallant and handsome young fellow, and the people of New Orleans ought to do something in favor of the standard bearer."[17]

Bates arrived in Milwaukee in 1869; it was noted, "Bates . . . is at present in Milwaukee. That city honors the distinguished gentleman with a complimentary benefit at the rink, and he amuses the quiet people of that village with an exhibition of the trophies of his march."[18]

In July 1881, Bates was speaking on the Morris, Illinois, public square and fell from the stage. His misstep caused Bates to break his leg.[19] No other information about this exists.

By October 1883, Bates had evidently planned another march. An article announced that Bates and his son would leave Chicago in mid-October for a journey "to Atlanta, Ga., and from thence to Charleston, S. C." Bates intended to make speeches as his son and he made their trek.[20]

Additional, yet limited, insight into Bates's 1880s march with his son appeared in a clipping from March 1884:

Sergeant Bates, the great American flag carrier . . . has just reached Washington from Savannah. He started from Chicago on the 15th of October last with his son Frank . . . carried the stars and stripes through Illinois, Indiana, Kentucky, Tennessee, Alabama, and Georgia, traveling 1,150 miles on foot, reaching Savannah on the 24th of January, addressing 119 public meetings en route. He evidently had a tough time of it during his tramp, for he was mobbed on several occasions, and, although he proclaimed his mission to be that of peace and good will, he was not cordially greeted.[21]

Almost two decades after Bates completed his Southern march, he continued to be mentioned in the same respect. The article ascribed, "All intelligent readers will recall Sergeant Bates . . . does speak, and the following is what he says." At that point in the write-up, the information included a letter Bates had written to an Iowa resident surnamed Tuttle.[22]

James Madison Tuttle was born in Ohio but moved to Iowa as a child. He held a variety of jobs, including sheriff, recorder, and treasurer of his county before joining the Second Iowa Infantry as a twenty-seven-year-old officer. He encountered action at Fort Donelson, narrowly avoided capture at Shiloh's Hornet's Nest, and later took part in the Vicksburg Campaign. He embezzled large sums of money during the Civil War and returned to Iowa almost a year before the struggle ended. He was an Iowa legislator in the postwar years, and he also dabbled in real estate, mining, and the meat-packing business.[23]

The letter said, "To General Tuttle, Iowa. . . . A friend of mine, a former resident of Iowa, has shown me a copy of . . . your great Fourth of July speech, in which . . . you foresee and foretell another rebellion in the factories, furnaces, iron and coal mines and cotton fields of the South."[24]

Bates added, "Your great speech has caused great uneasiness in this part of the Nation. . . . We have no factories, furnaces, iron nor coal mines . . . so that should you conclude to dynamite the factories and furnaces . . . it would work but little harm to us, and might insure the safety of the nation and remove the apprehensions of the Grand Army of the Republic."[25]

Additional words from Bates's letter were,

What troubles us is: What shall we raise or make that will not be contraband of war? We can not raise corn, this writer subsisted thirty days on parched corn during the late rebellion, and on corn meal during the war . . . the Georgia rebels lived on sweet potatoes all through the rebellion . . . it is an ascertained melancholy fact that Jeff Davis is fond of peanuts and eats a quart of them every day . . . persimmons were the daily rations of the North Carolina rebels. . . . Our soil and climate are admirably adapted to the production of cow peas, but they are a South Carolina product.[26]

Bates continued, "We are here in a splendid country. We are here in a splendid country. While God's people are sweltering in Iowa the lungs of these Florida rebels are filled with the finest breezes from the sea. . . . We assure you . . . we are very loyal, and never intend to beat our plough-shares into words, nor our pruning hooks into spears. . . . We hardly know what to eat or what to drink for fear of unwillingly bringing on another rebellion."[27]

As Bates concluded, he wrote, "You will please excuse my not addressing you by your Christian name, as I have never heard it; indeed, it is only quite recently that any of us heard of you by any name. I have inquired about you of several former citizens of Iowa . . . But as there never was and never will be but one General Tuttle, you will doubtless receive this letter."[28]

CHAPTER TWENTY-TWO

Bates Marches across England

REGARDLESS OF NEGATIVE NEWS SURROUNDING HIM FOR HAVING marched across the South and those who questioned his incentive, Gilbert Henderson Bates was given a new challenge in the late summer of 1872. At that time, Thomas J. Warren, a merchant in Saybrook, Illinois, the town in which Bates then resided, offered Bates $1,000 to $100 from Bates that carrying the Stars and Stripes "from the Scottish border to the Mansion House in London" could not be accomplished under the same conditions Bates was given when he completed his Southern expedition.[1]

Bates recalled the British-related wager in a September 5, 1872, letter to the editor of the *New York Herald*: "I forward you an article . . . giving a correct account of the origin of a journey I intend to make with the American flag through England. Whether I am right or wrong in my opinion of the English people is a question I hope to decide soon. However, as to myself, I firmly believe, and shall until demonstrated to the contrary, that I am right."[2]

As he had dealt with at the onset of his Southern sojourn, Bates stood firm that "a majority of the people of this country believe . . . that there is but very little friendship in the English heart for Americans. I am confident that I can and will prove such an idea to be erroneous."[3]

Another article added that the conversation between Bates and Mr. Warren, who was erroneously noted as being a resident of Faybrook, Illinois, hinged upon Bates's comment "nations are nearer together than is commonly supposed, and offered as an example his tour through the South." Warren reportedly retorted, "I will bet you $1,000 to $100 that you can't do that in England." A response from Bates was, "Done." At that point, the contract between Bates and Warren was "drawn up, signed, sealed, and delivered in the presence of witnesses."[4]

When Bates was asked the reasons for undertaking a trudge across England, he noted two answers. First, "being a man of little means, I desire to secure the amount Mr. Warren risks upon the result for the benefit of my family." Bates held the second point or rationale as "believing that the journey, properly conducted on my part, will increase, to some extent, the friendly feeling now existing between the people of England and America."[5]

In his account of the British trip, Bates restated his second reason, "the prime object of my coming to England at all, was to establish the friendliness of England to the United States."[6]

Bates was also quick to state that he firmly felt he had the right to undertake such a task, in that he had "a right to carry the American flag through England on a friendly mission" while he also believed that "no power exists with authority to prevent my doing so except the people of England. If they say not, I shall never tramp the soil of Old England under the folds of the American flag; otherwise I shall."[7]

In addition to explaining his reasons for undertaking the march across England and the right to do so, Bates added,

> I make the above brief statement in hopes you will publish the same in the columns of the Herald; for, no doubt, the motives which actuate me in this matter will be as greatly misrepresented as were the motives which actuated me when making the journey with the national flag through the late Confederacy. In this case, as in that, I assumed the obligation on the impulse of the moment. In that case, my judgement did not mislead me. . . . However, it seems to me that, by crossing the Atlantic in the character I propose, I simply return to the old homestead to see my mother.[8]

The *New York Herald* also published an article that William Van Voris wrote in relation to the wager Bates and Warren made. Van Voris stated, "A contract has been made and duly signed by and between Gilbert H.

Bates and Thomas J. Warren, of Saybrook, McLean County, Illinois on a wager of $1,000 against $100 that the said Bates cannot carry the flag of the United States in the daytime and on foot, said flag to be of large size and displayed from a nine-foot flag staff, from the dividing line between Scotland and England to the Mayor's Hall in the city of London, without molestation or insult to him or the flag."[9]

Bates agreed to obtain a certified voucher from each town he entered as a means of verifying that he had safely visited the same. In turn, Bates would enable himself to secure the wager of $1,000 which Warren had bet.[10]

Van Voris added that the origin of the wager stemmed from a conversation between Warren and Bates in which "the subject of the English people towards the United States in connection with the Alabama Claims came up. . . . Mr. Warren remarked the English people entertained feeling of hatred towards this country, and if the arbitrators at Geneva decided in favor of the United States that it would renew the old animosities."[11]

The Alabama Claims to which Van Voris referred originated during the War Between the States and would be settled in 1872, the year Bates walked across England. The claims centered upon the construction of Confederate warships that were built as merchant vessels to avoid England negating its neutrality during the war. One historian of the claims wrote, "The peaceful resolution of these claims seven years after the war ended set an important precedent for solving serious international disputes through arbitration, and laid the foundation for greatly improved relations between Britain and the United States."[12] This dispute between England and the United States had also added to the view many Americans held that England had favored the Confederate States of America during the Civil War. Bates desired to attempt to diminish that tension and the feelings of pro-Confederate sentiments on the part of England.

A Nashville publication made reference to the Alabama issue in writing, "Now that the Alabama muddle has been smoothed over, Sergeant Bates wants to march through England carrying the American flag from one end of the country to its other, as he carried it through the Southern States four years ago."[13]

Van Voris added, "Bates thought otherwise, and said that the masses of the people of England were friendly towards this country, and to show how people are mistaken sometimes in reference to public sentiment said that when he proposed to make the trip through the South many told him he would be murdered before he had travelled fifty miles when Mr. Warren said, while it was true that he had made the trip successfully through a single borough in England."[14]

"Mr. Bates, thinking he could make the journey in four weeks and at an expense of $400, and leave him $600, he closed the bargain, and the parties at once came to my office, and I drew up the contract in due form, when the parties signed the same in the presence of two witnesses, of which the following is a synopsis:"[15]

Van Voris elaborated,

> *Mr. Bates agrees on his part to go to England and with a flag of the United States of regulation size to commence his journey at some point on the north line of England, to proceed on foot, in the daytime, to travel to the Mayor's Hall in the city of London, with the flag displayed at full view during the entire trip, and return before the 1st day of January, A. D. 1873, with the vouchers of the municipal officers of the towns and boroughs that he may pass through on his journey aforesaid, that he has received no violence to himself or flag in said town, and upon presentation of the proofs is to receive $1,000. But it said should Bates be insulted, or the flag be dishonored or fails to perform the journey, he is to forfeit $100.*[16]

Papers as far away as Knoxville, Tennessee, printed news of Bates's contract. A daily from that city said, "Sergeant Gilbert H. Bates, who carried the stars and stripes through the South . . . proposes to carry the flag through England on a wager. He says he has a perfect right to do so if the people of England don't object. He thinks it will be the means of bringing about a better state of feeling between the United States and Great Britain."[17]

A Maine daily newspaper noted, "Sergeant Bates, who carried the United States flag through the Southern States three or four years ago, had found a daring person in Illinois, who wages $1,000 to $100 that he cannot carry the starry banner from the Scottish border to the mayor's Hall in London . . . offer is accepted."[18]

The *Chicago Tribune* announced,

> *Bates, who trotted through the South after the war . . . announces that he has bargained to repeat that gallant deed, with England instead of Dixie as the base of operations. There is no special objection to a man's making a fool of himself, as long as he harms nobody else, but it is very absurd to trumpet this trick of a charlatan as a great feat. There is no perceptible heroism in a man's arraying himself in a red coat, white vest, and blue pantaloons, and walking through England. We are unable to see why his carrying those colors in his hand, in the shape of a flag, instead of on his body, in the shape of clothes, introduces the heroic element into his achievement.[19]*

A Memphis, Tennessee, tabloid, upon learning of Bates's plans, published, "Some years ago, an inspired idiot named Sergeant Bates performed a tour of the Southern States. . . . Bates now proposes to carry the American flag from one end of England to the other. Bates should be polite and invite some true Englishman to carry the banner of St. George from Maine to California. . . . Should the Bates emblem receive like treatment in England, the blood of both countries would grow hot. . . . Bates must be stopped immediately."[20]

By October 1872, news of Bates's proposed trip was becoming more widespread. A Montana weekly paper proclaimed, "Gilbert H. Bates, the vagarious gentleman who carried the United States flag through the Southern States after the close of the war, is now going to test the feeling of the English people in their 'tight little island' by a similar per-formance."[21]

An October 3, 1872, article in the *Daily Dispatch* announced Bates's departure from his home, an event that had occurred a few days ear-lier. The article admonished, "Sergeant Gilbert H. Bates, who travelled through the South with the American flag unfurled at a perilous period . . . left Saybrook, Illinois on the 30th . . . en route for New York and

England, through which latter country he proposes to march under the flag the same as he did through the South."[22]

Saybrook had been founded in 1856 under the direction of Isaac Polk. Originally known as Cheney's Grove, the town's name was changed to Saybrook in 1865. Legend holds that that took place due to many of the people coming into the area because of nearby railroad construction had renamed it after Old Saybrook, Connecticut. The 1870 census revealed a population of 389 for the settlement the Bates family considered their home.[23]

An announcement in a Nevada paper voiced, "Late telegram . . . announces the departure of the famous and irrepressible Sergeant Bates for Europe, on a self-appointed, proud, and somewhat novel mission, being simply for the purpose of carrying the national flag . . . through England and Scotland. Ireland would have been included . . . , but this was deemed unnecessary, that country being considered well-inclined toward Americanism, and the people in their exuberant zeal might make public demonstrations not compatible with their loyalty toward the government under which they live."[24]

The decision to march to specific locations was explained, "Scotland, too, although more loyal to English rule, might not object to the old flag, but England was the objective point."[25]

A reporter for the *New York Herald* offered, "Sergeant Bates . . . had . . . a desire for pedestrian exercise, and a laudable wish to practically test the feeling of the people of England towards these United States." The journalist explained that those conditions "are impelling him to visit that country and carry the American flag through its length."[26]

One paper projected, "Under the peculiar circumstances and conditions of this bet . . . Bates, if he rightly manages the matter, might in place of exciting any antagonistic feeling, awaken a generous spirit of national admiration and chivalrous enthusiasm which would result in himself with his precious charge being received with public demonstrations in the hearty, whole-souled vein peculiar to the Anglo-Saxon race when occasion requires. The progress of the old flag through the United Kingdom will be regarded with interest by all nations."[27]

Full of errors and insults, an article from a Maine publication stated, "Sergeant Bates, who carried an American flag from Texas to New York in 1868 to show that the ex-rebels would not insult it, now proposes to try the same test upon the English people. . . . We suspect the Sergeant is so near a fool that he is of no use for any common labor, else he would not be striving for so cheap a notoriety."[28]

A late October article made an announcement about a critical phase of Bates's trip in exclaiming, "Next week the Sergeant leaves for Liverpool by the steamer *Manhattan* to carry the American flag from the boundary line between England and Scotland to the Guildhall in London."[29]

An update in relation to Bates's excursion announced, "Sergeant Bates starts for Europe on Wednesday. He will endeavor to carry the American flag floating above his head throughout England."[30]

When the day arrived for Bates's departure, the *New York Herald* reported, "Sergeant Bates will today embark for Europe to carry the American flag through England, in pursuance of a recent wager. He will, this morning, march with his flag from Union square down Broadway and through Dey Street to the steamship *Iowa*.[31]

An acknowledgement from New York City, dated October 20, 1872, stated, "Sergeant Bates sailed for Europe yesterday, after flapping his flag through the streets on his way to the steamer. . . . The Sergeant says he was robbed of $185 at the theater in this city . . . which will render him penniless when he lands in England. He depends now on British hospitality."[32]

Bates continued his elaboration on how to recover from the robbery, "I am in good health and expect to win the wager. I will raise money some way, if I have to dance the Highland Fling under the flag. I will go from Glasgow to Edinburg, and I will then go to the English border near Carlisle, I will then go by way of Kendall to Lancaster, thence to Manchester through Birmingham and Warwick to Oxford, and thence along the Thames Road to London. I expect to walk the entire distance in 18 days."[33]

The distance of Bates's British march was calculated at approximately three hundred miles. Another description of his route noted it as being "from the north line of England to the Lord Mayor's Hall, in London."

For that distance, he was to carry a flag measuring six feet by six feet atop the nine-foot staff.[34]

A short announcement of Bates's departure appeared in a New York City column, "Sergeant Bates has determined to 'flag' England, and for that purpose left Union Square, nearly an hour behind time, at five minutes before eleven o'clock yesterday morning. . . . He was clad in an army uniform of regulation cut, gaily trimmed with scarlet and gold and decked with navy buttons, and he wore the shako of an artillery officer."[35]

A small parade occurred at that point, and

the flag continually flapped in the faces, and wiped the eyes, mouths and noses of the passersby as the gallant non-commissioned raised or lowered it according as there were awnings or no awnings in his path. For several blocks its folds gracefully enveloped the dark-ly-beautiful features of a lady of African descent, who hailed it as an impromptu bandanna, and not the reverse, as it will probably be called in England. . . . Four boys continued with the procession to the wharf, and stared after the retreating form of the sergeant with a blank expression, when they were stopped at the entrance to the covered pier.[36]

An Indiana publication elaborated upon Bates's exodus from the United States and his personal costs in a negative manner: "Sergeant Bates, who earns a frugal living by carrying the American flag in the most daring manner through peaceful rural neighborhoods, has sailed for England. . . . Bates proposes to sacrifice his vote this fall to the interests of business."[37]

A much shorter announcement was, "Sergeant Bates has gone to England on the flag carrying wager."[38]

The *Chicago Daily Tribune* threw a negative slant toward Bates by saying, "There will be a very general feeling of relief that Mr. Sergeant Bates . . . has sailed from New York and is now on his way thither to carry out his plan. It is sincerely to be hoped that if the hard-headed Scotchmen clap him into an insane asylum no one in this country will be absurd enough to interfere and correct that natural proceeding. The despairing remark of

Macbeth, 'Time was that when the brains were out the man would die,' will derive new force from Sergeant Bates's Scottish journey."[39]

Bates wrote of his departure, "I remember very distinctly the faces and the speech of those who were gathered around me and followed me on my march down Broadway. Some were very incredulous of my success, and predicted that I would get into as nice a little mess as had ever entangled a fool-hardy human being. . . . Others, again, complimented me on my pluck, as they chose to call it; others chide me for my rashness; a few predicted for me a triumphant issue to the whole undertaking."[40]

A strong sign of support came from Benjamin Wood. That gentleman told Bates, "If you should find yourself at any time in Europe at a disadvantage, sick, or in need of money, apply to me, and the funds shall be forthcoming." At that point, Wood gave Bates $100 and offered to up the gift to $1,000.[41]

It is likely that the Benjamin Wood of which Bates spoke was born in Kentucky but moved to New York as a child. He served three terms as a congressman, and, as the editor of the *New York Daily News*, made the publication the highest-circulating daily publication of its day. His brother, a Democrat, was also the mayor of New York.[42]

Rather than boarding *Manhattan* as had been earlier predicted, Bates boarded *Europa*, "one of the Anchor lines of steamers." Bates paid $33.00 for what he labeled as "intermediate passage." A relatively new vessel, the 290-foot-long *Europa* had been built in Glasgow in 1867. A product of Alexander Stephen & Sons, its maiden voyage was from Glasgow to New York. It functioned until July 1878 when it with collided with the *Saffa* twenty-five miles north of Cape Finisterre.[43]

A large crowd of sightseers and well-wishers attended Bates's departure. He recalled, "After saying farewell to the many friends . . . who crowded the quay to see me off, I embarked, flag and all . . . and obtained a bunk for myself."[44]

A New York reporter exclaimed, "His name became a byword of heroism, and he retired after winning honors of which a noble soldier might well feel proud. Sergeant Bates is once more on the road to honor. Hearty and confident as before, he now sets out to perform a feat which, for novelty at least, has no parallel case on record."[45]

Bates reminisced, "The most remarkable thing about the *Europa* was the admirable precision and order which characterized all the proceedings on board. I never heard an angry utterance nor, that I recollect, an oath from either officers or crew." He also fondly recalled that "We were not long clear of land when Captain Archibald Campbell . . . came to me and asked if I would do him the honor to become his guest in the cabin during the voyage. Feeling that this was a tribute to the flag a much as to myself, I thankfully accepted his offer."[46]

While at sea, Bates read, played a variety of games, "lolled about on deck," and looked for approaching ships. He wrote, "When a ship hove in sight, we got out the telescopes and puzzled ourselves as to her nationality, name, crew, and destination. We used to ask such ridiculous questions of the officers that their good nature was racked to the utmost."[47]

From a spiritual standpoint, it was noted, "Sunday was observed most religiously on board. . . . I believe the Scotch are noted for their strict and reverential regard for the Sabbath, and this Scotch ship was eminently national in this respect."[48]

Bates saw the Irish coast, and one of the sailors told Bates that fourteen years had passed since he had set foot upon his native soil. Sadly, storms of the evening negated any passengers from disembarking at Moville. Bates recalled, "We made direct for the Clyde . . . and the Highland scenery of the adjacent coasts. How beautiful is Scotland!"[49]

Bates penned, "As we sailed up the Clyde, we saw the ship-building yards which have given Glasgow its world-wide reputation as the world's greatest ship-building mart. . . . Glasgow swarms with a busy, bustling population, every man of whom seems on business bent."[50]

Glasgow's origin can be traced to 1119, and its name, translated to English, means "Dear Green Place." The River Clyde cuts the city in half along an east-west line. Therefore, an accurate saying throughout the city's history has been "Glasgow made the Clyde and the Clyde made Glasgow." At the time Bates visited the city, the population was approximately 500,000.[51]

The River Clyde was the location of the launching for the world's first steamship in 1812. That event provided a catalyst for Glasgow to be a major shipbuilding location. The area was the site of manufacturing of ships sold to the North and South during the Civil War. Flowing a distance of 106 miles, the Clyde is the second-longest river in Scotland.[52]

Another set of impressions Glasgow made upon Bates centered upon the structures and the poverty. He wrote, "The first thing that struck me . . . on this, the first city of the old world I had visited, was the antiquity of the place. The buildings were big . . . weather-stained, smoke-begrimed . . . melancholy in aspect. . . . But I saw much of poverty, also, in Glasgow. Bare-footed women and children, a phenomenon happily very rare in our country . . . dirty lanes and squalid back courts."[53]

Bates stayed at the Waverly Hotel in Glasgow. He said it was "well-conducted and comfortable." In turn, Bates complimented Buchanan and Argyle Streets as "noble" in his eyes.[54]

The November 8, 1872, issue of the *New York Herald* hailed Bates's exit from Glasgow, "Sergeant Bates . . . set out from Glasgow on Tuesday . . . in the costume . . . adopted in America."[55]

From Glasgow, Bates traveled to Edinburgh, "the Metropolis of Scotland . . . unrivaled for its happy combination of rural and urban scenery." Bates noted the views from areas such as Calton Hill and how he perceived Princes Street as "level, broad, and straight as an arrow, with colossal structures on one side . . . monuments and gardens . . . on the other," causing Bates to feel as if he "had suddenly alighted on some city of the gods."[56]

By 600, Edinburgh was referred to as "Fort of Eidyn." Edinburgh replaced Scone as the capital of Scotland in 1437, and by 1500 over-population became an issue. The Old Town area of Edinburgh is largely located on volcanic rock, where it was originally formed.[57]

As he departed Edinburgh "for the Scottish borders at Gretna Green," Bates had a feeling of guilt as he did not unfurl his flag. He lamented, "My Scottish friends felt hurt that they had no opportunity of testifying their good feeling to the banner which waves over so many of their kindred in homes beyond the Atlantic." Bates assured those with whom he spoke that he would relay their affection to the residents of the United States.[58]

At Gretna Green, Bates was impressed with "the world-wide celebrity as the altar where so many runaway couples plighted their troth."

The beauty of the location added to a sense of uncertainty for Bates as he recalled that the marriage laws of the region made him think "it seemed to me to be so delightfully easy to get married in Scotland, that the difficulty in that country must be to know when one is not in the state of holy matrimony."[59]

Gretna Green grew in popularity after a 1754 law, Lord Hardwicke's Marriage Act, made it illegal for anyone under the age of twenty-one to marry in England. Because Scotland maintained the legal marriage age of fifteen, Brits routinely made the trek to Gretna Green, "possibly the most romantic place in Scotland, if not in the UK."[60]

CHAPTER TWENTY-THREE

Crossing England

BATES RECALLED THAT HIS NOON ARRIVAL AT GRETNA GREEN ENABLED him to visit a four-hundred-year-old structure called Sark Bridge and the River Sark. The latter landmark was significant one for Bates; he wrote, "The center of the River Sark is, for some distance, the dividing line between Scotland and England." Under the direction of Thomas Telford, the Sark Bridge, located on the Carlisle to Glasgow Turnpike Road, had been built in 1814.[1]

Astounding words from Bates included, "From this bridge my journey through England with the Stars and Stripes began. I paused awhile on the bank of the stream before I entered on the bridge and unfurled the flag . . . before me was England, our Mother Country, the home of the English language, the freest and most peaceable country in Europe. I now stood on its threshold a stranger with the flag and in the uniform of a nation thousands of miles beyond the Atlantic."[2]

An act of heroic proportions then occurred: "I was glad that I had freed myself from the taint of mercenary motive by posting my wager. . . . With no quiver of fear . . . but with a heart full of gladness, I stepped upon the bridge, and uncovering, gave the star-spangled banner to the breeze."[3]

The weather Bates encountered as he entered England was similar to that he had endured on numerous days during his march across the South. He wrote, "The weather was inauspicious. Heavy rains and strong winds prevailed all day. The dear old flag looked not the less lovely as it streamed in the breeze. . . . A few merry rustics were gathered around me, and . . . gave me some hearty cheers, a happy omen of the welcome greetings which were afterwards all through England to attend me."[4]

Some four miles outside of Carlisle, Bates met a group of men who were hunting, and he was invited to participate in their "Border Hare Coursing." Since a condition of Bates's journey was "that I should travel by daylight," he was forced to decline the gentlemen's offer. Bates added, "Their warm welcome put me in the best of spirits, and I entered Carlisle very well pleased. . . . I did not cause much stir in Carlisle. My march was as yet little known."[5]

Carlisle is a city rich in military history, making it an appropriate location for Bates to visit. It was originally a Roman town called Luguvalium. The Celts later gave it the name Caer Luel, and Vikings as well as Saxons eventually fought for its control. In 1092, King William Rufus rebuilt the city, and for the next several decades it changed hands many times. By 1851, the population grew to 25,000, due primarily to the arrival of Irish and Scottish immigrants.[6]

That evening, Bates reached Carlisle, where nothing "more important happening to me than a rigid cross-examination by an excited old woman . . . soon as she was satisfied that I was only a mad Yankee with a silly freak in his head, she insisted on my entering her house and drinking a glass of ale, which I did." Bates soon departed the elderly lady's home and carried with him her "best wishes for the success" of his journey as well as the memory of her telling him about friends she had in the United States.[7]

As the evening approached, Bates made his way to the Bush Hotel, "where a party of commercial gentlemen, good souls all of them, gave me a right hearty British welcome." Bates went on to say that he appreciated "these gentlemen for the courteous reception they gave the flag of my country." He recalled that the cities these men represented were Liverpool, Birmingham, Newcastle-on-Tyne, Hull, Langholm, London, and Gateshead-on-Tyne.[8]

Among the Carlisle locations Bates visited was Carlisle Castle, "one of the oldest keeps in England, once a place of confinement for prisoners of State." Built in 1092, it served as the headquarters of the Border Regiment, one of the oldest in the British army, at the time of Bates's visit. Individuals such as Wallace, Mary Queen of Scots, and Bruce had reportedly been held in the facility. More profoundly, Bates proposed, "No foreign soldier, carrying a foreign flag alone had ever gone, unmolested, so near it before. That I was now permitted to visit it in peace, seemed to me a good omen of that universal peace which I hope may long reign on earth."[9]

After one day at Carlisle, Bates left for Penrith. The only incidents he recorded from this portion of the English adventure began with Bates's encounter with a "moneyless" Irishman who walked with Bates "for a mile or two" until Bates outdistanced the man due to the latter's "sore feet." At that time, the "genial Irishman" saluted Bates "with many parting blessings on myself, my flag, and my country."[10]

Bates also noticed "a mansion house" from which he "saw white handkerchiefs waved from the windows." After saluting the home with his flag, Bates proceeded to "High Hesket," a village in Cumbria County, for lunch before arriving at Penrith at 6:00 p.m. He recalled that he "was entertained in the evening by leading citizens" and that "song, sentiment, and toast were kept up till a late hour." The sites Bates recorded as visiting were Beacon Tower, a fifty-foot-tall structure erected in 1846, and "situated on a high hill, and from which there is a magnificent prospect of the surrounding country," and King Arthur's Table, "a round piece of earthwork, enclosed in an arena for spectators."[11]

Bates marched from Penrith to the village of Shap; along the way he "had a fine view of Brougham Hall." Arriving in Shap at 4:00 p.m., Bates spent the night at Greyhound. No events were noted from that night, but Bates left Shap at 9:00 a.m. the following morning. He recalled receiving a rousing reception from granite workers who "seeing my flag winding its way up the opposite hill, mounted the jagged peaks of the quarries, and cheered me lustily.... For a few minutes the cheers were kept up; the flag the meanwhile fluttering bravely in the wind."[12]

As he made his way toward Kendal, Bates remarked, "For two or three hours, my journey was over a bleak, desolate moorland, where I met no one, and had no other eyes on the flag save those of a few harmless sheep.... I entered Kendal that afternoon. It was market day, and the streets were more than ordinarily thronged. So long as the flag appeared, it was welcomed with cheers."[13]

The *Manchester Guardian* reported in its November 14, 1872 edition, "When Sergeant Bates and his flag arrived in Kendall, all the public men of the town who were not pressingly engaged attended, and, after repast, speeches were delivered in which strong sympathy was expressed with Bates and his mission."[14]

Seemingly in disgust or protest of messages regarding Bates's progress being sent to the United States, a Washington, D.C. paper said, "We will thank the enterprising cableist on the other side not to send us any more about that intolerable flag-parading bore, Sergeant Bates. If he will forward us authentic information of Bates' timely end through softening of the brain, spontaneous combustion, or any other likely cause, we will cheerfully print it, not otherwise."[15]

Bates spent several days in Kendal after securing lodging at King's Arms Hotel, an establishment that opened in 1753. Making his presence there from Saturday through Monday, Bates's 4:30 p.m. arrival "did not attract so much attention as it would, had it been earlier, and people had been aware that he was coming." Liverpool author Samuel M. Harrison, Captain Bateson of the Navy, and Windermere Hotel authority "Mr. Rigg" were among his visitors. It was also recorded that "A large number of gentlemen also called in the course of the evening to pay their respects to Sergeant Bates, amongst the rest being Mr. Atkinson, of the *Westmorland Gazette*."[16]

A manuscript also acknowledged, "Bates . . . said that no reception, however grand and formal, could be more satisfactory to him than the kind and friendly manner in which he was now being received. He was only a common man . . . he . . . considered it no more friendly or flattering than the present reception."[17]

It was also recorded, "Bates said he believed that the people of America were desirous that nothing but peaceful relations should exist between them and England. Mr. Swinglehurst said they all rejoiced to see Sergeant Bates and the American flag in Kendal . . . although he was sorry to say that some people in Sergeant Bates's country thought differently, there was, in Kendal, no disposition to treat the American flag with cautious reserve; and persons who had examined the American flag and . . . institutions had feelings only of friendship towards that flag and that country."[18]

On November 11, 1872, Bates's last day spent in Kendal, he inscribed, "On Sunday, after visiting several places on interest in . . . Kendal, I dined at Aynham Lodge, the beautiful mansion of Mr. Edgar Robinson. I also visited a monument inscribed, 'Sacred to Liberty,' and which was erected in the year 1788, in memory of the English Revolution, a century before."[19]

As he left Kendal for Lancaster, Bates recalled, "Precisely at nine o'clock [a.m.], I set out for Lancaster. For some time before starting, my flag and the Union Jack were exhibited together in front of the Hotel, and, on making my appearance, a round of hearty cheers, first for one flag and then for the other, was given."[20]

Outside Kendall, Bates visited Levens Hall, "and was conducted over the magnificent gardens by Mr. Craig, the head gardener." The gardens at Levens Hall comprise ten acres and are regarded as "the world's oldest topiary gardens." Bates also took time to speak to the housekeeper of Levens Hall, a lady who, "on being informed by one of our party of the purport of my visit, she laughed heartily at the idea of anybody molesting 'so harmless an individual, with so harmless a thing as a flag.'" At that point, Bates continued the twenty-two-mile march to Lancaster under the accompaniment of Mr. Robert M. Dixon.[21]

Arriving in Lancaster at 5:00 p.m., Bates was escorted to the King's Arms Hotel where he was "put up for the night." Bates was intrigued by the establishment; Dickens dealt with it "in his story 'The Two Idle Apprentices,'" which Bates explained "describes it as a curious old house, teeming with ancient and elaborately-carved features." Bates spent the night in "a bedroom . . . known as King James the Second's Bedroom."[22]

Bates left Lancaster at 9:00 the next morning, and "an immense crowd" lined Market Street and cheered for his flag. He recalled, "They followed me to the outskirts of the town . . . after a deal of hand-shaking, I bade my good friends adieu and set off at a good steady pace for Preston."[23]

The November 13, 1872, issue of the *Preston Herald* provided an account of Bates's travels from Lancaster to Preston: "Quite a sensation was created in Preston yesterday afternoon by the entrance into the town of Color-Sergeant Bates, of the American Army, with a flag bearing the

Stars and Stripes, unfurled. The streets were lined with interested spectators, who cheered the Sergeant for his pluck, and gave him a cordial welcome to the ancient and honorable borough of Proud Preston."[24]

A period publication proclaimed, "The hearty people of that town . . . invited Sergeant Bates to the Royal Oak Hotel, where a sumptuous repast was provided; and whilst this was being enjoyed, the Church scholars were drawn up in line . . . and gave three hearty cheers for Sergeant Bates and the American flag. The streets were full of people, and an effort was made to induce him to remain with them all night, but . . . he was reluctantly compelled to decline their hospitality."[25]

It was also acknowledged, "Preston is a garrison town, but it is . . . an unusual thing to see a Sergeant dressed in his uniform, carrying an unfurled flag through the streets; and it is more unusual, we believe unprecedented, to see an American, dressed in regimentals of the Northern Army, bearing the flag of his great country with the familiar Stars and Stripes."[26]

While in Preston, Bates was asked how he had been treated to that point of his British march. Bates offered that he "had been favorably received, and had met with nothing more hostile on the road than one or two barking dogs." When he was asked what he would say constituted an insult, Bates said, "it would have to be in the nature of a public demonstration of disapprobation, or an open indication or dissatisfaction at his appearance on the part of some person or persons acting as representatives of the town passed through."[27]

Departing Preston at 9:00 a.m., Bates passed through Chorley, where "a large crowd awaited my arrival." After eating lunch, Bates headed toward Bolton. He stopped briefly approximately five miles outside of town for a drink at the Beehive Inn. He wrote, "all uncovering before the flag, a tribute of respect to my country for which I thanked them as I best could. . . . I arrived in Bolton about four p.m., and set up at the 'Swan.'"[28]

The twenty-mile journey between Preston and Bolton had been covered in only seven hours. By all reports, Bates's reception in Bolton was noted as "most cordial." Also, Bates was given a Union Jack and, according to a reporter, Bates "planned to carry it through the principal cities of the United States."[29]

A mid-December report sought to not only add to the origin of Bates's gift, but also to belittle Bates by saying, "That inflated specimen of humanity . . . who is now carrying the stars and stripes across England . . . has been presented . . . with a British Flag, which he will carry through the United States to show that no ill feeling exists against the 'Union Jack' in the 'Land of the Free.'"[30]

According to his 1873 memoir of the event, Bates "had a famous evening at the 'Swan,' as the good folks of Bolton seemed . . . to wish me success. The 'Swan' is a noted house in history. One of the Earls of Derby was beheaded in front of it."[31]

"Shortly after ten o'clock the next day, I unfurled my flag and proceeded on my march," Bates noted. Other departure details appeared in the November 14, 1872 issue of the *Bolton Chronicle*. It stated, "This morning . . . Sergeant Bates unfurled his flag at the door of the Swan Hotel . . . an immense crowd had gathered in Churchgate and Bradshawgate, rendering the streets almost impassable. . . . Bates . . . was loudly cheered, and was quickly surrounded by an eager crowd . . . the cheering being repeated at intervals. . . . Mr. William Thirlwind . . . presented him with a turtle dove . . . to . . . present it to President Grant."[32]

The *Bolton Evening News* said, "At Farnsworth . . . hundreds of persons were assembled in Market Street . . . manifesting the deepest interest in the arrival of the star-spangled banner. . . . On the arrival of Mr. Bates, there was more hand-shaking than we have ever seen bestowed on any person . . . every respect was shown to the flag of the great Republic. . . . Mr. Nathan Council . . . presented him with a piece of silver."[33]

In the midst of celebrations surrounding Bates and his triumphal march in England, a D.C. reporter penned, "*The New York Times*, animated evidently by a disposition to welcome Sergeant Bates to a hospitable grave, invites him to undertake to carry the English flag through the Irish Sixth ward of that city. Do it, Bates; that's a good fellow."[34]

From Vermont, word of Bates yielded, "Sergeant Bates, of flag-carrying notoriety . . . started from Gretna Green ten days ago, and a telegram today says he has arrived at Stockport, a few miles south of Manchester. Crowds always collect in the towns and villages through which he passes."[35]

A short announcement in the *New York Herald* hailed, "Sergeant Bates has reached Manchester."[36]

Bates recalled that "there was an immense reception on arriving at Manchester . . . the crowd was so dense that the open carriage I had been obliged . . . could scarce make headway." Additional information about Bates's Manchester entry, "The streets . . . were lined with curious and wondering spectators . . . he and his flag were . . . paraded through Market Street, Piccadilly, Portland Street, York Street, and Mosley Street to the Royal Hotel. Here, whatever his wishes might have been, the hero . . . was not allowed to take his ease at his inn."[37]

Bates countered the earlier report regarding his obtainment of the Union Jack and stated that it was at Manchester where he was given the banner. He said, "In the course of the evening, I was presented with a Union Jack by Mr. Jeremiah Bibby."[38]

An article in the *Chicago Daily Tribune* remarked, "We are not through with Sergeant Bates yet. In Manchester . . . he was presented with the Union Jack, which he intends to carry all over the American continent."[39]

Similarly, an American newspaper noted, "Here is another horror to be met. At Manchester, Sergeant Bates was greatly lionized, and was compelled to speak from a hotel balcony. Sergeant Bates was given an English flag . . . and announces his intention of carrying it all over the American continent. We trust his pedestrian powers will finally flag first."[40]

While in Manchester Bates "visited several of the leading warehouses" before he left early on Saturday morning. The *Manchester Examiner* stated, "The more anxious of our citizens will give a sigh of relief on learning that the star-spangled banner has been paraded through our streets without leading to breech of the peace. . . . No sane man anywhere, least of all in this part of England ever doubted the admiration with which we regarded the American nation."[41]

Leaving Manchester, Bates was given "the same hearty ovations which greeted me on my entry to Manchester." Bates recalled, "The crowd kept slapping me on the shoulders, shaking hands . . . slipping money in my pockets, hurrahing, singing, and even dancing with joy, before our glorious old flag. . . . A young lady and her little brother . . . accompanied me out of Manchester. . . . The girl's devotion to the flag was all the more welcome that she was an English subject."[42]

The next event for Bates was "at Macclesfield, I had another ovation. I was tendered the hospitalities of the Angel Hotel, and treated like a prince. On Sunday, I dined with the staff of the 2nd Royal Cheshire Militia, supped . . . with the Mayor. . . . Later in the evening, I was also entertained at the Punchbowl Inn, by quite a crowd."[43]

Bates added,

> *On Monday morning, I left Macclesfield, and arrived at Congleton at half-past eleven o'clock. I was conducted to the courtroom, which was crowded, and the Mayor introduced me in a neat little speech . . . several of the magistrates entertained me to luncheon. I was then escorted to the Lion and Swan, where another feast was spread. After a short sojourn, I set out amid deafening cheers, and arrived that evening at Burslem, where I was put up at the Leopard. The landlord . . . said he would feel insulted if I said a word about my bill.[44]*

The next day, Bates went to Stafford and was given a room at the Swan. The next night found Bates at Wolverhampton where he stayed at the Star and Garter. He elaborated, "Quite an ovation again. From this town to Birmingham, my march was like that of a triumphal warrior. The crowds at my heels . . . in military order, and tramped along to the singing of the national anthem."[45]

When Bates arrived in Birmingham, it was late afternoon, and he was "escorted by a crowd composed of all classes and all ages." He was given a room at the Hen and Chickens, where the proprietor, Mr. Oldfield, told Bates to "consider the house, wine cellar, cash drawer, everything your own while you are here." That night Mr. Oldfield carried Bates to the theater, and the following day Bates visited the American Consul.[46]

The *Portland Daily Press* of Portland, Maine mentioned, "The London agent of the Associated Press telegraphs us that Sergeant Bates 'has been well received in Birmingham.' If he had told us Bates had been well licked, it would have afforded us much more satisfaction."[47]

Leaving Birmingham and reaching the mid-point toward Warwick, Bates met Payton Pigott, who drove him toward the next village and ordered lunch. After viewing a set of stocks, "those old instruments of punishment," Bates stood "amid a crowd of assembled villagers ... happy speeches were made, full of complimentary allusions to the United States." Bates also stuck his flagstaff on the stocks, "and gave the folds of the banner of liberty to the breeze."[48]

Bates stayed at Warwick Arms after having found "several parties awaiting me," and on Sunday he visited Warwick Castle. At the castle Bates saw a helmet of Cromwell's and viewed portraits of several distinguished Englishmen. In the afternoon, Bates "drove to Stratford-on-Avon, and visited the house where Shakespeare first saw the light."[49]

In late November, a South Carolina paper proudly denounced Bates by saying, "That muscular idiot, Sergeant Bates, is tramping over England with the American flag in his hands. What a pity that bipeds are exempted from the ravages of the epizootic."[50]

Following a brief visit in Southam, Bates made his way toward Banbury and "encountered a fearful storm of wind and rain. Some poor moneyless people were tramping to Portsmouth, and with them we sought shelter for a while in a small wayside hostelry, and lunched on bread and cheese."[51]

Proceeding toward Oxford, Bates reached a junction where one road led toward Woodstock. There, "an enthusiastic deputation from that town met us, and beseeched us to visit their quaint old town. . . . Oxford was waiting for me at four o'clock, and I had to decline. We 'liquored up,' however, and indulged in a few fraternal speeches ... a few miles from Oxford I was met by the first party of students ... they saluted me kindly."[52]

Nearer Oxford, Bates "was struck with the beauty of its towers and spires ... the high dome of the Radcliffe Library, the tower of Magdalen, and the College spires. . . . All sorts of folks were at my heels. Little boys in broadcloth ... Street Arabs fresh from the gutter ... College Dons .. . students in blue and white flannel boating suits, and others in the solemnly-looking square cap and black gown, surrounded me."[53]

Bates ate supper in the University College and ate breakfast at Trinity College. He wrote, "At eleven o'clock I set out for High Wycombe, mid a reception of the same cheering which welcomed me the previous evening. I passed over Shottover Hill . . . thank Oxford for its generous reception of myself and my country's flag."[54]

A note from Bates said, "I reached Uxbridge at five o'clock on Thursday . . . a band of itinerant musicians on one of the side-walks struck up 'Yankee Doodle' so soon as my flag appeared, and I marched to the Chequers Inn . . . in the evening the crowd was so great that I had to be barricaded. . . . Detachments of visitors were let in to see me, shake hands, make speeches, and then pass out, so that others might follow suit."[55]

The next morning, Bates "set out for Shepherd's Bush. The crowd was very great. . . . I now began to enter London, as from this point I was never without an extraordinary number of followers. . . . Passing through the village of Haines, I was met by a bevy of pretty boarding-school young ladies . . . all of them saluted the American standard."[56]

A British newspaper recorded information about Bates: "As he neared London, the numbers of those who came to greet him increased . . . a few of the inhabitants . . . pressed him to drink. He refused with many thanks; but his entertainers would not take no for an answer . . . the gallant Sergeant and his flag were captured and borne . . . into the Viaduct Inn where he was pledged in champagne . . . the band of the London Central District Schools was drawn up and performed in honor of the stranger."[57]

Writings of the time added, "At the hotel at Ealing, the Stars and Stripes were hung out beside the Union Jack, and to each of those ensigns the Sergeant duly lowered his flag. . . . Mr. Richard Deane, representing the parochial authorities of Ealing, welcomed Sergeant Bates and invited him to drink a glass of champagne." Bates made additional stops at King's Arms and Askew Arms where he indulged in fellowship with other Brits.[58]

Spending the night at Shepherd's Bush, Bates planned to leave the following morning "for a walk to Guildhall by way of Oxford Street, Bond Street, St. James's Street, Pall Mall, Cockspur Street, Charing Cross, the Strand Fleet Street, Ludgate Hill, Cannon Street to Queen Street, and to Guildhall where he will finally salute the British flag and furl the Stars and Stripes."[59]

Bates crossed Long Bridge in his approach to Washington, D.C.

Wisconsin senator James Reed Doolittle.

President Andrew Johnson was in office when Bates arrived in D.C.

Martha Johnson Patterson, President Andrew Johnson's daughter, served as First Lady during her father's tenure and was an associate of Bates.

Metropolitan Hotel, Washington, D.C., a location Bates patronized.

Wisconsin representative
Charles Augustus Eldredge.

Ohio senator William Mungen.

Nathaniel Michler served as superintendent of public buildings and grounds in
the District of Columbia.

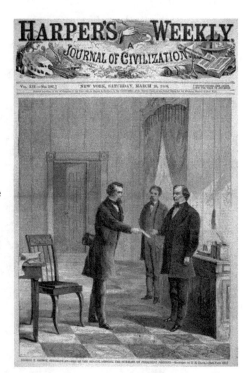

This depiction of Sergeant at Arms George Brown appeared on the cover of the March 28, 1868, issue of *Harper's Weekly* and is the only known image of him.

Nehemiah George Ordway served as Sergeant at Arms of the United States House of Representatives at the time Bates visited the city.

Bates viewed Washington Monument while it was under construction.

Edwin Oscar Perrin held a number of political posts in numerous locations.

Captain Mayne Reid, a novelist, is shown in this 1863 oil canvas.

James Madison Tuttle was an Iowa native and a politician.

St. Vincent Place.   Waverley Hotel.   Crow Hotel. Clarence Hotel. Globe Hotel.

This view shows the range of hotels which occupied the west side of George Square before the Bank of Scotland Buildings and Merchants' House were built.

The Waverly Hotel was located in Glasgow.

Gretna Green.

Sark Bridge as shown on a postcard.

Bush Hotel offered a location of rest for Bates.

Bates visited Carlisle Castle while in Europe.

Bates toured the area of Guild-hall.

Charles Spurgeon, the famous British Baptist preacher.

Bates held Wanstead Orphanage dear to his heart.

Bates traveled aboard the RMS *Atlantic*, a vessel of the White Star Line.

An artist's rendering of Bates arriving at Guildhall.

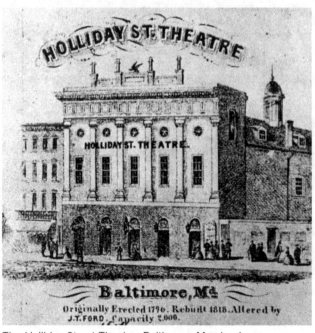

The Holliday Street Theatre, Baltimore, Maryland.

Buffalo Bill in 1875.

Annie Oakley in London.

Bates is depicted presenting the U.S. flag to Queen Victoria.

Bates with a Native American woman.

Bates is seen at the top center of this group photograph of Buffalo Bill's Wild West Show.

Head Chiefs of the Pawnee Nation.
Eagle Chief. Knife Chief. Brave Chief. Young Chief. (Serg't Bates.)

Head Chiefs of the Sioux Nation.
American Horse. Rocky Bear. Long Wolf. Flies Above.

Bates was photographed with a group of Native Americans.

CHAPTER TWENTY-FOUR

London and the Aftermath

A BRITISH NEWSPAPER RECORDED INFORMATION ABOUT BATES AS THE Federal veteran approached London, "the numbers of those who came to greet him increased . . . a few of the inhabitants . . . pressed him to drink. He refused with many thanks; but his entertainers would not take no for an answer . . . the gallant Sergeant and his flag were captured and borne . . . into the Viaduct Inn where he was pledged in champagne . . . the band of the London Central District Schools was drawn up and performed in honor of the stranger."[1]

Writings of the time added, "At the hotel at Ealing, the Stars and Stripes were hung out beside the Union Jack, and to each of those ensigns the Sergeant duly lowered his flag. . . . Mr. Richard Deane, representing the parochial authorities of Ealing, welcomed Sergeant Bates and invited him to drink a glass of champagne." Bates recalled making stops at King's Arms and Askew Arms where he indulged in fellowship with other Brits.[2]

Spending the night at Shepherd's Bush, Bates, according to a period publication, planned to leave the following morning "for a walk to Guild-hall by way of Oxford Street, Bond Street, St. James's Street, Pall Mall, Cockspur Street, Charing Cross, the Strand Fleet Street, Ludgate Hill, Cannon Street to Queen Street, and to Guildhall where he will finally salute the British flag and furl the Stars and Stripes."[3]

Bates's progress was noted in papers around America, with a Nashville, Tennessee, tabloid adding, "Sergeant Bates is getting along bravely in England with his light load of American bunting. The contemplation of the consequences, however, should any one snicker at him over the left shoulder, is enough to appall the strongest heart."[4]

From Washington, D.C., an announcement harshly titled "The Fool and the Flag" contained a London telegram that stated, "London, Nov. 30. Sergeant Bates, who has walked from Glasgow to London, carrying the American flag, will arrive at Guildhall this afternoon."[5]

A London journal said, "Today, Colour-Sergeant Bates . . . will complete his march from the northern boundary of England to the heart of the metropolis. He finished the penultimate stage at three yesterday, having walked . . . to Shepherd's Bush attended by a crowd which gathered all the way, and which . . . besieged the Telegraph Hotel. . . . Bates, leaving the Telegraph Hotel, this forenoon at eleven . . . will reach his civic destination at two."[6]

Reports continued, "having . . . entered London . . . the great impediment to his progress has been the enormous amount of hand shaking . . . from the limp and languid to the powerful and pitiless, that crunches the carpal bones into the size and semblance of a duck's foot."[7]

A November 30, 1872, telegram from London elaborated, "Sergeant Bates, the American traveler, arrived here today, having completed his pedestrian tour through Scotland and England. He entered the city bearing the Stars and Stripes . . . he halted and was loudly cheered by the people who immediately surrounded him in great numbers. . . . The unusual sight drew an immense crowd of spectators who followed the carriage for miles."[8]

Bates wrote, "By eleven o'clock on Saturday morning, an open carriage, pair of horses and postilion, were waiting me at the door of the Telegraph Hotel. . . . Mr. Holland mounted two fine flags of England and America on the carriage, and had the horse trappings suitably decorated with international symbols."[9]

He added, "The morning was dismally wet. Rain kept falling without intermission, but it in no ways damped the ardor of the crowds who were congregated around my head-quarters. Cheers for Bates, the Flag, the United States, the Republic, the Star-spangled Banner, were kept up unceasingly outside."[10]

The December 2, 1872, edition of the *Morning Post* noted, "On Saturday . . . Bates completed his self-imposed task, by carrying the Stars and Stripes through the Metropolis into the heart of the City of London. He had purposed accomplishing this last stage . . . on foot, but his friends represented to him that in such case it would be a matter of extreme difficulty to make his way through the crowds that were certain to attend his march."[11]

The *Post* article added, "The streets were also in an evil condition for a pedestrian, and had not been rendered more agreeable by the rain which had fallen during the night, so that the Sergeant was at length persuaded to avail himself of an open carriage, which had been kindly placed at his disposal. Sir John Bennett had kindly offered the use of his carriage, but an open carriage was the only one that could be used in conveying the flag and bearer through the streets so as to be seen by the people."[12]

The newspaper reporter continued to specify that in the morning of Bates's London arrival, "crowds began to assemble in the road, and these increased until many hundreds were gathered together near the hotel. At about half-past ten, the carriage, drawn by a pair of greys . . . drew up at the door. Rain began to fall heavily, and the carriage roof had to be closed for a time; but as the time for the departure drew near it was again opened, and two flags, the Union Jack and the Stars and Stripes, were placed at the back so as to hang out behind."[13]

Additional aspects disclosed were, "The rain was not so heavy when, at about half-past eleven, Sergeant Bates made his appearance and mounted the back seat of the carriage. His appearance was the signal for some rounds of hearty cheering, which he acknowledged by bowing and waving his hat to the crowd."[14]

As the carriage departed for Guildhall, it did so "at a foot pace." It was also noted, "The crowds became rather greater as the carriage came through Notting Hill, while down the cross streets came constantly working men by twos and threes, rushing through to seize the hand of the Sergeant. The crowd, for the most part, here consisted of decent working people . . . through Oxford Street, a large proportion appeared to belong to the classes in more easy circumstances, the windows and balconies along the route being also occupied by gazers of both sexes who waved handkerchiefs in token of welcome."[15]

More information included,

At Notting Hill was hung out the first Union Jack, and here, opposite the house of the loyal confectioner who had hoisted it, the carriage halted for a moment to allow the Sergeant to salute the English flag. At the same moment a handsome bouquet was thrown out of the window, and the hospitable owner of the house begged Sergeant Bates to descend and partake of a luncheon which he had prepared for him, and on his offer being declined with many thanks, he brought out some sherry, which was accepted, and he afterwards walked beside the carriage into town.[16]

Records of the London arrival announced, "The crowds in Oxford Street were very great, and . . . Bond Street . . . the reception was as enthusiastic as before . . . on reaching Pall Mall, the Sergeant saluted the Royal Palace, halts being made for a moment for the same purpose at Marlborough House, . . . not many flags were displayed along the line . . . a salute was given in honor of the City of London."[17]

"Guildhall Yard . . . was a dense mass of people . . . the men who drew the carriage . . . dragged it right in under the porch and up to the steps entering the Guildhall. The scene that ensued beggars description; the police were in small force and were utterly powerless to effect anything, and when the occupants of the carriage dismounted, with a view of entering the hall, the place was . . . too full to admit of any increase in the number of its occupants."[18]

Unable to safely return to the carriage and speak from it, Bates was thrown into a state of panic. Someone noted, "those next to the Sergeant lifted him upon their shoulders and hoisted him bodily, flag and all, into the carriage, while the rest of the party, by a succession of violent efforts, managed to regain their former positions, none the worse for the pressure they had experienced."[19]

Once the crowd grew silent, Bates, now able to stand on the seat of the carriage, said, "Englishmen, I have but a few words to say to you, for

I am not a man of many words, and it needs not many to explain to you the origin of the journey which I have undertaken.... I was right ... and [thank you for the] kindness with which you have received me ... and for the way in which you have received the Flag of America."[20]

Loud cheers ensued upon the conclusion of Bates's speech, and the "carriage was drawn out of the Guildhall Yard." That night, Bates dined at the Savage Club, where a member not only invited him to visit, but also paid for his food. Sadly, it was noted, "During the return journey . . . somewhere near Smithfield Market, the brass spearhead which surmounted the flag staff dropped off.... Bates values this much, it is hoped that the finder will forward it to the Langham Hotel for him. He will be happy to reward the restorer of what is now to him a precious relic." Bates noted that he never saw or heard of the spearhead again.[21]

Some of the London locations Bates visited during his stay included:

the public buildings of the city ... no one so impressed me as St. Paul's Cathedral.... Westminster Abbey I visited often.... I stood over the grave of Charles Dickens.... The Crystal Palace.... I went to hear Mr. Spurgeon. All we Americans do, and we are never disappointed. His voice is so mellifluous and yet so powerful.... It was my pleasure to meet Mr. Spurgeon, by his special invitation, in his study ... after the close of his Sunday morning service.... Spurgeon also presented me with copies of his two works.... The congregational singing in this church was the finest I have ever heard.[22]

Bates expressed a sad aspect of the trip: "I was pretty much annoyed by relic-hunters, who could they have had their way, would soon have whittled my flagstaff into imperceptible pieces, and rive the banner into a thousand shreds. I gave a piece of my flag and my boots to the Wax Work Temple of the Messrs. Tussaud, as a small offering to those of the British public who worship such things, and who find at Madame Tussaud's perhaps the best field for the satisfaction of their curiosity."[23]

Bates remarked upon completing his British march, "I furled my flag amid the plaudits of as enthusiastic a crowd as ever surrounded any foreigner, if after all an American can be called one, in the streets of

London. My work was done. I was glad my mission had been so triumphant a success."[24]

His appreciation for the British citizens was printed in a late December periodical, "A letter from Sergeant Bates thanking the people of England for the respect shown the American flag, and for the generous and unreserved greeting he received during his march through the country, is published in the London papers."[25]

A December 1872 *Memphis Daily Appeal* article contained an excerpt from the *New York Daily Tribune*:

Referring to the letter of Sergeant Bates to a London paper, "There is in this letter, however, one statement which is encouraging, given though it may be in language of exasperating elegance and beauty. Medical men informed me, writes . . . Bates, that an injury which I received in my chest during the late war will, before many years, send me marching over the gloomy trails leading to the thorny jungles of the condemned, or along the bright ways leading to the flowery kingdom of a beautiful and indestructible world, in the flower-strewn valleys of which lie the encampments of the forgiven."[26]

For no known reason, hurtful remarks toward Bates became more prevalent almost as quickly as he left London. A West Virginia publication quipped, "Sergeant Bates will still further immortalize himself next spring by marching through the State of New Jersey with the tail of his shirt fluttering in the breeze. He does this upon a wager of sixty cents that the youth of Jersey will not molest him, nor volunteer the information that he has a letter in the post office."[27]

Bates's recent accomplishment in England yielded adverse comments from across the Atlantic. One article alleged, "A British journal suggests that Sergeant Bates is carrying around the American bunting as a preliminary to the announcement of some quack medicine. This is the 'most unkind cut of all,' as it involves an intimation that a greater quack than Bates is possible, and he is merely one howling in the wilderness."[28]

The *Camden Journal* of Camden, South Carolina, noted in the January 9, 1873, edition, "Sergeant Bates, the champion dead beat of North

America . . . has just taken in another bet of a thousand dollars, by marching solus through Scotland and England, from Glasgow to Guildhall
. . . bearing aloft the same banner he carried throughout the Southern
States."[29]

Sarcastic sentiments toward Bates also appeared in a Washington,
D.C., paper:

*A London paper contains this remarkable 'personal' reference to that
impudent humbug and imposter who made himself notorious for
marching through the Southern States . . . and then by achieving the
same exploit through England. . . . "Mr. Sergeant Bates, who bears
the stars and stripes across England," it solemnly informs the British
people, "is of distinguished kin. A brother of the late Hon. Attorney
General under . . . Lincoln, and connected with the late Joshua Bates,
the great banker, he first entered the public service as an advocate of
distinguished qualities, appearing as attorney in the . . . famous case
of the United States vs. George Alfred Townsend. He gradually rose
to eminence . . . became one of the ornaments to the American bar. His
fondness for British institutions led him to adopt the title of Serjeant,
not Sergeant, Bates."[30]*

Quoting statements from the *Detroit Union*, an article titled "Did
Not Know What It Was" stated,

*Sergeant Bates, it appears, has accomplished his feat of carrying the
American flag, unfurled, from John O'Groat's to Land's End, and
without molestation. The English papers are disposed to treat the matter
as quite an event, and to claim great credit for the English people for
their treatment of our flag. The Detroit Union is not disposed to allow
them much credit for their forbearance. It says the fact is they do not
know what it was. It has been so many years since the English people
have seen an American flag that they have quite forgotten how it looked
. . . our flag is a rare sight in any foreign port; and the English people are
entitled to neither credit nor blame for not being aware that the piece
of bunting which [he]carried was the emblem of the land of the free.[31]*

Bates noted the success and productivity of his British march by writing, "I should submit to the public of both countries, the varied and often singular occurrences on my march, which go to prove beyond all question, the depth of the affection of the English people for their English-speaking brethren across the Atlantic. If I have received ovations wherever I have carried the flag; if corporations have feted me and voted me public addresses; if individuals have given me presents for our officials in the United States, what matters it if no public record thereof is given to both countries?"[32]

Bates also explained, "I shall ever regard with pride that in 1872 I succeeded in bringing the two great nations' hearts near to each other till they seemed to beat in unison. . . . God grant that work so begun may not willingly be let die."[33]

For those reasons, Bates produced and published a hurried account of his march across England. Interestingly, all of the profits from the sale of the manuscript were designated to go to the Wanstead Orphanage in England. Bates remarked, "If my book shall, by its sale, help the . . . poor little ones who are gathered like so many bleating lambs . . . it shall rejoice my heart when I am again in my Western home, and I shall look even with brighter hope and greater joy into the faces of my own little ones."[34] Bates's generosity and compassion for others continued; some six hundred children, residents of the home, benefited from the money the printed version of his recollections generated.

As a side note, Bates forfeited his earnings at the conclusion of his trip. He wrote, "The wager I afterwards gave up as the true bearings of the magnificent project I had undertaken dawned upon me; and before I left Scotland, or placed foot on English soil, I was able to say that no mercenary motive had aught to do with my pilgrimage through England with the flag."[35]

A cruel editorial appeared in January 1873 and offered a glimpse into the deep animosity some individuals held for Bates. In part, it said, "Persons wishing to sign a petition to the Queen of England to pardon the man who killed Sergeant Bates can be accommodated. . . . It is true that nobody has yet . . . but it seems so natural and proper that some one should, that we think it would be a very fitting and graceful thing to have a petition, ready signed, with a blank for the insertion of the prisoner's name, so that it could be forwarded by the first steamer after his arrest."[36]

Another insult that appeared after Bates completed his London trip was in the *Public Ledger* of Memphis, Tennessee. The January 29, 1873, article announced, "An English hotel proprietor recently asked Sergeant Bates to pay in advance because he had no luggage but the Stars and Stripes. The warrior refused and left the establishment."[37] The validity of that accusation is questionable.

Another article indicating an altercation with the proprietor of a British hotel offered, "An English landlord did not think a box of paper collars and the stars and stripes would pay his bill in the morning, and so refused him meals and lodging."[38] Bates made no mention of either of these incidents.

Substantiating Bates's acquisition of an English flag, an American newspaper presented a negative report: "The woeful intimation is given that Sergeant Bates has got a British Union Jack and is coming over to carry it across the American continent."[39]

A Washington, D.C., periodical added, "Sergeant Bates is now called the 'international idiot.'"[40]

Little information related to Bates's return to America exists, but a short statement in a New Orleans paper erroneously offered, "Bates came to New York last week in the *Atlantic*, of the White Star line. He carried the Stars and Stripes in England, unmolested and unnoticed."[41]

Another reference, although derogatory, to Bates's homecoming stated, "The White Star Line ... unkindly offers to bring Sergeant Bates back to America gratis. Is there no more refined way for the White Star Line Co. to show its disrespect for the country."[42]

Lastly, an article also in a Maine paper said, "The inhabitants of an Illinois town ... gave a public reception to their distinguished townsman on his arrival home, the other day."[43]

CHAPTER TWENTY-FIVE

Incidents after England

As noted in two earlier chapters, Gilbert Henderson Bates was the regular recipient of comments, positive and negative, in regard to his march across the South. Rumors of his financial instability, health issues, and attempted suicide were the primary references he was given in the aftermath of the event. Bates evidently sought to use his newfound fame to his advantage, but the likelihood of making a suitable living for a family numbering approximately half a dozen was difficult to achieve through the practice of making speeches and selling autographed photographs.

Flag historian Marc Leepson noted in a paragraph about Bates that in the summer after Bates's trek across the deep South, the sergeant appeared at a variety of venues such as the Holiday Street Theatre in Baltimore. There, the flag-carrying veteran charged admission for those inclined to hear his words of patriotism. Sadly, according to Leepson, Bates attempted to repeat an act of notoriety at the New York Democratic Convention but did not receive any recognition from those in attendance. In turn, Bates chose to remove himself from the situation after a short time and walked from the convention "unattended and unnoticed."[1]

Bates's sojourn across England, his poorly documented unsuccessful efforts to walk across Canada, and his collection of unrealized marches were noted in snippets of media in the decades that followed his historic Southern trek. In addition, references to the superior work ethic of at least one of Bates's siblings attempted to belittle the accomplishments

Bates had made, and would make, in the years after the American Civil War.

For example, an Iowa paper offered, "It is suggested . . . that Sergeant Bates, instead of carrying the flag of the free through various foreign lands, would be more profitably employed in the alternate propulsion and attraction of a common metallic implement with serrated edges, used for the separation of specimens of the highest development of vegetable growth into convenient lengths for culinary combustion, commonly called a wood saw."[2]

A Maine publication proposed, "A brother of Sergeant Bates, the flag-bearer, is at Terre Haute in a line of business similar to the sergeant's. He shoulders a hod full of mortar, and marches from one end of a ladder to the other with it, without molestation from anybody."[3]

Another defaming commentary upon Bates in the approximate time-frame of his British trudge said, "Sergeant Bates has a brother in Indianapolis who is quite respectable, and engaged in the forwarding and commission business. He is commissioned to forward a hod full of bricks and mortar to the top of a ladder, making as many trips a day as he can, and receiving a moderate income for his services."[4]

Facetiously proposing a possible means of income for Bates in the midst of his financial issues, a reporter penned, "Numerous Western editors are trying to induce Sergeant Bates to march through the lava beds, bearing the American flag, and although they offer him the odds on bets of $1,000 to $1, he hangs back and refuses to undertake the enterprise."[5]

A June 4, 1873, Delaware pamphlet added, "Heartless cynics will rejoice to learn that Sergeant Bates has become so poor that he has been forced to lay down his flag and go to work like a common mortal to obtain bread for his family. Indeed, the case is so bad that the sergeant is unable to publish a book of his travels."[6]

A New Orleans paper continued the negative remarks about Bates: "We should suggest Corporal punishment for him but for the fact that Sergeant Bates is a living monument of the inefficiency of promotion in such cases."[7]

In 1874, there was a push for Bates to undertake a third trip, one resembling in principle his Southern and British efforts. Titled "The Latest Fool's Errand," a write-up stated,

An interesting cavalcade will pass through the Continent this summer. Sergeant Bates, it is said, will on May 10th leave the United States for Europe with two ex-soldiers of France and Germany, and after passing through England will proceed to Calais. In London, engagements are to be made with an ex-soldier of each of the other countries of Europe to join him in the Grand International March of the Nineteenth Century. The sergeant and ex-soldiers, each bearing the standards of his own country, are to march from Calais to St. Petersburg through all the Capitals of the Continent. Negotiations are in progress to persuade an Irish home ruler to carry the green flag of Erin. A white silk banner, with the motto, "Peace on Earth," is also to be carried. . . . The progress of these standard bearers will be a magnificent spectacle, and will be watched with the deepest interest by the civilized world; but to render [the march] . . . a really striking success, Sergeant Bates and his companions should pay a visit . . . to some regular blood-thirsty barbarians. Why not land on the west coast of Africa and march straight to Coomassie, taking Europe on the return journey, King Koffee bringing up the procession with his umbrella, lent by the South Kensington Museum.[8]

Less than two weeks later, a Pennsylvania paper added,

Sergeant Bates is planning a grand sensation for the world. While in Chicago recently, he announced his program . . . neatly arranged, and he leaves for London in about ten days . . . America, England, France, Spain, Germany, Russia, Belgium, Denmark, Holland, Switzerland, Austria, Sweden, and Italy will each furnish one ex-soldier of their respective armies to make a grand peace march through the countries' names. Each soldier will be mounted on a black horse, bearing the flag of his country, . . . leading the battalion will be one on a white horse, who will carry a white banner labeled, "Peace on earth, and good will to men." This cavalcade . . . led by Sergeant Bates, will start from Amsterdam, and will visit in turn Hamburg, Stockholm, St. Petersburg, Berlin, Dresden, Vienna, Venice, Rome, Florence, Geneva, Paris, London, and some other places in Europe. They will then embark at Liverpool for the United States, and after visiting Washington, will commence a walk . . . West, passing through New York, Pennsylvania, Ohio, Indiana, and Illinois to Chicago. The march will probably not begin until next spring. . . . London parties desire to start at once. . . . Bates expects to reach Chicago in about five months from the time his flags are unfurled at Amsterdam.[9]

For some unknown reason or reasons, this trip failed to take place.

Limited documentation exists in regard to Bates's walk across Canada, but an 1875 pamphlet announced, "Sergeant Bates, don't swear; we only wish to mention the fact that he is alive, and that he proposes to start from Windsor, Ontario, on May 17th, to carry the stars and stripes unfurled to Toronto."[10]

Additional insight into Bates's Canadian march and the unfounded animosity individuals held toward him reads, "Sergeant Bates is on a tramp from Windsor to Montreal, carrying the stars and stripes, and passing through the principal cities. If any Canadian feels disposed to give the flag-bearing nuisance a thorough drubbing, he may be assured that the American people will freely forgive the constructive disrespect to their colors."[11]

Almost two years after Bates's English trek and his failure to attract several nations to participate in a European march, a small portion of insight was provided: "We are glad to learn . . . the Sergeant Bates business of carrying the Star-Spangled Banner into England is not contemplated, and hope that this sensible view of the case will be a lesson to all who imagine that dramatic art can ever be truly served by sensational encouragement of national rivalries."[12]

The accuracy of an announcement in a Washington paper can be questioned, but if true, there are indications of Bates having obtained a source of employment that many of his distractors would have deemed credible. The Washington paragraph proclaimed, "Sergeant Bates no longer totes flags around the country, but carries bricks in Chicago. Of the many shrinkages in value, this Bates all."[13]

In May 1878, Bates was in Gibson City, Illinois, a town located approximately eleven miles from his home in what was identified as "Slaybrook." Unfortunately, he was once again the victim of a crime while in Gibson City. It was noted, "Bates has been robbed of a $37 diamond. . . . The American flag was saved."[14]

Bates's activities were obviously delayed due to an accident noted in an Illinois periodical: "Last Saturday night, Sergeant Bates, the American flag carrier, addressed an audience on the public square at Morris. In stepping from the platform, he slipped in such a manner as to break his leg below the knee."[15]

Approximately a year after breaking his leg, Bates returned to the speaking circuit, continuing to pursue the idea of making a living from giving speeches. A Missouri paper proclaimed, "Sergeant Bates . . . has been stumping at various points in North Missouri . . . giving Kirksville the benefit of his views. He speaks from a dry goods box in the street. Not having heard either of the two speeches . . . we are not prepared to give an opinion thereon."[16]

It is clearly seen that a low level of material and information exist in regard to Bates, outside of his famous marches. Sarcastic comments about Bates carrying bricks and/or applying to work for the U.S. Post Office have also been provided. Sadly, the rumors of his death, suicide attempts, and statements concerning his financial issues and chemical dependency have also been given. Bates spent a great deal of his postwar life promoting his books and served as a guest lecturer on period political and social issues. Unfortunately, any additional insightful information regarding his activities outside of those related to the praises and insults that compiled earlier chapters is largely nonexistent.

Chapter Twenty-Six

Bates on Tour with Buffalo Bill

It appears that Gilbert Henderson Bates overcame his reported issues with abuse of laudanum and was able to move from the poor living conditions that were his residence in the years following his two landmark marches. Sadly, information related to those situations is more available than is that of his successes. Among the primary achievements of his later years was his association with the famous showman Buffalo Bill.

William Frederick Cody was born to Isaac and Mary Ann Laycock Cody on February 26, 1846, in Le Claire, Iowa. His father died when Cody was only eleven, and young William took it upon himself, as the oldest male in the family, to provide for his mother and siblings. He gained employment as a teamster and cattle drover and made trips to the West with military supply trains. In 1864, he joined the Seventh Kansas Volunteer Cavalry and served in that unit for more than a year. Four years later, Cody began a job with the military as a guide, hunter, and eventually a scout, with his income rising to $75 per month. Actions against Native Americans in the ensuing years led to his 1872 receipt of the Medal of Honor for his strong performance as a civilian scout. Claiming to have killed more than four thousand buffalo as food for railroad workers, Cody was given the nickname "Buffalo Bill." The success of dime novels centering upon his actions, as well as his tendency toward showmanship, eventually led to his establishment of a troupe of individuals portraying various aspects of the Wild West and Americana.[1] That organization welcomed Bates into its fold in the mid-1880s.

Bates's biography from the Cody Archives website concludes with the sentence, "Sergeant Bates appeared as the Color-bearer for Buffalo Bill's Wild West during the 1886 and 1887 seasons, presenting the American flag to Queen Victoria at the American Exhibition in London in May 1887." In addition, the program that circulated at the shows indicated the significance of Bates in noting, "Colour Bearer, SERGT. BATES and 'The Old Flag' The identical one carried in America and Europe."[2] It is noteworthy that the show was only three years old at the time Bates joined its ranks.

A July 3, 1886 issue of *Richmond County Advance* of West New Brighton, New York mentioned Bates by saying, "On Sunday morning last, Sergeant Gilbert Bates, the great U.S. World Flag carrier . . . attended the morning service at the Mariners' Harbor Baptist Church, with a body of Indians from the Wild West Show." As the article continued, it exclaimed, "In the evening Hon. W. F. Cody, with some thirty-five braves, attended the same church. . . . Buffalo Bill gave . . . a donation in the sum of $35 towards extinguishing church debt."[3]

In October 1886, a South Dakota paper published the following, which had effects upon Bates, "Hon. W. F. Cody, Buffalo Bill, and Nate Salisbury, proprietors of the Great Wild West Show, have secured six acres of space at the American Exhibition in London, 1887, and will take over their entire outfit, consisting of 240 Indians, Mexicans, cowboys, and assistants, and more than 150 Indian ponies, Mexican mustangs, buffalo, elk, antelope, deer, and Texas steers, and all the appliances to completely illustrate frontier life."[4]

"The Indians are of the Sioux, Pawnee, Ute, Oglala, and other tribes, and among them are such noted chiefs as American Horse, Rocky Bear, Flies Above, Eagle Chief, Knife Chief, Brave Chief, Long Wolf, Young Chief. . . . The transportation, grand stands, stables, and preliminary expenses of this magnificent retinue will cost $100,000, and its current expenses are over $1,600 daily. The contract covers a period of six months, commencing May 2, 1887."[5]

More prestige for Bates and his fellow members of Buffalo Bill's Wild West Show were expressed in a London-based paragraph, "The Prince and Princess of Wales, their daughters, the Marquis of Lorne, and the Princess Louise and the Comtesse de Paris, accompanied by a brilliant suite, visited the 'Wild West' show and the grounds of the American exhibition yesterday. Buffalo Bill and his company gave a special performance for the benefit of the royal guests, and they were surprised and delighted."[6]

Regarding the spectacle the royals reviewed, an articled announced,

Behold, in the first place, Buffalo Bill himself in knightly fashion saluting our Prince and Princess. Save in the matter of teasing and goading bulls—at which we most of us winced—the Hon. Bill Cody was apparently quite a Bayard. He lightly yet firmly sat his little horse like a North American Ivanhoe. He sped like lightning over the tan track to give the opening signal. With whirlwind rapidity did the painted and be-feathered. Sioux, Cheyenne, and Arapaho Indians and bands of Mexican Vaqueros and American Cowboys then sweep in, the Redskins waking the echoes with their wild war-screams! This rousing display of the wild horsemanship of the prairies is the strangest sight London has seen for many a long day, I assure ye. The Star-Spangled Banner! The Cowboy band aptly plays this inspiring air in welcome to Sergeant Bates . . . gallant bearer of the Stars and Stripes stirs martial ardor by riding round with the flag of Freedom in hand.[7]

Another news snippet added, "The Queen . . . attended a special performance of the Wild West this afternoon. Her majesty was delighted with the exhibition, and expressed her pleasure by frequent applause. After the performance, Buffalo Bill . . . and a number of the squaws attached to the show were presented to her Majesty."[8]

Comments about the show and Bates appeared in a May 1887 article,

As we took our places in one of the little boxes which edge the arena in the grounds of the American Exhibition, where Buffalo Bill's Wild West Show is given, we could not help being struck with the effectiveness of the scene before us. . . . There were the various tribes of Indians in their war-paint and feathers, the Mexicans, the ladies, and the cow-boys, and a fine array they made, with the chiefs of each tribe, the renowned Sergeant Bates, the equally celebrated Buffalo Bill, the stalwart Buck Taylor, and others who were introduced by Mr. Frank Richmond, who, from the top of an elevated platform, described the show as it proceeded. . . . The next sensation was created by Miss Annie Oakley, who did some wonderful things with her rifle.[9]

An article titled "Buffalo Bill in England," reported, "Buffalo Bill . . . deviated from the usual custom of less illustrious travelers. Instead of putting himself at once into the hands of London's tailor, Poole, as soon as he arrived, he chose to supply himself with a liberal outfit in America, and he landed on the other side with any amount of 'store clothes.' One suit, in which he intends to pay his respects to the Queen, is of dark gray; another, in which he will appear at the queen's jubilee as Nebraska's representative, is two shades of blue."[10]

An 1887 periodical titled the *Dramatic Review* contained information related to Bates:

So great has been the rush to see the Wild West Camp even before the show opens, so vast has been the noble army of deadheads seeking admission, the Executive of the American Exhibition have had to print a polite form of refusal to grant admittance to the countless applicants whose only claim was a not unnatural curiosity. . . . Nevertheless, the camp is all ready and so are the campers. One or two rehearsals have been run and galloped through. Miss Annie Oakley has been getting her shooting-hand in and only the bucking horses' part of the programme has not been practised. "They need no rehearsing," said Sergeant Bates to me grimly. This member of the big show is one of the most interesting personages there. He will be remembered as the man that carried the American flag through Great Britain in 1872. "A bit of a crank," as he calls himself, I am bound to say that I found him to be one of the most intelligent and interesting men I have met. He has all the charm of the really nice American.[11]

Another mention of Bates, and the significance the show held for the English people was,

> the "boss" of the Company, handsome Buffalo Bill, on a choice flea-bit-
> ten grey, of which, with his splendid seat, he seemed part and parcel.
> The broad-brimmed hats, breeches, boots, and belts of the Mexicans
> and cowboys; the painted warriors, clad in robes, skins, and feathers of
> pronounced colours; and the wiry little horses, not much to look at, but
> demons to go, made up a striking spectacle, truly novel to an English
> eye. The Red Indians greeted their leader, Buffalo Bill, with piercing
> shrieks. Thereafter their voices were often raised in mimic anger or joy,
> but it was always the same shrill falsetto, with never a hint of bass
> in the shout. We should not omit to mention that in the preliminary
> parade figured Sergeant Bates, who, years gone by, tramped through
> this country (and some few others) with the flag of the Union over his
> shoulder. There were nineteen entries on the programme, and it took
> two hours to get through with them.[12]

In a letter from London, praises were given to the man who served as Bates's boss for a brief period. The correspondence offered, "Buffalo Bill . . . the Hon. W. F. Cody, as he is called here, has taken London by storm. He is the guest of the aristocracy, and on Sunday . . . he will dine with Albert Edward. . . . While the future King of England and the noble peers of the realm are hobnobbing with the Hon. Mr. Cody . . . baronets and knights are glad enough to secure the genial cowboy to dine with them and meet their families and spoil some of them."[13]

Bates was a part of the latter group whose members were subjected to dining and being spoiled.

The impact of the Wild West crew members upon London society were indicated, "For the moment, the cowboys have the town and the royal family. There is a hint here for traveling Americans this year. Lay in a stock of broad-brimmed white hats, let your hair grow long, and don't be too aesthetic. The pendulum has swung to the other extreme."[14]

More insight into Bates's employer and the program in which he participated was given in a Wichita periodical:

In company with the correspondent of the New York World and a capitalist from Chicago we paid a visit to the American exhibition . . . outlay buildings covering several acres of ground have been constructed to accommodate not only a display of American manufacture but Buffalo Bill's mammoth Wild West show, and institution greater than the exhibition itself, of which it is an appendage. From the opening day of this wonderful show up to the present time vast crowds have been attracted thither. On one day, with the best seats selling at five dollars each, no less than sixty-four thousand people witnessed the performance which is held twice a day rain or shine. Buffalo Bill . . . has taken the English people by storm. I think I am perfectly safe in saying that no American has met with the same favor in the eyes of Londoners as he. The entertainment he gives dwarfs anything in the show line I have ever witnessed.[15]

Bates presented the American flag in the Wild West shows, but the Wichita article adds insight into another part he played in the demonstration in saying, "Among the celebrities that are with him is Sergeant Bates who, on a wager of two thousand dollars, carried the news of Mr. Lincoln's election by pony express to San Francisco in a given time, and won the bet."[16]

As Bates had encountered in his marches, he dealt with negative comments as a part of the Buffalo Bill entourage. A Nevada newspaper noted,

Hearing it insinuated in certain quarters that Buffalo Bill's boom in London was being overrated, the Appeal telegraphed yesterday to its regular London correspondent to investigate. . . . The following dispatch was received. . . . I called upon Buffalo Bill at his dressing rooms this evening but had to wait some time as Queen Victoria was there swapping anecdotes with him while he fixed up for the show.

. . . It is rumored that the Queen is hard at work making Bill an embroidered night gown to take back to America. The young ladies of the royal family knit a pair of socks for Bill every week, which he wears once and then sells to the crème of British society for $10 a pair, unwashed at that.[17]

Some of the sites Bates and his comrades were able to visit in England were mentioned in a write-up from August 1887:

Some of the Indians and American cowboys from Buffalo Bill's Wild West Show visited Windsor Castle yesterday. The party, which included the Sioux chieftain Red Shirt, six other chiefs, most of the warriors, and several women and children, was under the charge of Serjeant Bates, who, 15 years ago, carried the United States flag from the Scottish Border to the Metropolis. The Indians were attired in their bright-coloured native costumes, several carried Japanese fans, and all had their faces painted. Buck Taylor, the Chief of the Cowboys, is still suffering from the effects of his accident, and was compelled to use crutches. Arriving in the Royal borough soon after ten o'clock in the morning, the Red Men and their companions were taken to the Castle, and shown through the State apartments, with whose magnificence they were greatly impressed. They also ascended to the battlements of the Round Tower, promenaded the Palace terraces, and walked through the Royal stables, which were, unfortunately, some- what empty, many of the Queen's horses having been sent to Balmoral for the use of the Court, and others being in the Isle of Wight. The Indians after a couple of hours' sightseeing appeared fatigued, and half a dozen at a time would suddenly seat themselves upon the pavement to rest, while their companions continued their inspection. From the mews the party proceeded to the Albert Chapel and St. George's, where the visit terminated. They subsequently returned to the Great Western Station and thronged the refreshment bar until the time for the return train to start.[18]

Showing the significance Bates held in respect to the personnel of Buffalo Bill's show, the arrangement of the camp was described in the 1887 program. It stated,

> *The Cowboy band has been organized from those Cowboys who have cultivated a natural talent for music to while away the idle hours of camp life. On the left are the staff tents and the quarters of Sergeant Bates, who carried the American Flag throughout the Civil War, and afterwards throughout the Southern States and Great Britain. On the brow of a small hill facing the entire encampment is pitched the Official Headquarter tent of the Wild West Company. It is occupied by Mr. N. Salisbury, who is business manager and vice-president of the Company. To Mr. Salisbury's skill as a manager is due, in a great measure, the financial success of the enterprise. In the centre of the camp, at the foot of the bluff, is the headquarter tent of Col. William F. Cody, known all over the world as "Buffalo Bill."*[19]

The success of the show in which Bates played a pivotal role was indicated when the act completed its run. The *London Advertiser* announced, "This week terminates the career of the Wild West exhibition at Earl's Court. After that it will, so far as London is concerned, be numbered among the wonders that were. . . . What Mr. Cody, in his picturesque dialect, terms 'dust,' had been gathered in beyond the wildest dreams of avarice. . . . Since the Exhibition of 1851, London has never seen a show that so completely took it by storm as this one, which illustrates some of the phases of Western life."[20]

A note added, "Perhaps there never was a show, even in London, that was so matter of fact, and that owed to little of its attractiveness to stage effect and theatrical artifice. It was an honest effort to let people see . . . what the frontier life of adventure which they had read so much about in their story books was really like . . . as far as popularity was concerned, Mr. Cody's exhibition might apparently have gone on exhibiting in London for the rest of his natural life."[21]

A final sign of praise for Cody's show in which Bates participated can be seen in a December 1887 article that said, in part, "The . . . phenomenal success of Buffalo Bill in London prompts the *Chicago Tribune* to say that the difference between the Englishmen and Americans is that Americans prefer brains and Englishmen sport. In proof of this is cited the fact Buffalo Bill with a company of Indians, cowboys and hoodlums . . . are wined, dined, and feted by the British aristocracy."[22]

No indication is given as to why or under what circumstances Gilbert Henderson Bates ceased his relationship with Buffalo Bill's show. However, almost immediately upon the return of the troupe to the United States, offers were made to purchase the show from Mr. Cody. A period paper stated, "W. F. Cody had netted . . . $350,000 out of his Buffalo Bill season in London. He is willing to sell out his Wild West show for $162,000. He has been offered [approximately] $99,000 and refused."[23]

The logistics of the show were formidable. By the late 1890s, Cody's show often used as many as five hundred cast and staff members who were fed three hot meals a day. Expenses could reach as much as $4,000 per day as the show fed, paid, and housed its members, generated its own electricity, and maintained a fire department. Performers were housed inside wall tents for lengthy stays while railroad sleeping cars were provided for frequent moves between cities. In the decade before World War I, ticket sales declined as people became more prone to attend movies. Sadly, Buffalo Bill's show went bankrupt in 1913.[24]

Chapter Twenty-Seven

Bates's Final Years

POLITICAL ACTIVISM SEEMS TO HAVE SEIZED THE MAJOR INTEREST OF Gilbert Henderson Bates with the approach of the new century. His tendency to give large numbers of patriotic-themed speeches, free of charge, came to an end. Health issues were rumored to have taken a toll on Bates, limiting his travels and appearances.[1] Aside from a 1917 article in the *Pantagraph* of Bloomington, Illinois, little is written about his later years.

One of the final exhibitions of Bates's mindset, this one against American Imperialism, appeared in a May 24, 1899, issue of *Kansas Agitator* of Garnett, Kansas. The Spanish-American War had ended the previous August, but Bates's editorial entry had been submitted June 6, 1898, the approximate mid-point of the conflict.

The editorial, titled "What Does the Aggression Mean?" began, "It means the conquest through great sacrifice of blood and treasure of Cuba, Puerto Rico, Hawaii, the Philippines and other territory that the chances of war may give us. It means the active and ever-present service of from 100,000 to 150,000 soldiers to control the inhabitants of these possessions and protect them from internal disorder. It means foreign death and ... graves for many thousand Americans, and destroyed health and happiness for still more through the climatic influences of these possessions."[2]

Bates continued, "It means that, in case of foreign complications, which these possessions are most certain to bring, a standing army of 300,000 in time of peace, and an army three to five times as great in time

of war, and the increase of our navy to several times its present strength
. . . a vast increase of taxation and burden upon labor far greater and more
lasting than that imposed by . . . all prior American wars . . . a burden
upon a burden . . . greater upon the smaller already existing."[3]

Additional remarks from Bates were, "It means the adoption into the
American political family of 11,000,000 foreign people . . . antagonistic
to and opposite to the American in race, character, habits, customs, and
religion. It means opening the doors for the entrance of a steady and
increasing flood of cheap and ignorant Asiatic and South American
laborers already sorely oppressed and distressed by and excess of cheap
European labor."[4]

Bates added, "It means a strong and stronger growing . . . irresistible
aristocracy of wealth and political power to rule and direct their own,
irrespective of the interests of the common people. It means a much more
rapid increase of poverty, crime, and disorder . . . police, police stations,
prisons, and asylums for the poor and insane."[5]

Concluding comments from Bates were, "It means the repudiation
of the policies and principles that created and brough the republic to its
present greatness and power. It means the abuse and misapplication of
this power and disappearance of the republic as an example to and influence for good over the liberty-loving people of the whole world."[6]

An article about Bates appeared in Honolulu's the *Pacific Commercial
Advertiser* on September 7, 1899. Ironic in its place of origin in relation
to its subject matter, the article began, "Sergeant Bates, many years ago,
desired to make the American flag manifest to all nations . . . in exe-
cution of this patriotic mission, humbly carried it around the world on
foot, yielding only to transportation on highways. This . . . gave extreme
satisfaction to those who regarded the exhibition of the bunting as more
creditable to American civilization than the exhibition of a picturesque
national character, and a reputation for establishing the brotherhood of
men."[7]

The Hawaii article continued, "He was known in all of the Grand
Army posts, in the taverns, on the railways upon which he was usually
dead-headed, and the small boys followed him wherever on his grand
tour he entered the towns, covered with dust . . . always dramatically

waving the Flag. It was said that he carried an eagle on his back, but the eagle one day mistook his ear for a sandwich, and made a humble meal of a portion of it. He pronounced the eagle a treacherous ally of the Flag, liquidated his account with him, and traded him off to the keeper of a restaurant."[8]

Additionally, the Hawaii commentary stated, "Bates now announces to his millions of constituents that he is opposed to Imperialism, and has withdrawn confidence in President McKinley's policy regarding the Philippines. He pronounces this policy to be 'hysterical politics,' and wicked Jingoism . . . and it forces him to set the Flag at half-mast so long as the President indulges in the policy of expansion which he calls 'militarism and greed.'"[9]

Completing its discussion of Bates and his thoughts, the article noted,

He believed that Flag waving was a more valuable educational force than character-building of the nation, but a thorough and spectacular self-education . . . has finally landed him among the anti-expansionists, and warns his fellow countrymen against erecting flagstaffs on any spot . . . not connected with the Mainland. The moral of it is, that the character of the man has more to do with national progress than visible gymnastics with the Flag. The murderer who was executed with the flag in his hand, displayed much emotion at the sight of it, but it had failed to keep him off the scaffold.[10]

Sadly, the next information related to the final years of Gilbert Bates bears a more tragic form. With eighteen years elapsed, a 1917 Illinois paper contained an article titled "He Carried Our Flag to Many Lands" as well as a photograph of Bates holding the U.S. flag. The ominous words that began the write-up were, "Gilbert Henderson Bates . . . better known . . . as Sergeant Bates, died on Saturday afternoon at his home in Saybrook."[11]

A fragment of insight into the last years Bates spent on earth added, "He had been in failing health for a long time, during which he had short periods of slight improvement." Having passed away on February

17, 1917, Bates was interred in Cheney Grove Township Cemetery in Saybrook, Illinois. He was eighty-one years old.[12]

In a true indication of a spouse being heartbroken over the loss of her longtime husband, Anna Bates, seventy-one years old, passed away March 22, 1917, approximately one month after Sergeant Bates. It was noted in Anna Bates's obituary that she had been sick for ten days and fell victim to "pneumonia and debilities of old age." She was buried next to Sergeant Bates.[13]

Three of the four surviving Bates children, adults at the time of their parents' passing, lived several more years. Hattie Bates Brokaw, born in 1865, lived until 1953. Nellie Bates Means lived from 1867 to 1936. Addie E. Bates lived until 1944, at which point she was in her early seventies. Frank Bates, the only son of Gilbert and Ann Bates, died the year after his parents in his late forties.[14]

Having served his country as an artilleryman during the deadliest war of its history, Gilbert Henderson Bates had risen to the rank of sergeant, a title that would follow him the remainder of his life. He accepted a challenge to march 1,400 miles across territory that was hostile to him only three years earlier. He not only faced the challenge, but conquered it, earning a massive mixture of acclaimers and antagonists along the way. Financially struggling throughout his adult life, Bates managed to march across England in a second effort to show that the respect of the United States and for his beloved Stars and Stripes was not only confined to the onetime nemesis of the Southern United States, but was also present in the hearts and minds of the British people, citizens of the Mother Country, and a land which had launched two wars against the American people. A showman with Buffalo Bill, an author of two books and numerous articles, Bates spent his final years as he died, in relative obscurity. Sadly, he has been largely forgotten in the annals of American history. The mission of unity and reconciliation is one that most modern Americans would agree is needed to this day. Unfortunately, the ridicule and negative comments Bates received would be indicative of someone who sought to instill those ideals upon many of the current citizens of the United States. It is the intention of the author of this manuscript that the message of Bates, and the healing he strove to instill, should never be forgotten.

NOTES

INTRODUCTION

1. "Gilbert Henderson Bates," https://www.ancestry.com/boards/topics.obits2/23960/ mb.ashx; *Madison, Dane County, and Surrounding Towns* (Madison, WI: William J. Park), 1877; "City of Edgerton," https://www.cityofedgerton.com/visitor-information.
2. Ibid.; "He Carried Our Flag to Many Lands," *Pantagraph* (Bloomington, IL), February 17, 1917, 8.
3. "He Carried Our Flag to Many Lands."
4. Ibid.; "Roster of Company H," n.d.; "Bates, Gilbert H." https://wisvetsmuseum. pastperfectonline.com/byperson?keyword=Bates%2C+Gilbert+H; "1st Regiment, Wisconsin Heavy Artillery," https://www.nps.gov/civilwar/search-battle-units-detail. htm?battleUnitCode=UW10001RAH; "1st Wisconsin Heavy Artillery History," https:// www.wisconsinhistory.org/Records/Article/CS2320.
5. Ibid.
6. "He Carried Our Flag to Many Lands"; "Gilbert Henderson Bates," https://www. findagrave.com/memorial/28320774/gilbert-henderson-bates.
7. "Sergeant Bates," *Edgefield Advertiser* (Edgefield, SC), March 18, 1868, 1.

CHAPTER 1

1. "Gilbert Henderson Bates," https://www.findagrave.com/memorial/28320774/gil-bert-henderson-bates; "Sergeant Bates," *Ottawa Free Trader* (Ottawa, IL), February 22, 1868, 1; "Sergeant Bates, His Walk from Vicksburg to Washington," *Daily Phoenix* (Columbia, SC), February 16, 1868, 1.
2. Gilbert H. Bates, *Sergeant Bates' March: Carrying the Flag from Vicksburg to Washington* (New York: B. W. Hitchcock, 1868), 3. (Hereafter referred to as Bates, *Sergeant . . . to Washington.*)
3. Ibid.
4. Ibid.; "Sergeant Bates: His March Through the South with the Old Flag Unfurled," *Edgefield Advertiser* (Edgefield, SC), March 18, 1868, 1.
5. "Sergeant Bates . . . Unfurled."
6. Ibid.
7. Ibid.
8. Ibid.
9. Bates, *Sergeant . . . to Washington*, 3.

10. "Sergeant Bates ... Unfurled."

11. Ibid.

12. Ibid.; "Sergeant Bates," *Ottawa Free Trader* (Ottawa, IL), February 22, 1868, 1; "Sergeant Bates, His Walk from Vicksburg to Washington," *Daily Phoenix* (Columbia, SC), February 16, 1868, 1.

13. "Sergeant Bates ... Unfurled."

14. "Sergeant Bates, His Walk from Vicksburg to Washington," *Daily Phoenix* (Columbia, SC), February 16, 1868, 1.

15. "Sergeant Bates ... Unfurled."

16. Ibid.

17. Ibid.; "Sergeant Bates, His Walk from Vicksburg to Washington," *Daily Phoenix* (Columbia, SC), February 16, 1868, 1.

18. Ibid.

19. "Sergeant Bates ... Unfurled."

20. Bates, *Sergeant ... to Washington*, 3–4.

21. Ibid.; "Patriotic Movement, on Foot," *Western Democrat* (Charlotte, NC), December 31, 1867, 1.

22. "Sergeant Bates, His Walk from Vicksburg to Washington," *Daily Phoenix* (Columbia, SC), February 16, 1868, 1.

23. "Sergeant Bates," *Plymouth Weekly Democrat* (Plymouth, IN), February 13, 1868, 2.

24. "The Flag March from Vicksburg," *Daily Milwaukee News* (Milwaukee, WI), January 15, 1868, 5.

25. Milton Lomask, "Sergt. Bates March: Carrying the Stars and Stripes Unfurled, from Vicksburg to Washington, and Gretna Green to London," *American Heritage* 16, no. 6 (October 1965): 1.

26. "He Carried Our Flag to Many Lands."

27. *Shasta Courier* (Shasta, CA), February 8, 1868, 4.

28. *National Republican* (Washington, D.C.), January 7, 1868, 3.

CHAPTER 2

1. "Patriotic Movement, on Foot," *Western Democrat* (Charlotte, NC), December 31, 1867.

2. Gilbert H. Bates, *Sergeant Bates' March: Carrying the Flag from Vicksburg to Washington* (New York: B. W. Hitchcock, 1868), 4. (Hereafter referred to as Bates, *Sergeant ... to Washington*.)

3. Ibid.

4. "Sergeant Bates, His Walk from Vicksburg to Washington," *Daily Phoenix* (Columbia, SC), February 16, 1868, 1.

5. "The Flag March from Vicksburg," *Daily Milwaukee News* (Milwaukee, WI), January 15, 1868, 5.

6. Milton Lomask, "Sergt. Bates March: Carrying the Stars and Stripes Unfurled, from Vicksburg to Washington, and Gretna Green to London," *American Heritage* 16, no. 6 (October 1965): 2.

7. "Sergeant Bates: What he Proposes to Do, and How He Intends to Do It," *Evening Argus* (Rock Island, IL), February 3, 1868, 2.

8. Ibid.

9. Bates, *Sergeant . . . to Washington*, 4.

10. Larry M. Logue, "Mississippians in Confederate Army," https://mississippiencyclopedia.org/entries/mississippians-in-confederate-army.

11. Lynda Lasswell Crist, "Jefferson Davis, 1808–1889," http://mshistorynow.mdah.state.ms.us/articles/287/jefferson-davis-1808-1889.

12. "Reconstruction Era: 1865–1877," https://www.howard.edu/library/reference/guides/reconstructionera.

13. Jason Phillips, "Reconstruction," https://mississippiencyclopedia.org/entries/reconstruction.

14. Ibid.

15. "Sergeant Bates," *Ottawa Free Trader* (Ottawa, IL), February 22, 1868, 1.

16. *Daily Clarion* (Jackson, MS), January 31, 1868, 3.

17. "Sergeant Bates," *Ottawa Free Trader* (Ottawa, IL), February 22, 1868, 1.

18. Bates, *Sergeant . . . to Washington*, 4.

19. Ibid.

20. "The Prentiss House," *Daily Commercial Herald* (Vicksburg, MS), January 18, 1891, 5.

21. Ibid.

22. Ibid.; "Gen. McMakin of the Prentiss House," *Vicksburg Weekly Sentinel* (Vicksburg, MS), May 16, 1849, 2.

23. Ibid.

CHAPTER 3

1. Randy Bishop, *Mississippi's Civil War Battlefields* (Gretna, LA: Pelican, 2010), 229–76.

2. US Census 2018, ACS 5-year Survey Table 803002.

3. "Sergeant Bates, His Walk from Vicksburg to Washington," *Daily Phoenix* (Columbia, SC), February 16, 1868, 1.

4. "The Flag March from Vicksburg," *Daily Milwaukee News* (Milwaukee, WI), January 15, 1868, 5.

5. Gilbert H. Bates, *Sergeant Bates' March: Carrying the Flag from Vicksburg to Washington* (New York: B. W. Hitchcock, 1868), 4. (Hereafter referred to as Bates, *Sergeant . . . to Washington*.)

6. Ibid.

7. Ibid.

8. Ibid.

9. Ibid., 5.

10. Ibid.

11. Ibid.; "George Washington Ball House," https://visitvicksburg.com/george-washington-ball-house.

12. Bates, *Sergeant . . . to Washington*, 5; *Des Arc Weekly Citizen* (Des Arc, AR), February 1, 1868, 2.

13. "Original Surrender Monument," https://www.nps.gov/vick/planyourvisit/surmonu-ment.htm; Bates, *Sergeant . . . to Washington*, 5.

14. *Des Arc Weekly Citizen*; Bates, *Sergeant . . . to Washington*, 6.

15. Bates, *Sergeant . . . to Washington*, 5–6.

16. Ibid.

17. Ibid., 6.

18. *Alexandria Gazette* (Alexandria, VA), January 29, 1868, 1.

19. *Daily Dispatch* (Richmond, VA), January 29, 1868, 1.

20. "Mississippi Items," *Memphis Daily Appeal* (Memphis, TN), February 1, 1868, 1.

21. Mark Twain, *Territorial Enterprise* (Virginia City, NV), February 27, 1868, 1.

CHAPTER 4

1. Gilbert H. Bates, *Sergeant Bates' March: Carrying the Flag from Vicksburg to Washington* (New York: B. W. Hitchcock, 1868), 6. (Hereafter referred to as Bates, *Sergeant . . . to Washington*); "Vicksburg & Meridian," http://www.msrailroads.com/V&M.htm.

2. See https://meridianspeedway.weebly.com/history-of-the-av.html.

3. Ibid.

4. Ibid.

5. Bates, *Sergeant . . . to Washington*, 6.

6. Ibid.

7. Ibid.

8. *Nashville Union and Dispatch* (Nashville, TN), January 30, 1868, 2.

9. *Dodgeville Chronicle* (Dodgeville, WI), February 28, 1868, 2.

10. Bates, *Sergeant . . . to Washington*, 6.

11. Ibid.

12. Ibid.

13. Ibid.

14. Ibid., 7.

15. Ibid.

16. "A Place in History, A Place in Your Future," http://www.townofedwards.com/history.htm.

17. Bates, *Sergeant . . . to Washington*, 7.

18. Rebecca Blackwell Drake, "Kaleidoscope of History: Raymond," http://raymondhistory.org/history/kaleidoscope.htm.

19. Ibid.

20. Bates, *Sergeant . . . to Washington*, 7.

21. Ibid.

22. Mark Twain, *Territorial Enterprise* (Virginia City, NV), February 27, 1868, 1.

23. Bates, *Sergeant . . . to Washington*, 7.

24. Ibid., 7–8.

25. "Gilbert H. Bates," *Daily Clarion* (Jackson, MS), January 30, 1868.

CHAPTER 5

1. *Daily Clarion* (Jackson, MS), January 31, 1868, 3; Gilbert H. Bates, *Sergeant Bates' March: Carrying the Flag from Vicksburg to Washington* (New York: B. W. Hitchcock, 1868), 8. (Hereafter referred to as Bates, *Sergeant . . . to Washington.*)

2. "Sergeant Bates," *Ottawa Free Trader* (Ottawa, IL), February 22, 1868, 1.

3. *South-Western* (Shreveport, LA), February 5, 1868; *New Orleans Republican* (New Orleans, LA), February 21, 1868, 1; *Daily Dispatch* (Richmond, VA), January 29, 1868, 1.

4. "Carrying the Flag of the Union," *Evening Argus* (Rock Island, IL), February 3, 1868, 2.

5. "Mr. and Mrs. Jefferson Davis, Sergeant Bates, and the Pedestrian," *Daily Dispatch* (Richmond, VA), February 1, 1868, 3.

6. Timothy B. Smith, "Jackson: The Capital City and the Civil War," http://mshistorynow.mdah.state.ms.us/articles/337/jackson-the-capital-city-and-the-civil-war.

7. Ibid.

8. Ibid.

9. Ibid.; "Jackson," https://www.nps.gov/abpp/battles/ms008.htm.

10. Smith, "Jackson."

11. Ibid.

12. Ibid.

13. Bates, *Sergeant . . . to Washington*, 8.

14. "Arrival of Gilbert H. Bates," *Daily Clarion* (Jackson, MS), January 31, 1868, 1.

15. "Mississippi State Convention," *Daily Clarion* (Jackson, MS), January 31, 1868, 1.

16. *Daily Clarion* (Jackson, MS), January 31, 1868, 3.

17. Bates, *Sergeant . . . to Washington*, 8.

18. "Sergeant Bates," *Ottawa Free Trader* (Ottawa, IL), February 22, 1868, 1.

19. *Daily Clarion*, (Jackson, MS), January 31, 1868, 3.

20. Ibid.

21. Bates, *Sergeant . . . to Washington*, 8.

22. Ibid.

23. Ibid.

24. Ibid., 9.

25. Ibid.

26. Ibid.

27. Ibid.

28. Ibid.

CHAPTER 6

1. Gilbert H. Bates, *Sergeant Bates' March: Carrying the Flag from Vicksburg to Washington* (New York: B. W. Hitchcock, 1868), 9. (Hereafter referred to as Bates, *Sergeant . . . to Washington.*)

2. Ibid.

3. Ibid.; A. J. Brown, "The Town of Hickory." https://www.nchgs.org/html/town_of_hickory.html.

4. Ibid.

5. Ibid.
6. Ibid.
7. Bates, *Sergeant . . . to Washington*, 9.
8. Ibid.
9. Ibid.
10. Ibid.
11. "Sergeant Bates," *Anderson Intelligencer* (Anderson Court House, SC), February 19, 1868, 4.
12. "Meridian and the Civil War," https://www.visitmeridian.com/plan-your-trip/meridians-history/.
13. Ibid.
14. "Sherman Enters Meridian, Mississippi," https://www.history.com/this-day-in-history/sherman-enters-meridian-mississippi.
15. Ibid.
16. Ibid.; "Civil War Trail," https://www.visitmeridian.com/explore/historic-trail-markers/civil-war/.
17. Bates, *Sergeant . . . to Washington*, 9–10.
18. Ibid., 10.
19. Ibid.
20. Ibid.
21. "The Great Walk: Sergeant Bates on His Travels, His Doings at Meridian," *Charleston Daily News* (Charleston, SC), February 21, 1868, 1.
22. Ibid.
23. Ibid.
24. Ibid.; Bates, *Sergeant . . . to Washington*, 10.
25. Ibid.
26. Ibid.
27. Philip Leigh, "Union Leagues," https://www.abbevilleinstitute.org/blog/union-leagues.
28. Sergeant G. H. Bates, "Editor Raleigh Sentinel," *Daily Register* (Carson City, NV), May 13, 1871, 1.
29. Ibid.

CHAPTER 7

1. G. Ward Hubbs, "Civil War in Alabama," http://www.encyclopediaofalabama.org/article/h-1429.
2. Gilbert H. Bates, *Sergeant Bates' March: Carrying the Flag from Vicksburg to Washington* (New York: B. W. Hitchcock, 1868), 10. (Hereafter referred to as Bates, *Sergeant . . . to Washington*.)
3. James P. Kaetz, "Cuba," http://www.encyclopediaofalabama.org/article/h-3772.
4. Ibid.
5. Bates, *Sergeant . . . to Washington*, 10.
6. Ibid., 10–11.
7. Ibid., 11; *Daily Clarion* (Jackson, MS), February 20, 1868, 2.

8. Bates, *Sergeant . . . to Washington*, 11; Keith S. Hebert, "Battle of Selma," http://www. encyclopediaofalabama.org/article/h-3442.

9. Hebert.

10. "The Battle of Selma," https://battleofselma.com/history-of-the-battle/.

11. Ibid.

12. Ibid.

13. Ibid.

14. Bates, *Sergeant . . . to Washington*, 11; Herbert Lewis, "Selma," *Encyclopedia of Alabama*, http://www.encyclopediaofalabama.org/face/Article.jsp?id=1635.

15. Bates, *Sergeant . . . to Washington*, 11.

16. Ibid.

17. Leah Rawls Atkins, "Andrew B. Moore," http://www.encyclopediaofalabama.org/article/h-1454.

18. Sarah Woolfolk Wiggins, "Lewis Eliphalet Parsons 1865," http://www.encyclopediaofalabama.org/article/h-1169.

19. Ibid.

20. Bates, *Sergeant . . . to Washington*, 11; "Progress of Serg't Bates," *Daily Argus* (Mount Vernon, NY), February 14, 1868, 1.

21. Ibid.

22. Bates, *Sergeant . . . to Washington*, 11.

23. *Charleston Daily News* (Charleston, SC), February 17, 1868, 2.

24. Bates, *Sergeant . . . to Washington*, 11.

25. Ibid.

26. Ibid.

27. James P. Kaetz, "Benton," http://encyclopediaofalabama.org/article/h-3541.

28. Bates, *Sergeant . . . to Washington*, 11.

29. Ibid.

30. Ibid., 11–12.

31. Ibid., 12.

32. *Manitowoc Tribune* (Manitowoc, WI), February 13, 1868, 1.

33. Ibid.

CHAPTER 8

1. *Emporia News* (Emporia, KS), February 21, 1868, 2.

2. Gilbert H. Bates, *Sergeant Bates' March: Carrying the Flag from Vicksburg to Washington* (New York: B. W. Hitchcock, 1868), 12. (Hereafter referred to as Bates, *Sergeant . . . to Washington*.)

3. "Montgomery, Ala., Feb. 18," *Alexandria Gazette* (Alexandria, VA), February 18, 1868, 1.

4. "From Montgomery," *Weekly North Carolina Standard* (Raleigh, NC), February 19, 1868, 3.

5. Mary Ann Oglesby Neeley, "Montgomery," http://www.encyclopediaofalabama.org/article/h-1833.

6. Ibid.

7. Ibid.

8. Bates, *Sergeant . . . to Washington*, 12.

9. "The Old Flag at Montgomery," *Edgefield Advertiser* (Edgefield, SC), March 18, 1868.

10. Bates, *Sergeant . . . to Washington*, 12; "Montgomery, Ala., Feb. 18," *Alexandria Gazette* (Alexandria, VA), February 18, 1868, 1.

11. Bates, *Sergeant . . . to Washington*, 12.

12. Ibid.

13. Ibid.

14. Ibid.; "From Montgomery," *Weekly North Carolina Standard* (Raleigh, NC), February 19, 1868, 3.

15. Bates, *Sergeant . . . to Washington*, 12; *New Orleans Republican* (New Orleans, LA), February 21, 1868, 1.

16. Bates, *Sergeant . . . to Washington*, 12.

17. Sergeant G. H. Bates, "Editor Raleigh Sentinel," *Daily Register* (Carson City, NV), May 13, 1871, 1.

18. Ibid.

19. "James Holt Clanton," https://www.findagrave.com/memorial/8757/james-holt-clanton.

20. "Montgomery, Ala. Feb. 18," *Alexandria Gazette* (Alexandria, VA), February 18, 1868, 1.

21. "Sergeant Bates," *Native Virginian* (Orange Court House, VA), February 21, 1868, 1.

22. "Sergeant Bates and the Flag," *Richmond Dispatch* (Richmond, VA), February 15, 1868, 1.

23. Ibid.

24. Ibid.

25. Ibid.

26. "The March to Washington," *Daily News* (Charleston, SC), February 29, 1868, 1.

27. Ibid.

28. Ibid.

29. *Evening Argus* (Rock Island, IL), February 26, 1868, 2.

30. Ibid.

31. Ibid.

32. Ibid.

33. Bates, "Editor Raleigh Sentinel."

34. Sarah Lawless, "Tuskegee," http://www.encyclopediaofalabama.org/article/h-2051.

35. Bates, *Sergeant . . . to Washington*, 12.

36. Ibid.

37. Ibid., 13.

CHAPTER 9

1. William Harris Bragg, "Reconstruction in Georgia," https://www.georgiaencyclopedia.org/articles/history-archaeology/reconstruction-georgia.

2. Gilbert H. Bates, *Sergeant Bates' March: Carrying the Flag from Vicksburg to Washington* (New York: B. W. Hitchcock, 1868), 13. (Hereafter referred to as Bates, *Sergeant . . . to Washington.*)

3. Ibid.

4. "Sergeant Bates," *Daily Phoenix* (Columbus, SC), March 3, 1868, 1.

5. Ibid.

6. "History of Columbus, Georgia," https://www.columbusga.gov/history.

7. George J. Burnes, "Columbus as It Was During the War, 1861–65," https://www.columbusga.gov/history/history.pdf.

8. "Battle of Columbus," http://www.americancivilwarstory.com/battle-of-columbus.html.

9. "Sergeant Bates," *Daily Phoenix* (Columbus, SC), March 3, 1868, 1.

10. Bates, *Sergeant . . . to Washington*, 13.

11. Mike Stucka, "Macon Played Pivotal Role in Civil War in Georgia," *Telegraph* (Macon, GA), April 12, 2011.

12. Bates, *Sergeant . . . to Washington*, 13.

13. "City of Milledgeville," https://www.milledgevillega.us/index.php/our-history.

14. Bates, *Sergeant . . . to Washington*, 13.

15. Ibid., 14.

16. Ibid., 13–14.

17. Ibid., 14; "Census of Population and Housing," Census.gov, archived from the original on May 12, 2015.

18. Bates, *Sergeant . . . to Washington*, 14.

CHAPTER 10

1. Gilbert H. Bates, *Sergeant Bates' March: Carrying the Flag from Vicksburg to Washington.* (New York: B. W. Hitchcock, 1868), 14. (Hereafter referred to as Bates, *Sergeant . . . to Washington.*)

2. John Rozier. "Sparta." https://www.georgiaencyclopedia.org/articles/counties-cities-neighborhoods/sparta.

3. Ibid.

4. Bates, *Sergeant . . . to Washington*, 14.

5. Ibid.

6. Ibid.

7. Ibid.

8. Ibid.

9. Ibid.

10. Ibid.

11. Ibid., 15.

12. Ibid.

13. Ibid.; "Arrival of Sergeant Bates at Augusta," *Daily Ohio Statesman* (Columbus, OH), March 13, 1868, 1.

14. "The Flood at the South," *Daily Dispatch* (Richmond, VA), January 23, 1865, 1; "Southern News," *Alexandria Gazette* (Alexandria, VA), April 21, 1863, 1; "Walker,

Pendleton and Broadman Ad," *Abbeville Press* (Abbeville, SC), April 27, 1866, 2; "Screven House," *Daily Phoenix* (Columbia, SC), April 17, 1868, 1.

15. "History of Augusta, Georgia," https://www.u-s-history.com/pages/h2735.html; Rebecca Rogers, "History of Augusta," https://www.nps.gov/nr/travel/augusta/historyaugustaoverview.html; "Civil War in Augusta," https://www.visitaugusta.com/things-to-do/civil-war/.

16. Edward J. Cashin, "Augusta," https://www.georgiaencyclopedia.org/articles/counties-cities-neighborhoods/augusta.

17. Rogers, "History of Augusta, Georgia."

18. Bates, *Sergeant . . . to Washington*, 15.

19. Ibid.

20. Ibid.

21. Ibid.

22. Sergeant G. H. Bates, "Editor Raleigh Sentinel," *Daily Register* (Carson City, NV), May 13, 1871, 1.

CHAPTER 11

1. Gilbert H. Bates, *Sergeant Bates' March: Carrying the Flag from Vicksburg to Washington* (New York: B. W. Hitchcock, 1868), 15. (Hereafter referred to as Bates, *Sergeant . . . to Washington*.)

2. Ibid.

3. Tom Downey, "Hamburg," https://www.scencyclopedia.org/sce/entries/hamburg/; Charles Seabrook, "Savannah River," https://www.georgiaencyclopedia.org/articles/geography-environment/savannah-river.

4. "Local Items," *Daily Phoenix* (Columbia, SC), March 18, 1868, 2.

5. Bates, *Sergeant . . . to Washington*, 15–16.

6. "History of Columbia," https://columbiasc.net/about-columbia.

7. "Sergeant Bates in Columbia," *Anderson Intelligencer* (Anderson Court House, SC), March 25, 1868, 1.

8. "Arrival of Sergeant Bates, His Reception at the Capital of South Carolina," *Daily Phoenix* (Columbia, SC), March 19, 1868, 1.

9. Ibid.

10. "Sergeant Bates," *Yorkville Enquirer* (Yorkville, SC), March 26, 1868, 3.

11. Ibid.

12. Bates, *Sergeant . . . to Washington*, 16.

13. Sergeant Bates, *Yorkville Enquirer*.

14. Ibid.

15. Tom Elmore, *Columbia Civil War Landmarks* (Charleston, SC: The History Press, 2011), 19.

16. "Arrival of Sergeant Bates, His Reception at the Capital of South Carolina."

17. Ibid.; Bates, *Sergeant . . . to Washington*, 16.

18. *Daily Phoenix* (Columbia, SC), March 20, 1868, 1.

19. Ibid.; The Angel of Marye's Heights. https://civilwartalk.com/threads/the-angel-of-marye%E2%80%99s-heights.167413/page-2.

20. Bates, *Sergeant . . . to Washington*, 16.
21. "Sergeant Bates," *Yorkville Enquirer*.
22. "Sherman Sacks Columbus, South Carolina," https://www.history.com/this-day-in-history/sherman-sacks-columbia-south-carolina.
23. Bates, *Sergeant . . . to Washington*, 16.
24. "About the Daily Phoenix," https://chroniclingamerica.loc.gov/lccn/sn84027008/.
25. Ibid.
26. Bates, *Sergeant . . . to Washington*, 16.
27. *Daily Phoenix* (Columbia, SC), March 22, 1868, 1.
28. *Daily Ohio* (Columbus, OH), March 25, 1868, 1.
29. "Sergeant Bates," *Yorkville Enquirer*.
30. Ibid.

CHAPTER 12

1. *Daily Phoenix* (Columbia, SC), March 24, 1868, 1.
2. "Town of Winnsboro," https://discoversouthcarolina.com/products/10078; J. D. Lewis, "A History of Winnsboro, South Carolina," https://www.carolana.com/SC/Towns/Winnsboro_SC.html; "Winnsboro History." http://www.townofwinnsboro.com/winsboro-history.
3. *Daily Phoenix* (Columbia, SC), March 21, 1868, 1.
4. Gilbert H. Bates, *Sergeant Bates' March: Carrying the Flag from Vicksburg to Washington* (New York: B. W. Hitchcock, 1868), 16. (Hereafter referred to as Bates, *Sergeant . . . to Washington*.)
5. Ibid.
6. Ibid.
7. Ibid., 16–17.
8. Ibid., 17.
9. Ibid.
10. Ibid.
11. Ibid.
12. Ibid., 17–18.
13. *Daily Phoenix* (Columbia, SC), March 27, 1868, 1.
14. Bates, *Sergeant . . . to Washington*, 18.
15. Matthew A. Lockhart, "Rock Hill," https://www.scencyclopedia.org/sce/entries/rock-hill/; "York County History, An Introduction." https://www.yclibrary.org/ychistory.
16. Bates, *Sergeant . . . to Washington*, 18.
17. Ibid., 18–19.
18. Ibid., 19.
19. "Fort Mill, South Carolina," https://fortmillsc.gov/?SEC=F13B2B44-D121-4B1B-9C0D-5787B1C02256; "Historic Markers Across South Carolina," http://lat34north.com/HistoricMarkersSC/SC_Index; "South Carolina Historical Markers in York County, 1936–Present," https://www.cityofrockhill.com/home/showdocument?id=1279.
20. Bates, *Sergeant . . . to Washington*, 19.
21. Ibid.

CHAPTER 13

1. "The History of Charlotte," https://www.charlottesgotalot.com/articles/history/the-history-of-charlotte; "History of Charlotte, North Carolina," https://www.u-s-history.com/pages/h3876.html.

2. David C. Williard, "North Carolina in the Civil War," https://dev.ncpedia.org/history/cw-1900/civil-war.

3. "Look at Buxbaum and Lang's Price List," *Charlotte Democrat* (Charlotte, NC), June 2, 1868, 3; Gilbert H. Bates, *Sergeant Bates' March: Carrying the Flag from Vicksburg to Washington* (New York: B. W. Hitchcock, 1868), 19. (Hereafter referred to as Bates, *Sergeant . . . to Washington*.)

4. Bates, *Sergeant . . . to Washington*, 19.

5. Ibid.

6. Ibid.

7. Ibid.

8. "Concord: Historic Facts," https://www.concordnc.gov/visitor/historic-facts.

9. Bates, *Sergeant . . . to Washington*, 19–20.

10. Ibid.

11. Ibid.

12. Ibid.

13. Ibid.

14. Jonathan Martin, "Rowan County," https://northcarolinahistory.org/encyclopedia/rowan-county-1753; "A History of Salisbury, North Carolina," https://www.carolana.com/NC/Towns/Salisbury_NC.html.

15. Betty Dan Spencer, "In Its Heyday, Boyden House Had a Central Role in Salisbury Social Life," *Salisbury Post* (Salisbury, NC), September 11, 2016, 1.

16. Bates, *Sergeant . . . to Washington*, 20.

17. Mrs. John T. Cramer, "Recollections of the Founding and Growth During the Early Years of Thomasville," *Chairtown News* (Thomasville, NC), July 28, 1921, 1.

18. Ibid.

19. Bates, *Sergeant . . . to Washington*, 20.

20. Ibid.

21. Ibid.

22. J. W. Cannon, "Old School for Girls Has Place in History Despite Hectic Career," *Greensboro Daily News*, January 3, 1932, 1; Mary Green Matthews, *Wheels of Faith and Courage: A History of Thomasville, North Carolina* (Thomasville, NC: Hall Printing Company), 1952.

23. Ibid.

CHAPTER 14

1. Gilbert H. Bates, *Sergeant Bates' March: Carrying the Flag from Vicksburg to Washington* (New York: B. W. Hitchcock, 1868), 20. (Hereafter referred to as Bates, *Sergeant . . . to Washington*.)

2. Ibid., 20–21.

3. "Prior 1830s: The Early Years," https://www.greensboro-nc.gov/departments/police/about-gpd/history; "Greensboro History," https://www.visitgreensboronc.com/about-us/greensboro-history.

4. "The Civil War in Greensboro: Key Sites in the Action," https://greensboro.com/news/the-civil-war-in-greensboro-key-sites-in-the-action/article_cfed1093-58d5-5b1e-aeb5-9f468620d312.html.

5. Ibid.; https://americanhistory.si.edu/.

6. Sergeant G. H. Bates, "Editor Raleigh Sentinel," *Daily Register* (Carson City, NV), May 13, 1871, 1.

7. Ibid.

8. Jerry L. Cross, "William Woods Holden," https://ncpedia.org/holden-william-woods-research; Sai Srikanth, "William Woods Holden," https://northcarolinahistory.org/encyclopedia/william-woods-holden-1818-1892/.

9. *Western Democrat* (Charlotte, NC), June 13, 1865, 1.

10. W. W. Holden, "Proclamation," *Western Democrat* (Charlotte, NC), June 27, 1865, 1.

11. "North Carolina Election," *Tarboro Southerner* (Tarboro, NC), April 23, 1868, 1.

12. Bates, *Sergeant . . . to Washington*, 21.

13. "History of Raleigh." https://raleighnc.gov/history-raleigh.

14. "Raleigh, N.C., and the Civil War," https://www.visitraleigh.com/things-to-do/history/civil-war/.

15. Ibid.

16. "History of Raleigh"; "Raleigh, N.C., and the Civil War"; Chick Jacobs, "The Lesser-Known Story of How the Civil War Ended in North Carolina," *Fayetteville Observer* (Fayetteville, NC), March 22, 2015, 3.

17. Bates, *Sergeant . . . to Washington*, 21.

18. "The Flag in the South," *Daily Phoenix* (Columbia, SC), April 8, 1868, 1.

19. Ibid.

20. Bates, *Sergeant . . . to Washington*, 20–21; "Jonathan Worth," https://www.carolana.com/NC/Governors/jworth.html; "Jonathan Worth," https://www.nga.org/governor/jonathan-worth/.

21. Bates, *Sergeant . . . to Washington*, 21.

22. Ibid.

23. Ibid.

24. Ibid.

25. Ibid.

26. Ibid.

27. Ibid., 22.

28. Ibid.

29. Ibid.

30. Ibid.

31. Ibid.

32. Ibid.

CHAPTER 15

1. Gilbert H. Bates, *Sergeant Bates' March: Carrying the Flag from Vicksburg to Washington* (New York: B. W. Hitchcock, 1868), 22. (Hereafter referred to as Bates, *Sergeant . . . to Washington.*)

2. "Early Danville History," http://danvillehistory.org/history.html.

3. Ibid.; Catherine M. Wright, "Danville During the Civil War," https://www.encyclopediavirginia.org/Danville_During_the_Civil_War.

4. Ibid.

5. Ibid.

6. Bates, *Sergeant . . . to Washington*, 22.

7. Historical Census Browser, University of Virginia Library; "Sergeant Bates at Pettusville, Va.—Mr. Nasby is Present When He Arrives," *Jackson Standard* (Jackson Court House, OH), May 7, 1868, 1.

8. "Nasby, Petroleum V." https://pfaffs.web.lehigh.edu/node/54257.

9. "Sergeant Bates at Pettusville, Va."

10. Ibid.

11. Ibid.

12. Ibid.

13. Ibid.

14. Ibid.

15. Ibid.

16. Ibid.

17. Ibid.

18. "Sergeant Bates and the Flag of the Union," *Daily Dispatch* (Richmond, VA), April 8, 1868, 1.

19. Bates, *Sergeant . . . to Washington*, 22.

20. "Co-partnership." *Daily Dispatch* (Richmond, VA), July 17, 1861, 1; "Confederate States District Court," *Daily Dispatch* (Richmond, VA), October 21, 1864, 1; "The Courts," *Daily Dispatch* (Richmond, VA), December 18, 1868, 1.

21. "The Fourth at Oakwood," *Daily Dispatch* (Richmond, VA), July 6, 1866, 1; "Notice: Mr. Joseph Cance," *Daily Dispatch* (Richmond, VA), June 15, 1867, 1; "Valuable Bakery and Fixtures," *Daily Dispatch* (Richmond, VA), July 26, 1867, 1; "List of Letters," *Daily Dispatch* (Richmond, VA), February 22, 1868, 1.

22. "Sergeant Bates in Richmond," *Daily Dispatch* (Richmond, VA), April 9, 1868, 1.

23. Bates, *Sergeant . . . to Washington*, 23.

24. Ibid.

25. Wayne Russell and Jeanette Porter, "Amelia Court House," *Cooperative Living*, January 2010, 32–35.

CHAPTER 16

1. "Sergeant Bates and the Flag of the Union," *Daily Dispatch* (Richmond, VA), April 8, 1868, 1.

2. Ibid.

3. Gilbert H. Bates, *Sergeant Bates' March: Carrying the Flag from Vicksburg to Washington* (New York: B. W. Hitchcock, 1868), 23. (Hereafter referred to as Bates, *Sergeant . . . to Washington.*)

4. "Sergeant Bates in Richmond," *Daily Phoenix* (Richmond, VA), April 9, 1868, 1.

5. Bates, *Sergeant . . . to Washington*, 23.

6. "Sergeant Bates in Richmond," *Daily Phoenix.*

7. Bates, *Sergeant . . . to Washington*, 23.

8. "Sergeant Bates in Richmond," *Daily Phoenix.*

9. "The Exchange Hotel Civil War Medical Museum," https://visitorangevirginia.com/step-into-history-the-exchange-hotel-civil-war-medical-museum/; "The Exchange Hotel Civil War Medical Museum: Gordonsville, Virginia." https://colonialghosts.com/the-exchange-hotel-civil-war-medical-museum/.

10. Mary DeCredico and Jaime Amanda Martinez, "Richmond During the Civil War," https://www.encyclopediavirginia.org/richmond_during_the_civil_war.

11. Ibid.

12. Ibid.

13. Ibid.

14. Bates, *Sergeant . . . to Washington*, 23.

15. "Sergeant Bates in Richmond," *Daily Phoenix.*

16. Bates, *Sergeant . . . to Washington*, 23.

17. Ibid.

18. "Sergeant Bates in Richmond," *Daily Phoenix.*

19. Ibid.

20. Ibid.

21. Bates, *Sergeant . . . to Washington*, 23-24.

22. "Sergeant Bates in Richmond," *Daily Phoenix.*

23. Ibid.; Bates, *Sergeant . . . to Washington*, 24; *Alexandria Gazette* (Alexandria, VA), April 10, 1868, 1.

24. "Sergeant Bates," *Alexandria Gazette* (Alexandria, VA), April 11, 1868, 1.

25. "Historic Hanover County, Virginia," https://www.hanovervirginia.com/explore-hanover/things-to-do/historic-sites/; "History: Hanover County, Virginia," http://www.hanovervirginia.com/explore-hanover/history/; Bates, *Sergeant . . . to Washington*, 24.

26. Bates, *Sergeant . . . to Washington*, 24.

27. Ibid.

28. "History of Fredericksburg," https://www.fredericksburgva.gov/202/History-of-Fredericksburg; "Battle of Fredericksburg," https://www.history.com/topics/american-civil-war/battle-of-fredericksburg.

29. Bates, *Sergeant . . . to Washington*, 24.

30. "Stonewall Jackson," https://www.biography.com/military-figure/stonewall-jackson.

31. Bates, *Sergeant . . . to Washington*, 24.

32. Ibid.; "Sergeant Bates," *Edgefield Advertiser* (Edgefield, SC), March 18, 1868, 1.

33. "History: Town of Dumfries," https://www.dumfriesva.gov/residents/history.php; "Historic Dumfries, Virginia," https://historicdumfriesva.org/about/history. Bates, *Sergeant . . . to Washington*, 24.

34. Ibid.

35. Ibid.

36. Ibid., 24–25.

37. Ibid., 25.

38. *Daily Clarion* (Jackson, MS), April 15, 1868, 1.

39. "Alexandria: The Crossroads of the Civil War," http://www.pbs.org/mercy-street/uncover-history/real-people-places/alexandria/#:~:text=In%20the%20spring%20of%201862,unprecedented%20and%20overwhelming%20scale%20of; "Alexandria During the Civil War," https://www.alexandriava.gov/CivilWar.

40. Brady Dennis, "The Federal Occupation of Alexandria in the Civil War Changed and Spared City," *Washington Post*, April 7, 2011; "Wayfinding: Marshall House," https://www.alexandriava.gov/historic/info/default.aspx?id=101305.

41. "Sergeant Bates," *Alexandria Gazette* (Alexandria, VA), April 14, 1868, 3.

42. Bates, *Sergeant . . . to Washington*, 25.

CHAPTER 17

1. "Sergeant Bates," *Alexandria Gazette* (Alexandria, VA), April 13, 1868, 3.

2. Ibid.

3. Gilbert H. Bates, *Sergeant Bates' March: Carrying the Flag from Vicksburg to Washington* (New York: B. W. Hitchcock, 1868), 25. (Hereafter referred to as Bates, *Sergeant . . . to Washington.*)

4. "The Arrival of Sergeant Bates at Washington City," *Spirit of Jefferson* (Charles Town, WV), April 21, 1868, 1.

5. Bates, *Sergeant . . . to Washington*, 25.

6. Robert Cohen, "History of the Long Railroad Bridge Crossing Across the Potomac River," http://www.dcnrhs.org/learn/washington-d-c-railroad-history/history-of-the-long-bridge; "Long Bridge Over the Potomac River," http://www.virginiaplaces.org/rail/longbridge.html.

7. "Washington, April 14," *Western Democrat* (Charlotte, NC), April 21, 1868, 1.

8. "Bates and his Banner," *Burlington Weekly Free Press* (Burlington, VT), April 24, 1868, 1.

9. "Sergeant Bates and the U.S. Flag," *Western Democrat* (Charlotte, NC), April 21, 1868, 1; "Sergeant Bates at Washington," *Yorkville Enquirer* (Yorkville, SC), April 23, 1868, 1.

10. Bates, *Sergeant . . . to Washington*, 25.

11. Ibid.

12. "Doolittle, James Rood." https://bioguide.congress.gov/search/bio/D000428; "James Rood Doolittle," https://www.findagrave.com/memorial/8795250/james-rood-doolittle; *Wood County Reporter* (Grand Rapids, WI), January 29, 1863, 1.

13. Bates, *Sergeant . . . to Washington*, 25.

14. "The United States Senatorship," *Chronicle* (Dodgeville, WI), December 4, 1868, 1.

15. Bates, *Sergeant . . . to Washington*, 25.

16. *Daily Phoenix* (Columbia, SC), April 15, 1868, 1.

17. "Bates and his Banner," *Burlington Weekly Free Press.*

18. Bates, *Sergeant . . . to Washington*, 25; "Arrival of Sergeant Bates at Washington City," *Spirit of Jefferson*.
19. "Bates and his Banner," *Burlington Weekly Free Press*.
20. Bates, *Sergeant . . . to Washington*, 26.
21. "Sergeant Bates," *Alexandria Gazette* (Alexandria, VA), April 14, 1868, 1.
22. Ibid.
23. Bates, *Sergeant . . . to Washington*, 26; "Arrival of Sergeant Bates at Washington City," *Spirit of Jefferson*.
24. "Unconstitutional Convention," *Staunton Spectator* (Staunton, VA), April 14, 1868, 1.
25. Ibid.
26. Ibid.
27. Ibid.
28. Bates, *Sergeant . . . to Washington*, 26; "Arrival of Sergeant Bates at Washington City," *Spirit of Jefferson*.
29. "Andrew Johnson," https://www.whitehouse.gov/about-the-white-house/presidents/andrew-johnson/
30. "Arrival of Sergeant Bates at Washington City," *Spirit of Jefferson*.
31. "The White House Building," https://www.whitehouse.gov/about-the-white-house/the-white-house.
32. Bates, *Sergeant . . . to Washington*, 26.
33. "East Room," http://www.whitehousemuseum.org/floor1/east-room.htm.
34. "Sergeant Bates at the Capitol," *South-Western* (Shreveport, LA), April 29, 1868, 1.
35. "Arrival of Sergeant Bates at Washington City," *Spirit of Jefferson*.
36. "Sergeant Bates at the Capitol," *South-Western*.
37. Ibid.
38. Ibid.
39. Ibid.
40. "Arrival of Sergeant Bates at Washington City," *Spirit of Jefferson*.
41. "Sergeant Bates at the Capitol," *South-Western*.
42. Bates, *Sergeant . . . to Washington*, 26; "Arrival of the Sergeant at Washington," *The New York Herald*, April 15, 1868, 5; "Arrival of Sergeant Bates at Washington City," *Spirit of Jefferson*.
43. "Martha Johnson Patterson: Hostess of the Andrew Johnson White House," https://www.whitehousehistory.org/martha-johnson-patterson-hostess-of-the-andrew-johnson-white-house.
44. "Summary of News," *Vermont Transcript* (St. Albans, VT), April 24, 1868, 2; "Bates and his Banner," *Burlington Weekly Free Press*.

CHAPTER 18

1. "The Metropolitan, aka Brown's Marble Hotel," http://www.streetsofwashington.com/2009/12/metropolitan-aka-browns-marble-hotel.html; Gilbert H. Bates, *Sergeant Bates' March: Carrying the Flag from Vicksburg to Washington* (New York: B. W. Hitchcock, 1868), 26. (Hereafter referred to as Bates, *Sergeant . . . to Washington*.)

2. Bates, *Sergeant . . . to Washington*, 26; "Washington, April 14," *Western Democrat* (Charlotte, NC), April 21, 1868, 1.

3. "Eldredge, Charles Augustus," https://www.wisconsinhistory.org/Records/Article/CS7388.

4. Bates, *Sergeant . . . to Washington*, 26.

5. Ibid.

6. Ibid.

7. Ibid.

8. Ibid.; "William Mungen," https://www.findagrave.com/memorial/8122776/william-mungen.

9. Bates, *Sergeant . . . to Washington*, 26.

10. "Sergeant Bates at the Capitol," *South-Western* (Shreveport, LA), April 29, 1868, 1; "The Arrival of Sergeant Bates at Washington City," *Spirit of Jefferson* (Charles Town, WV), April 21, 1868, 1.

11. Bates, *Sergeant . . . to Washington*, 27.

12. "Michler, Nathaniel," https://tshaonline.org/handbook/online/articles/fmi88.

13. "Sergeant Bates at the Capitol," *South-Western*.

14. Ibid.

15. "George T. Brown, Sergeant at Arms," https://www.senate.gov/about/officers-staff/sergeant-at-arms/SAA-George-Brown.htm; Bates, *Sergeant . . . to Washington*, 27.

16. Bates, *Sergeant . . . to Washington*, 27.

17. "Arrival of Sergeant Bates at Washington City," *Spirit of Jefferson*.

18. "Ordway, Nehemiah G.," https://history.house.gov/People/Listing/O/ORDWAY,-Nehemiah-G-/.

19. "Sergeant Bates at the Capitol," *South-Western*.

20. "Mr. J. Corson," *Alexandria Gazette* (Alexandria, VA), April 16, 1868, 1.

21. "Sergeant Bates at the Capitol," *South-Western*.

22. Bates, *Sergeant . . . to Washington*, 27.

23. Ibid.

24. Ibid.

25. Ibid., 28.

26. Ibid.

27. Ibid.

28. Ibid.

29. "Sergeant Bates in the Capital," *Charlotte Daily News* (Charlotte, NC), April 15, 1868, 1.

30. Bates, *Sergeant . . . to Washington*, 28.

31. "Sergeant Bates at the Capitol," *South-Western*.

32. "Sergeant Bates and His Flag," *Daily Phoenix* (Columbia, SC), April 19, 1868, 1.

33. Elizabeth Nix, "5 Things You Might Not Know About the Washington Monument," September 1, 2018. https://www.history.com/news/5-things-you-might-not-know-about-the-washington-monument.

34. Bates, *Sergeant . . . to Washington*, 28.

35. Ibid.; Hiram Calkins and DeWitt Van Buren, *Biographical sketches of John T. Hoffman and Allen C. Beach: The Democratic nominees for governor and lieutenant-governor of the state*

of New York: also, a record of the events in the lives of Oliver Bascom, David B. McNeil, and Edwin O. Perrin, the other candidates on the same ticket. (New York: New York Printing Company, 1868), 110.

36. "Arrival of Sergeant Bates at Washington City," *Spirit of Jefferson.*

37. Bates, *Sergeant . . . to Washington*, 28.

38. Ibid.

39. "Washington, April 14," *Western Democrat.*

40. Bates, *Sergeant . . . to Washington*, 29.

41. Ibid.

42. Pat Young, "Book Review: Edward Pollard's *The Lost Cause: A New Southern History of the War of the Confederates.*" https://civilwartalk.com/threads/the-lost-cause-a-new-southern-history-of-the-war-of-the-confederates-by-edward-pollard.140775.

43. Bates, *Sergeant . . . to Washington*, 29.

44. Ibid.

45. Ibid.

46. Ibid.

47. Ibid.

48. Ibid., 30.

49. Ibid.

50. Ibid.

51. Ibid.

52. Ibid.

53. Ibid.

54. Ibid.

55. Ibid.

56. Ibid., 31.

57. Ibid.

58. Ibid., 31–32.

59. Ibid., 32.

60. Ibid.

61. Ibid.

62. Ibid.

63. Ibid., 32–33.

64. "Arrival of Sergeant Bates," *Evening Argus* (Rock Island, IL), April 24, 1868, 1.

65. "Sergeant Bates and His Flag," *Aegis and Intelligencer* (Bel Air, MD), April 24, 1868, 1.

66. Ibid.

67. Ibid.

CHAPTER 19

1. Gilbert H. Bates, *Sergeant Bates' March: Carrying the Flag from Vicksburg to Washington* (New York: B. W. Hitchcock, 1868), 33. (Hereafter referred to as Bates, *Sergeant . . . to Washington*.)

2. "Sergeant Bates in the Capital," *Charlotte Daily News* (Charlotte, NC), April 15, 1868, 1.

3. Bates, *Sergeant . . . to Washington*, 33.

4. Ibid.

5. Ibid.

6. Ibid.

7. Ibid.

8. Ibid.

9. Ibid.

10. Ibid.

11. Ibid.

12. "Sergeant Bates at the Capitol," *South-Western* (Shreveport, LA), April 29, 1868, 1.

13. "Reid, Captain Mayne," https://www.ulib.niu.edu/badndp/reid_mayne.html.

14. Howard Miller, *The Student's Dream and Other Poems* (Louisville, KY: John P. Morton and Company, 1871), 38–43.

CHAPTER 20

1. *Evening Argus* (Rock Island, IL), April 25, 1868, 1.

2. "Insults to Our Soldiers and Insults to Our Flag," *Weekly Echo* (Lake Charles, LA), May 2, 1868, 1.

3. "The Conservative Soldiers and Sailors," *Carson Daily Appeal* (Carson City, NV), July 8, 1868, 2.

4. "Sergeant Bates and His Flag: A Played-Out Demagogue," *Watertown Republic* (Watertown, WI), July 29, 1868, 2.

5. "Political Items," *Dodgeville Chronicle* (Dodgeville, WI), January 29, 1869, 1.

6. *Wyandot County Republican* (Upper Sandusky, OH), January 7, 1869, 1.

7. "Then and Now," *Oxford Democrat* (Paris, ME), May 30, 1871, 1.

8. *Arizona Citizen* (Tucson, AZ), November 9, 1872, 1.

9. *Wilmington Journal* (Wilmington, NC), January 17, 1873, 1.

10. *Petroleum Centre Daily Record* (Petroleum Center, PA), March 15, 1873, 1.

11. "Sergeant Bates Challenged," *Democratic Advocate* (Westminster, MD), March 15, 1873, 1.

12. *Daily Phoenix* (Columbia, SC), June 6, 1873, 2.

13. "Carrying the Rebel Flag through the Northern States," *New York Herald*, June 12, 1873, 2.

14. Ibid.

15. Ibid.

16. *Jasper Weekly Courier* (Jasper, IN), November 8, 1873, 2.

17. "War with Spain," *Public Ledger* (Memphis, TN), December 18, 1873, 1.

18. *Wood County Reporter* (Grand Rapids, WI), February 1874, 4.

19. *Bolivar Bulletin* (Bolivar, TN), August 14, 1874, 1.

20. *Anti-monopolist* (Saint Paul, MN), May 20, 1875, 9.

21. *Hillsborough Recorder* (Hillsborough, NC), August 18, 1875, 1.

22. *Albany Register* (Albany, OR), September 24, 1875, 2.

23. *Pioche Daily Record* (Pioche, NV), October 7, 1875, 2.

24. *Essex County Herald* (Guildhall, VT), October 23, 1875, 1.

25. *Star of Pascagoula* (Pascagoula, MS), October 23, 1875, 2.

26. *New Orleans Republican* (New Orleans, LA), November 13, 1875, 5.

27. *New Orleans Republican* (New Orleans, LA), December 23, 1875, 2.

28. *Albany Register* (Albany, OR), December 31, 1875, 4.

29. *New Orleans Republican* (New Orleans, LA), April 9, 1876, 4.

30. *Watertown Republican* (Watertown, WI), June 14, 1876, 3.

31. "Wit and Humor." *Watertown Republican* (Watertown, WI), November 15, 1876, 6.

32. "Sergeant Bates," *Dallas Daily Herald* (Dallas, TX), January 25, 1877, 4.

33. "By Telegraph to the Gazette," *Daily Gazette* (Wilmington, DE), August 29, 1877, 2.

34. "Chicago, Aug. 29," *Cincinnati Daily Star* (Cincinnati, OH), August 29, 1877, 1.

35. Christina Tkacik, "'The Laudanum Evil': Maryland's 19th Century Opiate Epidemic," *Baltimore Sun*, January 13, 2019, 2.

36. *News and Herald* (Winnsboro, SC), September 11, 1877, 1.

37. *Wheeling Daily Intelligencer* (Wheeling, WV), December 21, 1877, 1.

38. "Sergeant Bates Turns up Again," *Newberry Herald* (Newberry, SC), January 26, 1878, 1.

39. "Sergeant Bates Robbed and Maltreated," *Evening Star* (Washington, D.C.), April 8, 1878, 4.

40. "Professional Tramps." *Puget Sound Weekly Argus* (Port Townsend, WA), July 25, 1878, 6.

41. *Alpena Weekly Argus* (Alpena, MI), August 28, 1878, 1.

42. *Morning Appeal* (Carson City, NV), December 20, 1878, 2.

43. "Wheelbarrow Idiocy," *Lake Charles Echo* (Lake Charles, LA), June 21, 1879, 6.

44. "Sergeant Bates," *Chicago Daily Tribune*, March 13, 1881, 12.

45. *Morning Appeal* (Carson City, NV), March 16, 1881, 2.

46. "Death of Sergeant Bates," *Eureka Daily Sentinel* (Eureka, NV), April 14, 1881, 1.

47. *New Ulm Weekly Review* (New Ulm, MN), April 20, 1881, 1.

48. *Savannah Morning News* (Savannah, GA), April 23, 1881, 2.

49. Ibid.

50. "Poor Sergeant Bates," *Watertown Republican* (Watertown, WI), July 29, 1881, 3.

51. *Daily Astorian* (Astoria, OR), October 25, 1882, 2.

52. *Savannah Morning News* (Savannah, GA), September 18, 1883, 2.

53. *Daily Globe* (St. Paul, MN), October 4, 1883, 1.

54. Ibid.

55. "Sergeant Bates Not Appreciated," Morning Appeal (Carson City, NV), October 13, 1883, 3.

56. "Sergeant Bates Is a Bummer." *Morning Appeal* (Carson City, NV), October 19, 1883, 1.

57. *Semi-weekly Bourbon News* (Paris, KY), November 2, 1883, 1.

58. *Semi-weekly South Kentuckian* (Hopkinsville, KY), November 23, 1883, 3.

59. *Semi-weekly Bourbon News* (Paris, KY), December 4, 1883, 4.

60. *Public Ledger* (Memphis, TN), December 20, 1883, 1.
61. *Milan Exchange* (Milan, TN), March 1, 1884, 1.
62. *Semi-weekly Interior Journal* (Stanford, KY), March 7, 1884, 2.
63. "Sergeant Bates and His Flag," *Eureka Daily Sentinel* (Eureka, NV), March 19, 1884, 2.
64. *Idaho Semi-Weekly World* (Idaho City, ID), December 26, 1884, 1.
65. *Indianapolis Journal* (Indianapolis, IN), January 2, 1885, 4.
66. *Kimball Graphic* (Kimball, SD), February 27, 1885, 6.
67. *River Press* (Fort Benton, MT), June 3, 1885, 6.

CHAPTER 21

1. Gilbert H. Bates, *Sergeant Bates's March from Gretna Green to the Guildhall* (London: George Routledge and Sons, 1873), 3–4.
2. *Daily Phoenix* (Columbia, SC), March 11, 1868, 2.
3. *Daily Phoenix* (Columbia, SC), March 13, 1868, 1.
4. "Sergeant Bates Offered Ten Thousand Dollars to Work for the Radicals," *Daily Dispatch* (Richmond, VA), April 9, 1868, 1.
5. *Wyoming Democrat* (Tunkhannock, PA), April 22, 1868, 1.
6. "From a Soldier in the Regular Army." *Wyandot Pioneer* (Upper Sandusky, OH), June 11, 1868, 1.
7. *Staunton Spectator* (Staunton, VA), May 26, 1868, 1.
8. "Letter from New York," *Evansville Journal* (Evansville, IN), July 13, 1868, 1.
9. Ibid.
10. *Daily Phoenix* (Columbia, SC), August 6, 1868, 3.
11. "Sergeant Bates' March," *Daily Phoenix* (Columbia, SC), August 7, 1868, 1.
12. "Sergeant Bates," *Daily Phoenix* (Columbia, SC), September 13, 1868, 1.
13. "Sergeant Bates." *Daily Ohio Statesman* (Columbus, OH), October 27, 1868, 3.
14. "Sergeant Bates Is in Grief." *New Orleans Republican* (New Orleans, LA), December 12, 1868, 3.
15. *New Orleans Republican* (New Orleans, LA), December 15, 1868, 3.
16. "Robberies," *New Orleans Crescent* (New Orleans, LA), December 15, 1868, 1.
17. *Wyandot County Republican* (Upper Sandusky, OH), January 7, 1869, 1.
18. *Spirit of Democracy* (Woodsfield, OH), May 25, 1869, 1.
19. *Vermont Phoenix* (Brattleboro, VT), July 1, 1881, 3.
20. "Sergeant Bates' New Tramp," *Daily Evening Bulletin*, October 4, 1883, 4.
21. *Press and Daily Dakotaian* (Yankton, Dakota Territory), March 1, 1884, 2.
22. "The South Startled," *Butler Weekly Times* (Butler, MO), August 17, 1887, 1.
23. "James Madison Tuttle." https://www.findagrave.com/memorial/5895024/james-madison-tuttle; Sanford W. Huff, "Brigadier-General James M. Tuttle," *The Annals of Iowa 1868* (1868): 233–37.
24. "The South Startled."
25. Ibid.
26. Ibid.
27. Ibid.
28. Ibid.

Chapter 22

1. "Sergeant Bates Again," *New York Herald*, September 10, 1872, 1.
2. Ibid.
3. Ibid.
4. "The Old Flag Marching On," *Evening News* (Gold Hill, NV), October 3, 1872, 1.
5. "Sergeant Bates Again."
6. Gilbert H. Bates, *Sergeant Bates's March from Gretna Green to the Guildhall* (London: George Routledge and Sons, 1873), 1.
7. "Sergeant Bates Again."
8. Ibid.
9. "A Novel Wager," *New York Herald*, September 10, 1872, 1.
10. Ibid.
11. Ibid.
12. "The Alabama Claims, 1862–1872." https://history.state.gov/milestones/1861-1865/alabama.
13. *Nashville Union and American* (Nashville, TN), September 18, 1872, 2.
14. "Novel Wager."
15. Ibid.
16. Ibid.
17. *Knoxville Daily Chronicle* (Knoxville, TN), September 15, 1872, 1.
18. *Portland Daily Press* (Portland, ME), September 13, 1872, 2.
19. *Chicago Tribune*, September 14, 1872, 4.
20. *Public Ledger* (Memphis, TN), September 18, 1872, 2.
21. "Sergeant Bates: The Flag-bearing Traveler Going to Exhibit the Bunting to John Bull," *Helena Weekly Herald* (Helena, MT), October 3, 1872, 1.
22. *Daily Dispatch* (Richmond, VA), October 3, 1872, 1.
23. "Cheney's Grove Township." http://genealogytrails.com/ill/mclean/history_cheneysgrove.html.
24. "Old Flag Marching On."
25. Ibid.
26. *New York Herald*, October 6, 1872, 8.
27. "Old Flag Marching On."
28. *Portland Daily Press.*
29. "The Invasion of England," *Beaufort Republican* (Beaufort, SC), October 24, 1872, 1.
30. *Juniata Sentinel* (Mifflintown, PA), October 16, 1872, 2.
31. *New York Herald*, October 9, 1872, 4.
32. *Helena Weekly Herald* (Helena, MT), October 24, 1872, 3.
33. Ibid.
34. Bates, *Sergeant Bates's March*, 12–13.
35. "Bates Over the Border," *New York Herald*, October 20, 1872, 11.
36. Ibid.
37. *Jasper Weekly Courier* (Jasper, IN), November 8, 1872, 2.
38. "Miscellaneous," *New North-west* (Deer Lodge, MT), October 26, 1872, 2.
39. *Chicago Daily Tribune*, October 24, 1872, 4.

40. Bates, *Sergeant Bates's March*, 9.
41. Ibid.
42. "Benjamin Wood." https://elections.harpweek.com/1872/bio-1872-Full. asp?UniqueID=35&Year=1872.
43. "Norway-Heritage Across the Sea: *S/S Europa*, Anchor Line, http://www.norway-heritage.com/p_ship.asp?sh=euro1; Bates, *Sergeant Bates's March*, 9.
44. Bates, *Sergeant Bates's March*, 9.
45. Ibid.
46. Ibid., 13.
47. Ibid., 14.
48. Ibid.
49. Ibid., 15.
50. Ibid.
51. "Historic Glasgow," https://peoplemakeglasgow.com/discover/historic-glasgow; "Victorian Glasgow," http://www.bbc.co.uk/history/scottishhistory/victorian/trails_victorian_glasgow.shtml.
52. "Clyde, River." https://www.scottish-places.info/features/featurefirst1125.html.
53. Bates, *Sergeant Bates's March*, 15–16.
54. Ibid., 16.
55. "Banner Bearing by Sergeant Bates," *New York Herald*, November 7, 1872, 7.
56. Bates, *Sergeant Bates's March*, 17.
57. Ben Johnson, "Edinburgh," https://www.historic-uk.com/HistoryMagazine/DestinationsUK/Edinburgh/.
58. Bates, *Sergeant Bates's March*, 17.
59. Ibid.
60. Ellen Castelow, "Gretna Green." https://www.historic-uk.com/HistoryUK/HistoryofScotland/Gretna-Green.

CHAPTER 23

1. Gilbert H. Bates, *Sergeant Bates's March from Gretna Green to the Guildhall* (London: George Routledge and Sons 1873), 19; "Sark Bridge," https://www.geograph.org.uk/photo/2636471.
2. Bates, *Sergeant Bates's March*, 19.
3. Ibid.
4. Ibid., 20.
5. Ibid.
6. Tim Lambert, "A Brief History of Carlisle, England," http://www.localhistories.org/carlisle.html.
7. Bates, *Sergeant Bates's March*, 20.
8. Ibid., 21.
9. Ibid., 22; "History of the Carlisle Castle." https://www.english-heritage.org.uk/visit/places/carlisle-castle/.
10. Bates, *Sergeant Bates's March*, 22.

11. Ibid., 23; "Pictures of High Hesket," https://www.picturesofengland.com/England/Cumbria/High_Hesket; Beacon Hill and Tower, https://www.dudley.gov.uk/things-to-do/parks-and-open-spaces/parks-in-the-borough/beacon-hill-and-tower/.

12. Bates, *Sergeant Bates's March*, 24.

13. Ibid.

14. *Manchester Guardian* (Manchester, England), November 14, 1872, 1.

15. *Evening Star* (Washington, D.C.), November 11, 1872, 2.

16. *Kendall Mercury* (Kendall, England), November 16, 1872, 1; "Welcome to the Kings Arms," https://kingsarmsburton.co.uk; *Sergeant Bates's March*, 24–26.

17. Bates, *Sergeant Bates's March*, 27.

18. Ibid., 29.

19. Ibid., 37.

20. Ibid., 38.

21. Ibid.

22. Ibid., 39.

23. Ibid.

24. Ibid., 40–41; *Preston Herald* (Preston, England), November 13, 1872, 1.

25. Bates, *Sergeant Bates's March*, 41.

26. Ibid.

27. "The Tour of the American Flag," *Memphis Daily Appeal* (Memphis, TN), December 15, 1872, 1.

28. Bates, *Sergeant Bates's March*, 42.

29. "The Tour of the American Flag."

30. "Sergeant Bates," *Watertown Republican* (Watertown, WI), December 18, 1872, 1.

31. Bates, *Sergeant Bates's March*, 42.

32. *Bolton Chronicle* (Bolton, England), November 14, 1872, 1.

33. *Bolton Evening News* (Bolton, England), November 14, 1872, 1.

34. *Evening Star* (Washington, D.C.), November 18, 1872, 2.

35. "Sergeant Bates and the Feeling in England Toward America," *Green-Mountain Freeman* (Montpelier, VT), December 18, 1872, 1.

36. "Telegram to the New York Herald," *New York Herald*, November 16, 1872, 7.

37. Bates, *Sergeant Bates's March*, 49; *Manchester Enquirer* (Manchester, England), November 15, 1872, 1.

38. Bates, *Sergeant Bates's March*, 49–50.

39. *Chicago Daily Tribune*, December 11, 1872, 8.

40. *Daily Phoenix* (Columbia, SC), December 20, 1872, 4.

41. Bates, *Sergeant Bates's March*, 54–56.

42. Ibid., 56–57.

43. Ibid., 57–58.

44. Ibid., 58.

45. Ibid., 59.

46. Ibid., 62.

47. *Portland Daily Press* (Portland, ME), November 27, 1872, 1.

48. Bates, *Sergeant Bates's March*, 71.

49. Ibid., 72–73.
50. "Courier Journalisms," *Daily Phoenix* (Columbia, SC), November 30, 1872, 4.
51. Bates, *Sergeant Bates's March*, 81.
52. Ibid., 85.
53. Ibid., 85–86.
54. Ibid., 88.
55. Ibid., 91.
56. Ibid., 92–93.
57. Ibid., 104.
58. Ibid., 105–6.
59. Ibid., 106.

Chapter 24

1. Gilbert H. Bates, *Sergeant Bates's March from Gretna Green to the Guildhall* (London: George Routledge and Sons, 1873), 104.
2. Ibid., 105–6.
3. Ibid., 106.
4. *Nashville Union and American* (Nashville, TN), December 1, 1872, 4.
5. "The Fool and the Flag," *Evening Star* (Washington, D.C.), November 30, 1872, 1.
6. Bates, *Sergeant Bates's March*, 108–9.
7. Ibid., 109.
8. "Sergeant Bates on His Tramp," *Wheeling Daily Register* (Wheeling, WV), December 2, 1872, 1.
9. Bates, *Sergeant Bates's March*, 123.
10. Ibid.
11. *Morning Post* (London), December 2, 1872, 1.
12. Ibid.
13. Ibid.
14. Ibid.
15. Ibid.
16. Ibid.
17. Ibid.
18. Ibid.
19. Ibid.
20. Ibid.
21. Ibid.; Bates, *Sergeant Bates's March*, 131, 135.
22. Bates, *Sergeant Bates's March*, 148–50.
23. Ibid., 147.
24. Ibid., 135.
25. *Marshall County Republican* (Plymouth, IN), December 26, 1872, 6.
26. *Memphis Daily Appeal* (Memphis, TN), December 29, 1872, 2.
27. *Wheeling Daily Register* (Wheeling, WV), December 30, 1872, 1.
28. *Wheeling Daily Register* (Wheeling, WV), January 3, 1873, 1.
29. "The Champion Dead Beat," *Camden Journal* (Camden, SC), January 9, 1873, 1.

30. *New National Era* (Washington, D.C.), January 23, 1873, 2.
31. "Did Not Know What It Was," *States Rights Democrat* (Albany, OR), January 24, 1873, 2.
32. Bates, *Sergeant Bates's March*, 1–2.
33. Ibid., 3.
34. Ibid., 1–3.
35. Ibid., 8.
36. "Editorial Notes," *Delaware State Journal* (Wilmington, DE), January 25, 1873, 2.
37. *Public Ledger* (Memphis, TN), January 29, 1873, 4.
38. *New Orleans Republican.* (New Orleans, LA), January 28, 1873, 4.
39. *Andrew County Republican* (Savannah, MO), January 24, 1873, 1.
40. *Evening Star* (Washington, D.C.), December 20, 1872, 1.
41. *New Orleans Republican* (New Orleans, LA), February 5, 1873, 4.
42. *Portland Daily Press* (Portland, ME), January 24, 1873, 1.
43. *Portland Daily Press* (Portland, ME), February 27, 1873, 2.

CHAPTER 25

1. Marc Leepson, *Flag: A Biography* (New York: Thomas Dunne Books, 2005), 200.
2. *Iowa Plain Dealer* (New Oregon, IA), December 6, 1872, 4.
3. *Portland Daily Press* (Portland, ME), December 21, 1872, 1.
4. *Bolivar Bulletin* (Bolivar, TN), January 3, 1873, 2.
5. *Daily Phoenix* (Columbia, SC), May 22, 1873, 2.
6. *Wilmington Daily Gazette* (Wilmington, DE), June 4, 1873, 1.
7. *New Orleans Bulletin* (New Orleans, LA), April 3, 1874, 2.
8. *Charlotte Democrat* (Charlotte, NC), May 11, 1874, 2.
9. *Centre Reporter* (Centre Hill, PA), May 21, 1874, 4.
10. *Worthington Advance* (Worthington, MN), May 14, 1875, 1.
11. "Current Topics," *Worthington Advance* (Worthington, MN), October 1, 1875, 1.
12. "American Actors in England," *New York Herald*, January 14, 1876, 4.
13. *Vancouver Independent* (Vancouver, WA), March 7, 1878, 9.
14. *Emporia News* (Emporia, KS), May 18, 1878, 1.
15. *Daily Cairo Bulletin* (Cairo, IL), July 3, 1881, 3.
16. *Weekly Graphic* (Kirksville, MO), July 21, 1882, 3.

CHAPTER 26

1. "Documenting the Life and Times of Buffalo Bill," https://codyarchive.org/life/.
2. "Bates, Gilbert Henderson," https://codyarchive.org/life/wfc.person.html#bates.g; Buffalo Bill's Wild West: America's National Entertainment (Hartford: Cody and Salsbury, May 31, 1886), McCracken Research Library, Buffalo Bill Center of the West, MS6.3274; Paul Fees, "Wild West Shows: Buffalo Bill's Wild West," https://centerofthehewest.org/learn/western-essays/wild-west-shows.
3. "Among the Churches," *Richmond County Advance* (West New Brighton, NY), July 3, 1886, 2.

4. *Mitchell Capital* (Mitchell, SD), October 1, 1886, 2.
5. Ibid.
6. "Visited Buffalo Bill's Show," *Fort Worth Daily Gazette* (Fort Worth, TX), May 7, 1887, 5.
7. "What Our Prince & Princess Saw of Buffalo Bill's Show," *Penny Illustrated Paper and Illustrated Times* (London, England), May 14, 1887.
8. "Queen Victoria and Buffalo Bill," *Indianapolis Journal*, May 12, 1887, 2.
9. "The Wild West Show," *The Era* (London, England), Buffalo Bill Center of the West; MS6, William F. Cody collection, MS6.3681.008.05 Oakley scrapbook. May 14, 1887.
10. "Buffalo Bill in England," *Pulaski Citizen* (Pulaski, TN), May 12, 1887, 1.
11. *Dramatic Review*, Buffalo Bill Center of the West; MS6, William F. Cody collection, MS6.3681.007.03 Oakley scrapbook, 1887.
12. "Opening of the American Exhibition," *Daily News* (London), May 10, 1887, 1.
13. "The Cowboy and the Peer," *Indianapolis Journal*, June 12, 1887, 3.
14. Ibid.
15. M. Stewart, "Rambles about Europe," *Wichita Eagle* (Wichita, KS), July 6, 1887, 1.
16. Ibid.
17. "Buffalo Bill: The Wide Swath He is Cutting in London," *Morning Appeal* (Carson City, NV), August 4, 1887, 2.
18. "The Provinces," *The Standard* (London, England), August 26, 1887, 1.
19. *Souvenir Album of the Visit of Her Majesty Queen Victoria to the American Exhibition*, James Wojtowicz Collection, McCracken Research Library, Buffalo Bill Center of the West, MS327, 1887.
20. "Buffalo Bill's Show in England," *Indianapolis Journal*, November 6, 1887, 4.
21. Ibid.
22. *Wichita Eagle* (Wichita, KS), December 1, 1887, 1.
23. *Daily Independent* (Elko, NV), November 4, 1887, 1.
24. Fees, "Wild West Shows: Buffalo Bill's Wild West.

Chapter 27

1. "He Carried Our Flag to Many Lands," *Pantagraph* (Bloomington, IL), February 17, 1917, 8.
2. Sergeant Bates, "What Does the Aggression Mean?" *Kansas Agitator* (Garnett, KS), May 24, 1899, 1.
3. Ibid.
4. Ibid.
5. Ibid.
6. Ibid.
7. "Too Much Flag," *Pacific Commercial Advertiser* (Honolulu, HI), September 7, 1899, 4.
8. Ibid.
9. Ibid.
10. Ibid.

11. "He Carried Our Flag to Many Lands," *Pantagraph* (Bloomington, IL), February 17, 1917, 8.

12. Ibid.; Gilbert Henderson Bates, https://www.findagrave.com/memorial/28320774/gilbert-henderson-bates.

13. "Ann E. Noe Bates," https://www.findagrave.com/memorial/68319772/ann-e_-bates.

14. "Hattie Bates," https://ancestors.familysearch.org/en/K8BZ-RZQ/hattie-bates-1865-1953.

Bibliography

"About the Daily Phoenix." https://chroniclingamerica.loc.gov/lccn/sn84027008/.
"The Alabama Claims, 1862–1872." https://history.state.gov/milestones/1861-1865/alabama.
Albany Register (Albany, OR), September 24, 1875, 2.
Albany Register (Albany, OR), December 31, 1875, 4.
"Alexandria During the Civil War." https://www.alexandriava.gov/CivilWar.
Alexandria Gazette (Alexandria, VA). January 29, 1868, 1.
Alexandria Gazette (Alexandria, VA). April 10, 1868, 1.
"Alexandria: The Crossroads of the Civil War." http://www.pbs.org/mercy-street/uncover-history/real-people-places/alexandria/#:~:text=In%20the%20spring%20of%201862,unprecedented%20and%20overwhelming%20scale%20of.
Alpena Weekly Argus (Alpena, MI), August 28, 1878, 1.
"American Actors in England." *New York Herald,* January 14, 1876, 4.
"Among the Churches." *Richmond County Advance* (West New Brighton, NY), July 3, 1886, 2.
Andrew County Republican (Savannah, MO), January 24, 1873, 1.
"Andrew Johnson." https://www.whitehouse.gov/about-the-white-house/presidents/andrew-johnson.
"The Angel of Marye's Heights." https://civilwartalk.com/threads/the-angel-of-marye%E2%80%99s-heights.167413/page-2.
"Ann E. Noe Bates." https://www.findagrave.com/memorial/68319772/ann-e_-bates.
Anti-monopolist (Saint Paul, MN), May 20, 1875, 9.
Arizona Citizen (Tucson, AZ), November 9, 1872, 1.
"Arrival of Gilbert H. Bates." *Daily Clarion* (Jackson, MS), January 31, 1868, 1.
"Arrival of Sergeant Bates." *Evening Argus* (Rock Island, IL), April 24, 1868, 1.
"The Arrival of Sergeant Bates at Washington City." *Spirit of Jefferson* (Charles Town, WV), April 21, 1868, 1.
"Arrival of the Sergeant at Washington." *New York Herald,* April 15, 1868, 5.
"Arrival of Sergeant Bates at Augusta." *Daily Ohio Statesman* (Columbus, OH), March 13, 1868, 1.
"Arrival of Sergeant Bates, His Reception at the Capital of South Carolina." *Daily Phoenix* (Columbia, SC). March 19, 1868, 1.
Atkins, Leah Rawls. "Andrew B. Moore." http://www.encyclopediaofalabama.org/article/h-1454.

"Banner Bearing by Sergeant Bates." *New York Herald*, November 7, 1872, 7.

Bassett, Thom. "Was the Burning of Columbia, S.C. a War Crime?" *New York Times*, Opinion Pages, March 10, 2015.

"Bates and His Banner." *Burlington Weekly Free Press* (Burlington, VT), April 24, 1868, 1.

Bates, Gilbert H. *Sergeant Bates' March: Carrying the Flag from Vicksburg to Washington.* New York: B. W. Hitchcock, 1868.

———. *Sergeant Bates's March from Gretna Green to the Guildhall.* London: George Routledge and Sons, 1873.

"Bates, Gilbert H." https://wisvetsmuseum.pastperfectonline.com/archive/9E480DFC -3B37-4E6C-B895-015345582400.

"Bates, Gilbert Henderson." http://codyarchive.org/life/wfc.person.html#bates.g.

"Bates Over the Border." *New York Herald*, October 20, 1872, 11.

Bates, Sergeant. "What Does the Aggression Mean?" Kansas Agitator (Garnett, KS), May 24, 1899, 1.

Bates, Sergeant G. H. "Editor Raleigh Sentinel." *Daily Register* (Carson City, NV), May 13, 1871, 1.

"Battle of Columbus." http://www.americancivilwarstory.com/battle-of-columbus.html.

"Battle of Fredericksburg." https://www.history.com/topics/american-civil-war/battle-of-fredericksburg.

"The Battle of Selma," https://battleofselma.com/history-of-the-battle/.

"Beacon Hill and Tower." https://www.dudley.gov.uk/things-to-do/parks-and-open -spaces/parks-in-the-borough/beacon-hill-and-tower.

"Benjamin Wood." https://elections.harpweek.com/1872/bio-1872-Full.asp?Unique ID=35&Year=1872.

Bishop, Randy. *Mississippi's Civil War Battlefields.* Gretna, LA: Pelican, 2010.

Bolivar Bulletin (Bolivar, TN), January 3, 1873, 2.

Bolivar Bulletin (Bolivar, TN), August 14, 1874, 1.

Bolton Chronicle (Bolton, England), November 14, 1872, 1.

Bolton Evening News (Bolton, England), November 14, 1872, 1.

Bragg, William Harris. "Reconstruction in Georgia." https://www.georgiaencyclopedia .org/articles/history-archaeology/reconstruction-georgia.

Brown, A. J. "The Town of Hickory." https://www.nchgs.org/html/town_of_hickory .html.

"Buffalo Bill in England." *Pulaski Citizen* (Pulaski, TN), May 12, 1887, 1.

"Buffalo Bill's Show in England." *Indianapolis Journal*, November 6, 1887, 4.

"Buffalo Bill: The Wide Swath He is Cutting in London." *Morning Appeal* (Carson City, NV), August 4, 1887, 2.

Buffalo Bill's Wild West: America's National Entertainment. Hartford: Cody and Salsbury, May 31, 1886. McCracken Research Library, Buffalo Bill Center of the West. MS6.3274.

Burnes, George J. "Columbus as It Was During the War, 1861–65." https://www .columbusga.gov/history/history.pdf.

"By Telegraph to the Gazette." *Daily Gazette* (Wilmington, DE), August 29, 1877, 2.

Calkins, Hiram, and DeWitt Van Buren. *Biographical sketches of John T. Hoffman and Allen C. Beach: The Democratic nominees for governor and lieutenant-governor of the state of New York: also, a record of the events in the lives of Oliver Bascom, David B. McNeil, and Edwin O. Perrin, the other candidates on the same ticket.* New York: New York Printing Company, 1868.

Cannon, J. W. "Old School for Girls Has Place in History Despite Hectic Career." *Greensboro Daily News*, January 3, 1932, 1.

Centre Reporter (Centre Hill, PA), May 21, 1874, 4.

"Carrying the Flag of the Union." *Evening Argus* (Rock Island, IL), February 3, 1868, 2.

"Carrying the Rebel Flag through the Northern States." *New York Herald*, June 12, 1873, 2.

Castelow, Ellen. "Gretna Green." https://www.historicuk.com/HistoryUK/Historyof Scotland/Gretna-Green.

"Census of Population and Housing." Census.gov. Archived from the original on May 12, 2015.

"The Champion Dead Beat." *Camden Journal* (Camden, SC), January 9, 1873, 1.

Charleston Daily News (Charleston, SC), February 17, 1868, 2.

Charlotte Democrat (Charlotte, NC), May 11, 1874, 2.

"Cheney's Grove Township." http://genealogytrails.com/ill/mclean/history_cheneys-grove.html.

"Chicago, Aug. 29." *Cincinnati Daily Star* (Cincinnati, OH), August 29, 1877, 1.

Chicago Daily Tribune, October 24, 1872, 4.

Chicago Daily Tribune, December 11, 1872, 8.

Chicago Tribune, September 14, 1872, 4.

"City of Edgerton." https://www.cityofedgerton.com/visitor-information.

"City of Milledgeville." https://www.milledgevillega.us/index.php/our-history.

"Civil War in Augusta." https://www.visitaugusta.com/things-to-do/civil-war/.

"The Civil War in Greensboro: Key Sites in the Action." https://greensboro.com/news/ the-civil-war-in-greensboro-key-sites-in-the-action/article_cfed1093-58d5-5b1e -aeb5-9f468620d312.html.

"Civil War Trail." https://www.visitmeridian.com/explore/historic-trail-markers/civ-il-war/.

"Clyde, River." https://www.scottish-places.info/features/featurefirst1125.html.

Cohen, Robert. "History of the Long Railroad Bridge Crossing Across the Potomac River." http://www.dcnrhs.org/learn/washington-d-c-railroad-history/history-of -the-long-bridge.

"Concord: Historic Facts." https://www.concordnc.gov/visitor/historic-facts.

"Confederate States District Court." *Daily Dispatch* (Richmond, VA), October 21, 1864, 1.

"The Conservative Soldiers and Sailors." *Carson Daily Appeal* (Carson City, NV), July 8, 1868, 2.

"Co-partnership." *Daily Dispatch* (Richmond, VA), July 17, 1861, 1.

"Courier Journalisms." *Daily Phoenix* (Columbia, SC). November 30, 1872, 4.

"The Courts." *Daily Dispatch* (Richmond, VA), December 18, 1868, 1.

"The Cowboy and the Peer." *Indianapolis Journal* (Indianapolis, IN), June 12, 1887, 3.
Cramer, Mrs. John T. "Recollections of the Founding and Growth During the Early Years of Thomasville." *Chairtown News* (Thomasville, NC), July 28, 1921, 1.
Crist, Lynda Lasswell. "Jefferson Davis, 1808–1889." http://mshistorynow.mdah.state.ms.us/articles/287/jefferson-davis-1808-1889.
Cross, Jerry L. "William Woods Holden." https://ncpedia.org/holden-william-woods-research.
"Current Topics." *Worthington Advance* (Worthington, MN), October 1, 1875, 1.
Daily Astorian (Astoria, OR), October 25, 1882, 2.
Daily Clarion (Jackson, MS), January 31, 1868, 3.
Daily Clarion (Jackson, MS), February 20, 1868, 2.
Daily Clarion (Jackson, MS), April 15, 1868, 1.
Daily Dispatch (Richmond, VA), January 29, 1868, 1.
Daily Dispatch (Richmond, VA), October 3, 1872, 1.
Daily Globe (St. Paul, MN), October 4, 1883, 1.
Daily Independent (Elko, NV), November 4, 1887, 1.
Daily Ohio (Columbus, OH), March 25, 1868, 1.
Daily Phoenix (Columbia, SC), March 20, 1868, 1.
Daily Phoenix (Columbia, SC), March 21, 1868, 1.
Daily Phoenix (Columbia, SC), March 22, 1868, 1.
Daily Phoenix (Columbia, SC), March 24, 1868, 1.
Daily Phoenix (Columbia, SC), March 27, 1868, 1.
Daily Phoenix (Columbia, SC), April 9, 1868, 1.
Daily Phoenix (Columbia, SC), April 15, 1868, 1.
Daily Phoenix (Columbia, SC), December 20, 1872, 4.
Daily Phoenix (Columbia, SC), May 22, 1873, 2.
Daily Phoenix (Columbia, SC), June 6, 1873, 2.
"Death of Sergeant Bates." *Eureka Daily Sentinel* (Eureka, NV), April 14, 1881, 1.
DeCredico, Mary, and Jaime Amanda Martinez. "Richmond During the Civil War." https://www.encyclopediavirginia.org/richmond_during_the_civil_war.
Dennis, Brady. "The Federal Occupation of Alexandria in the Civil War Changed and Spared City." *The Washington Post*, April 7, 2011.
Des Arc Weekly Citizen (Des Arc, AR), February 1, 1868, 2.
"Did Not Know What It Was." *States Rights Democrat* (Albany, OR), January 24, 1873, 2.
"Documenting the Life and Times of Buffalo Bill." http://codyarchive.org/life/wfc.bio.00001.html.
Dodgeville Chronicle (Dodgeville, WI), February 28, 1868, 2.
"Doolittle, James Rood." https://bioguide.congress.gov/search/bio/D000428.
Downey, Tom. "Hamburg." https://www.scencyclopedia.org/sce/entries/hamburg/.
Drake, Rebecca Blackwell. "Kaleidoscope of History: Raymond." http://raymondhistory.org/history/kaleidoscope.htm.
Dramatic Review. Buffalo Bill Center of the West: MS6, William F. Cody collection, MS6.3681.007.03 Oakley scrapbook. 1887.

"Early Danville History." http://danvillehistory.org/history.html.

"East Room." http://www.whitehousemuseum.org/floor1/east-room.htm.

"Editorial Notes." *Delaware State Journal* (Wilmington, DE), January 25, 1873, 2.

"Eldredge, Charles Augustus." https://www.wisconsinhistory.org/Records/Article/CS7388.

Elmore, Tom. *Columbia Civil War Landmarks*. Charleston, SC: The History Press, 2011.

Emporia News (Emporia, KS), May 18, 1878, 1.

Essex County Herald (Guildhall, VT), October 23, 1875, 1.

Evening Argus (Rock Island, IL), February 26, 1868, 2.

Evening Argus (Rock Island, IL), April 25, 1868, 1.

Evening Star (Washington, D.C.), November 11, 1872, 2.

Evening Star (Washington, D.C.), November 18, 1872, 2.

Evening Star (Washington, D.C.), December 20, 1872, 1.

"The Exchange Hotel Civil War Medical Museum." https://visitorangevirginia.com/step-into-history-the-exchange-hotel-civil-war-medical-museum/.

"The Exchange Hotel Civil War Medical Museum: Gordonsville, Virginia." https://colonialghosts.com/the-exchange-hotel-civil-war-medical-museum.

Fees, Paul. "Wild West Shows: Buffalo Bill's Wild West." https://centerofthewest.org/learn/western-essays/wild-west-shows.

"1st Regiment, Wisconsin Heavy Artillery." https://www.nps.gov/civilwar/search-battle-units-detail.htm?battleUnitCode=UW10001RAH.

"1st Wisconsin Heavy Artillery History." https://www.wisconsinhistory.org/Records/Article/CS2320.

"The Flag in the South." *Daily Phoenix* (Columbia, SC). April 8, 1868, 1.

"The Flag March from Vicksburg." *Daily Milwaukee News* (Milwaukee, WI), January 15, 1868, 5.

"The Flood at the South." *Daily Dispatch* (Richmond, VA), January 23, 1865, 1.

"The Fool and the Flag." *Evening Star* (Washington, D.C.), November 30, 1872, 1.

"Fort Mill, South Carolina." https://fortmillsc.gov/?SEC=F13B2B44-D121-4B1B-9C0D-5787B1C02256.

"The Fourth at Oakwood." *Daily Dispatch* (Richmond, VA), July 6, 1866, 1.

"From a Soldier in the Regular Army." *Wyandot Pioneer* (Upper Sandusky, OH), June 11, 1868, 1.

"From Mississippi." *New Orleans Republican* (New Orleans, LA), January 31, 1868, 1.

"From Montgomery." *Weekly North Carolina Standard* (Raleigh, NC), February 19, 1868, 3.

"Gen. McMakin of the Prentiss House." *Vicksburg Weekly Sentinel* (Vicksburg, MS), May 16, 1849, 2.

"George T. Brown, Sergeant at Arms." https://www.senate.gov/about/officers-staff/sergeant-at-arms/SAA-George-Brown.htm.

"George Washington Ball House." https://visitvicksburg.com/george-washington-ball-house.

"Gilbert H. Bates." *Daily Clarion* (Jackson, MS), January 30, 1868.

"Gilbert Henderson Bates." https://www.ancestry.com/boards/topics.obits2/23960/mb.ashx.

"Gilbert Henderson Bates." https://www.findagrave.com/memorial/28320774/
gilbert-henderson-bates.

"The Great Walk: Sergeant Bates on His Travels, His Doings at Meridian." *Charleston
Daily News* (Charleston, SC), February 21, 1868, 1.

"Greensboro History." https://www.visitgreensboronc.com/about-us/greensboro-history.

"Hattie Bates." https://ancestors.familysearch.org/en/K8BZ-RZQ/hat-
tie-bates-1865-1953.

Hebert, Keith S. "Battle of Selma." http://www.encyclopediaofalabama.org/article/
h-3442.

"He Carried Our Flag to Many Lands." *Pantagraph* (Bloomington, IL). February 17,
1917, 8.

Helena Weekly Herald (Helena, MT), October 24, 1872, 3.

Hillsborough Recorder (Hillsborough, NC), August 18, 1875, 1.

Historical Census Browser. University of Virginia Library.

"Historic Dumfries, Virginia." https://historicdumfriesva.org/about/history.

"Historic Glasgow." https://peoplemakeglasgow.com/discover/historic-glasgow.

"Historic Hanover County, Virginia." https://www.hanovervirginia.com/explore-ha-
nover/things-to-do/historic-sites.

"Historic Markers Across South Carolina." http://lat34north.com/HistoricMarkersSC/
SC_Index.

"History: Hanover County, Virginia." http://www.hanovervirginia.com/explore
-hanover/history/.

"History of Augusta." https://www.nps.gov/nr/travel/augusta/historyaugustaoverview
.html.

"History of the Carlisle Castle." https://www.english-heritage.org.uk/visit/places/
carlisle-castle/.

"The History of Charlotte." https://www.charlottesgotalot.com/articles/history/the
-history-of-charlotte.

"History of Charlotte, North Carolina." https://www.u-s-history.com/pages/h3876.
html.

"History of Columbia." https://columbiasc.net/about-columbia.

"History of Columbus, Georgia." https://www.columbusga.gov/history.

"History of Fredericksburg." http://www.hanovervirginia.com/explore-hanover/history/.

"History of Raleigh." https://raleighnc.gov/history-raleigh.

"A History of Salisbury, North Carolina." https://www.carolana.com/NC/Towns/Salis-
bury_NC.html.

"History: Town of Dumfries." https://www.dumfriesva.gov/residents/history.php.

Holden, W.W. "Proclamation." *Western Democrat* (Charlotte, NC), June 27, 1865, 1.

Hubbs, G. Ward. "Civil War in Alabama." http://www.encyclopediaofalabama.org/
article/h-1429.

Huff, Sanford W. "Brigadier-General James M. Tuttle." *Annals of Iowa* 1868 (1868):
233–37.

Idaho Semi-Weekly World (Idaho City, ID), December 26, 1884, 1.

Indianapolis Journal (Indianapolis, IN), January 2, 1885, 4.

"Insults to Our Soldiers and Insults to Our Flag." *Weekly Echo* (Lake Charles, LA), May 2, 1868, 1.

"The Invasion of England." *Beaufort Republican* (Beaufort, SC), October 24, 1872, 1.

Iowa Plain Dealer (New Oregon, IA), December 6, 1872, 4.

"Jackson." https://www.nps.gov/abpp/battles/ms008.htm.

Jacobs, Chick. "The Lesser-Known Story of How the Civil War Ended in North Carolina." *Fayetteville Observer* (Fayetteville, NC), March 22, 2015.

"James Holt Clanton." https://www.findagrave.com/memorial/8757/james-holt-clanton.

"James Madison Tuttle." https://www.findagrave.com/memorial/5895024/james-madison-tuttle.

"James Rood Doolittle." https://www.findagrave.com/memorial/8795250/james-rood-doolittle.

Jasper Weekly Courier (Jasper, IN), November 8, 1873, 2.

Johnson, Ben. "Edinburgh." https://www.historicuk.com/HistoryMagazine/DestinationsUK/Edinburgh/.

"Jonathan Worth." https://www.carolana.com/NC/Governors/jworth.html.

"Jonathan Worth." https://www.nga.org/governor/jonathan-worth/.

Juniata Sentinel (Mifflintown, PA), October 16, 1872, 2.

Kaetz, James P. "Benton." http://encyclopediaofalabama.org/article/h-3541.

———. "Cuba." http://www.encyclopediaofalabama.org/article/h-3772.

Kendall Mercury (Kendall, England), November 16, 1872, 1.

Kimball Graphic (Kimball, SD), February 27, 1885, 6.

Knoxville Daily Chronicle (Knoxville, TN), September 15, 1872, 1.

Lambert, Tim. "A Brief History of Carlisle, England." http://www.localhistories.org/carlisle.html.

Lawless, Sarah. "Tuskegee." http://www.encyclopediaofalabama.org/article/h-2051.

Leepson, Marc. *Flag: A Biography.* New York: Thomas Dunne Books, 2005.

Leigh, Philip. "Union Leagues." https://www.abbevilleinstitute.org/blog/union-leagues.

"Letter from New York." *Evansville Journal* (Evansville, IN), July 13, 1868, 1.

Lewis, Herbert. "Selma." *Encyclopedia of Alabama.* http://www.encyclopediaofalabama.org/face/Article.jsp?id=1635.

Lewis, J. D. "A History of Winnsboro, South Carolina. https://www.carolana.com/SC/Towns/Winnsboro_SC.html.

"List of Letters." *Daily Dispatch* (Richmond, VA), February 22, 1868, 1.

"Local Items." *Daily Phoenix* (Columbia, SC). March 18, 1868, 2.

Lockhart, Matthew A. "Rock Hill." https://www.scencyclopedia.org/sce/entries/rock-hill/.

Logue, Larry M. "Mississippians in Confederate Army." https://mississippiencyclopedia.org/entries/mississippians-in-confederate-army/.

Lomask, Milton. "Sergt. Bates March: Carrying the Stars and Stripes Unfurled, from Vicksburg to Washington, and Gretna Green to London." *American Heritage* 16, no. 6 (October 1965): 12–16.

"Long Bridge Over the Potomac River." http://www.virginiaplaces.org/rail/longbridge.html.

"Look at Buxbaum and Lang's Price List." *Charlotte Democrat* (Charlotte, NC), June 2, 1868, 3.

Madison, Dane County, and Surrounding Towns. Madison, WI: William J. Park, 1877.

Manchester Enquirer (Manchester, England), November 15, 1872, 1.

Manchester Guardian (Manchester, England), November 14, 1872, 1.

Manitowoc Tribune (Manitowoc, WI), February 13, 1868, 1.

"The March to Washington." *Daily News* (Charleston, SC), February 29, 1868, 1.

Marshall County Republican (Plymouth, IN), December 26, 1872, 6.

"Martha Johnson Patterson: Hostess of the Andrew Johnson White House." https://www.whitehousehistory.org/martha-johnson-patterson-hostess-of-the-andrew-johnson-white-house.

Martin, Jonathan. "Rowan County." https://northcarolinahistory.org/encyclopedia/rowan-county-1753.

Matthews, Mary Green. *Wheels of Faith and Courage: A History of Thomasville, North Carolina.* Thomasville, NC: Hall Printing Company, 1952.

Memphis Daily Appeal (Memphis, TN), December 29, 1872, 2.

"Meridian and the Civil War." https://www.visitmeridian.com/plan-your-trip/meridians-history/.

The Metropolitan, aka Brown's Marble Hotel." http://www.streetsofwashington.com/2009/12/metropolitan-aka-browns-marble-hotel.html.

"Michler, Nathaniel." https://tshaonline.org/handbook/online/articles/fmi88.

Milan Exchange (Milan, TN), March 1, 1884, 1.

Miller, Howard. *The Student's Dream and Other Poems.* Louisville, KY: John P. Morton and Company, 1871.

"Miscellaneous." *New North-west* (Deer Lodge, MT), October 26, 1872, 2.

"Mississippi Items." *Memphis Daily Appeal* (Memphis, TN), February 1, 1868, 1.

"Mississippi State Convention." *Daily Clarion* (Jackson, MS), January 31, 1868, 1.

"Mr. and Mrs. Jefferson Davis, Sergeant Bates, and the Pedestrian." *Daily Dispatch* (Richmond, VA), February 1, 1868, 3.

"Mr. J. Corson." *Alexandria Gazette* (Alexandria, VA), April 16, 1868, 1.

Mitchell Capital (Mitchell, SD), October 1, 1886, 2.

"Montgomery, Ala., Feb. 18." *Alexandria Gazette* (Alexandria, VA), February 18, 1868, 1.

Morning Appeal (Carson City, NV), December 20, 1878, 2.

Morning Appeal (Carson City, NV), March 16, 1881, 2.

Morning Post (London), December 2, 1872, 1.

"Nasby, Petroleum V." https://pfaffs.web.lehigh.edu/node/54257.

Nashville Union and American (Nashville, TN), September 18, 1872, 2.

Nashville Union and American (Nashville, TN), December 1, 1872, 4.

Nashville Union and Dispatch (Nashville, TN), January 30, 1868, 2.

National Republican (Washington, D.C.), January 7, 1868, 3.

Neeley, Mary Ann Oglesby. "Montgomery." http://www.encyclopediaofalabama.org/article/h-1833.

New National Era (Washington, D.C.), January 23, 1873, 2.

New Orleans Bulletin (New Orleans, LA), April 3, 1874, 2.

New Orleans Republican (New Orleans, LA), February 21, 1868, 1.

New Orleans Republican (New Orleans, LA), December 15, 1868, 3.

New Orleans Republican (New Orleans, LA), January 28, 1873, 4.

New Orleans Republican (New Orleans, LA), February 5, 1873, 4.

New Orleans Republican (New Orleans, LA), November 13, 1875, 5.

New Orleans Republican (New Orleans, LA), December 23, 1875, 2.

New Orleans Republican (New Orleans, LA), April 9, 1876, 4.

News and Herald (Winnsboro, SC), September 11, 1877, 1.

New Ulm Weekly Review (New Ulm, MN), April 20, 1881, 1.

New York Herald, October 6, 1872, 8.

New York Herald, October 9, 1872, 4.

Nix, Elizabeth. "5 Things You Might Not Know About the Washington Monument." September 1, 2018. https://www.history.com/news/5-things-you-might-not -know-about-the-washington-monument.

"North Carolina Election." *Tarboro Southerner* (Tarboro, NC), April 23, 1868, 1.

"Norway-Heritage Across the Sea: *S/S Europa*, Anchor Line. http://www.norway heritage.com/p_ship.asp?sh=euro1.

"Notice: Mr. Joseph Cance." *Daily Dispatch* (Richmond, VA), June 15, 1867, 1.

"Notice: Mr. Joseph Cance." *Daily Dispatch* (Richmond, VA), June 18, 1867, 1.

"Notice: Mr. Joseph Cance." *Daily Dispatch* (Richmond, VA), June 19, 1867, 1.

"A Novel Wager." *New York Herald*, September 10, 1872, 1.

"The Old Flag at Montgomery." *Edgefield Advertiser* (Edgefield, SC), March 18, 1868, 1.

"The Old Flag Marching On." *Evening News* (Gold Hill, NV), October 3, 1872, 1.

"Opening of the American Exhibition." *Daily News* (London), May 10, 1887, 1.

"Ordway, Nehemiah G." https://history.house.gov/People/Listing/O/ORDWAY,-Ne-hemiah-G-/.

"Original Surrender Monument." https://www.nps.gov/vick/planyourvisit/surmonument .htm.

"Patriotic Movement, on Foot." *Western Democrat* (Charlotte, NC). December 31, 1867, 1.

Petroleum Centre Daily Record (Petroleum Center, PA), March 15, 1873, 1.

Phillips, Jason. "Reconstruction." https://mississippiencyclopedia.org/entries/reconstruc-tion.

"Pictures of High Hesket." https://www.picturesofengland.com/England/Cumbria/ High_Hesket.

Pioche Daily Record (Pioche, NV), October 7, 1875, 2.

"A Place in History, A Place in Your Future," http://www.townofedwards.com/history .htm.

"Political Items." *Dodgeville Chronicle* (Dodgeville, WI), January 29, 1869, 1.

"Poor Sergeant Bates." *Watertown Republican* (Watertown, WI), July 29, 1881, 3.

Portland Daily Press (Portland, ME), September 13, 1872, 2.

Portland Daily Press (Portland, ME), October 11, 1872, 2.

Portland Daily Press (Portland, ME), November 27, 1872, 1.

Portland Daily Press (Portland, ME), December 21, 1872, 1.

Portland Daily Press (Portland, ME), January 24, 1873, 1.

Portland Daily Press (Portland, ME), February 27, 1873, 2.

"The Prentiss House." *Daily Commercial Herald* (Vicksburg, MS), January 18, 1891, 5.

Press and Daily Dakotaian (Yankton, Dakota Territory), March 1, 1884, 2.

Preston Herald (Preston, England), November 13, 1872, 1.

"Prior 1830s: The Early Years." https://www.greensboro-nc.gov/departments/police/about-gpd/history.

"Professional Tramps." *Puget Sound Weekly Argus* (Port Townsend, WA), July 25, 1878, 6.

"Progress of Serg't Bates." *Daily Argus* (Mount Vernon, NY), February 14, 1868, 1.

"The Provinces." *The Standard* (London, England), August 26, 1887, 1.

Public Ledger (Memphis, TN), September 18, 1872, 2.

Public Ledger (Memphis, TN), January 29, 1873, 4.

Public Ledger (Memphis, TN), December 20, 1883, 1.

"Queen Victoria and Buffalo Bill." *Indianapolis Journal*, May 12, 1887, 2.

Raleigh, N.C., and the Civil War." https://www.visitraleigh.com/things-to-do/history/civil-war/.

"Reconstruction Era: 1865–1877." https://www.howard.edu/library/reference/guides/reconstructionera.

"Reid, Captain Mayne." https://www.ulib.niu.edu/badndp/reid_mayne.html.

River Press (Fort Benton, MT), June 3, 1885, 6.

"Robberies." *New Orleans Crescent* (New Orleans, LA), December 15, 1868, 1.

Rogers, Rebecca. "History of Augusta, Georgia." https://www.u-s-history.com/pages/h2735.html.

"Roster of Company H," n.d.

Rozier, John. "Sparta." https://www.georgiaencyclopedia.org/articles/counties-cities-neighborhoods/sparta.

Russell, Wayne, and Jeanette Porter. "Amelia Court House." *Cooperative Living*, January 2010, 32–35.

"Sark Bridge." https://www.geograph.org.uk/photo/2636471.

Savannah Morning News (Savannah, GA), April 23, 1881, 2.

Savannah Morning News (Savannah, GA), September 18, 1883, 2.

"Screven House." *Daily Phoenix* (Columbia, SC), April 17, 1868, 1.

Seabrook, Charles. "Savannah River." https://www.georgiaencyclopedia.org/articles/geography-environment/savannah-river.

Semi-weekly Bourbon News (Paris, KY), November 2, 1883, 1.

Semi-weekly Bourbon News (Paris, KY), December 4, 1883, 4.

Semi-weekly Interior Journal (Stanford, KY), March 7, 1884, 2.

Semi-weekly South Kentuckian (Hopkinsville, KY), November 23, 1883, 3.

"Sergeant Bates." *Alexandria Gazette* (Alexandria, VA), April 11, 1868, 1.

"Sergeant Bates." *Alexandria Gazette* (Alexandria, VA), April 13, 1868, 3.

"Sergeant Bates." *Alexandria Gazette* (Alexandria, VA), April 14, 1868, 1.

"Sergeant Bates." *Alexandria Gazette* (Alexandria, VA), April 14, 1868, 3.

"Sergeant Bates." *Anderson Intelligencer* (Anderson Court House, SC), February 19, 1868, 4.

"Sergeant Bates." *Chicago Daily Tribune,* March 13, 1881, 12.

"Sergeant Bates." *Daily Ohio Statesman* (Columbus, OH), October 27, 1868, 3.

"Sergeant Bates." *Dallas Daily Herald* (Dallas, TX), January 25, 1877, 4.

"Sergeant Bates." *Daily Phoenix* (Columbus, SC). March 3, 1868, 1.

"Sergeant Bates." *Edgefield Advertiser* (Edgefield, SC). March 18, 1868, 1.

"Sergeant Bates." *Native Virginian* (Orange Court House, VA), February 21, 1868, 1.

"Sergeant Bates," *Ottawa Free Trader* (Ottawa, IL), February 22, 1868, 1.

"Sergeant Bates." *Plymouth Weekly Democrat* (Plymouth, IN), February 13, 1868, 2.

"Sergeant Bates." *Watertown Republican* (Watertown, WI), December 18, 1872, 1.

"Sergeant Bates." *Yorkville Enquirer* (Yorkville, SC), March 26, 1868, 3.

"Sergeant Bates Again." *New York Herald,* September 10, 1872, 1.

"Sergeant Bates and His Flag." *Aegis and Intelligencer* (Bel Air, MD), April 24, 1868, 1.

"Sergeant Bates and His Flag." *Daily Phoenix* (Columbia, SC). April 19, 1868, 1.

"Sergeant Bates and His Flag." *Eureka Daily Sentinel* (Eureka, NV), March 19, 1884, 2.

"Sergeant Bates and His Flag: A Played-Out Demagogue." *Watertown Republic* (Watertown, WI), July 29, 1868, 2.

"Sergeant Bates and the Feeling in England Toward America." *Green-Mountain Freeman* (Montpelier, VT), December 18, 1872, 1.

"Sergeant Bates and the Flag." *Richmond Dispatch* (Richmond, VA), February 15, 1868, 1.

"Sergeant Bates and the Flag of the Union." *Daily Dispatch* (Richmond, VA), April 8, 1868, 1.

"Sergeant Bates and the U.S. Flag." *Western Democrat* (Charlotte, NC), April 21, 1868, 1.

"Sergeant Bates at the Capitol." *South-Western* (Shreveport, LA), April 29, 1868, 1.

"Sergeant Bates at Pettusville, Va.—Mr. Nasby Is Present When He Arrives." *Jackson Standard* (Jackson Court House, OH), May 7, 1868, 1.

"Sergeant Bates at Washington." *Yorkville Enquirer* (Yorkville, SC), April 23, 1868, 1.

"Sergeant Bates Challenged." *Democratic Advocate* (Westminster, MD), March 15, 1873, 1.

"Sergeant Bates: The Flag-bearing Traveler Going to Exhibit the Bunting to John Bull." *Helena Weekly Herald* (Helena, MT), October 3, 1872, 1.

"Sergeant Bates: His March Through the South with the Old Flag Unfurled." *Edgefield Advertiser* (Edgefield, SC). March 18, 1868, 1.

"Sergeant Bates, His Walk from Vicksburg to Washington." *Daily Phoenix* (Columbia, SC). February 16, 1868, 1.

"Sergeant Bates in the Capital." *Charlotte Daily News* (Charlotte, NC), April 15, 1868, 1.

"Sergeant Bates in Columbia." *Anderson Intelligencer* (Anderson Court House, SC), March 25, 1868, 1.

"Sergeant Bates in Richmond." *Daily Dispatch* (Richmond, VA), April 9, 1868, 1.

"Sergeant Bates in Richmond." *Daily Phoenix* (Columbia, SC), April 9, 1868, 1.

"Sergeant Bates Is a Bummer." *Morning Appeal* (Carson City, NV), October 19, 1883, 1.
"Sergeant Bates Is in Grief." *New Orleans Republican* (New Orleans, LA), December 12, 1868, 3.
"Sergeant Bates not Appreciated." *Morning Appeal* (Carson City, NV), October 13, 1883, 3.
"Sergeant Bates on his Tramp." *Wheeling Daily Register* (Wheeling, WV), December 2, 1872, 1.
"Sergeant Bates Robbed and Maltreated." *Evening Star* (Washington, D.C.), April 8, 1878, 4.
"Sergeant Bates Turns up Again." *Newberry Herald* (Newberry, SC), January 26, 1878, 1.
"Sergeant Bates: What he Proposes to Do, and How He Intends to Do It." *Evening Argus* (Rock Island, IL), February 3, 1868, 2.
Shasta Courier (Shasta, CA), February 8, 1868, 4.
"Sherman Enters Meridian, Mississippi," https://www.history.com/this-day-in-history/sherman-enters-meridian-mississippi.
"Sherman Sacks Columbus, South Carolina." https://www.history.com/this-day-in-history/sherman-sacks-columbia-south-carolina.
Smith, Timothy B. "Jackson: The Capital City and the Civil War," http://mshistorynow.mdah.state.ms.us/articles/337/jackson-the-capital-city-and-the-civil-war.
"South Carolina Historical Markers in York County, 1936-Present." https://www.cityofrockhill.com/home/showdocument?id=1279.
"Southern News." *Alexandria Gazette* (Alexandria, VA). April 21, 1863, 1.
"The South Startled." *Butler Weekly Times* (Butler, MO), August 17, 1887, 1.
South-Western (Shreveport, LA), February 5, 1868.
Souvenir Album of the Visit of Her Majesty Queen Victoria to the American Exhibition. James Wojtowicz Collection, McCracken Research Library, Buffalo Bill Center of the West, MS327. 1887.
"Sparta." https://georgiahistory.com/ghml_marker_updated/sparta.
Spencer, Betty Dan. "In Its Heyday, Boyden House Had a Central Role in Salisbury Social Life." *Salisbury Post* (Salisbury, NC), September 11, 2016, 1.
Spirit of Democracy (Woodsfield, OH), May 25, 1869, 1.
Srikanth, Sai. "William Woods Holden." https://northcarolinahistory.org/encyclopedia/william-woods-holden-1818-1892/.
Star of Pascagoula (Pascagoula, MS), October 23, 1875, 2.
Staunton Spectator (Staunton, VA), May 26, 1868, 1.
Stewart, M. "Rambles about Europe." *Wichita Eagle* (Wichita, KS), July 6, 1887, 1.
"Stonewall Jackson." https://www.biography.com/military-figure/stonewall-jackson.
Stucka, Mike. "Macon Played Pivotal Role in Civil War in Georgia." *Telegraph* (Macon, GA), April 12, 2011.
"Summary of News." *Vermont Transcript* (St. Albans, VT), April 24, 1868, 2.
"Telegram to the New York Herald." *New York Herald*, November 16, 1872, 7.
"Then and Now." *Oxford Democrat* (Paris, ME), May 30, 1871, 1.
Tkacik, Christina. "'The Laudanum Evil': Maryland's 19th Century Opiate Epidemic." *Baltimore Sun*, January 13, 2019, 2.

"Too Much Flag." *Pacific Commercial Advertiser* (Honolulu, HI), September 7, 1899, 4.
"The Tour of the American Flag." *Memphis Daily Appeal* (Memphis, TN), December 15, 1872, 1.
"Town of Winnsboro." https://discoversouthcarolina.com/products/10078.
Twain, Mark. *Territorial Enterprise* (Virginia City, NV). February 27, 1868, 1.
"The United States Senatorship." *The Chronicle* (Dodgeville, WI), December 4, 1868, 1.
US Census 2018: ACS 5-year Survey Table 803002.
"Valuable Bakery and Fixtures." *Daily Dispatch* (Richmond, VA), July 26, 1867, 1.
Vancouver Independent (Vancouver, WA), March 7, 1878, 9.
"Vicksburg & Meridian." http://www.msrailroads.com/V&M.htm.
"Victorian Glasgow." http://www.bbc.co.uk/history/scottishhistory/victorian/trails_victorian_glasgow.shtml.
"Visited Buffalo Bill's Show." *Fort Worth Daily Gazette* (Fort Worth, TX), May 7, 1887, 5.
"Walker, Pendleton and Broadman." *Abbeville Press* (Abbeville, SC), April 27, 1866, 2.
"War with Spain." *Public Ledger* (Memphis, TN), December 18, 1873, 1.
"Washington, April 14." *Western Democrat* (Charlotte, NC), April 21, 1868, 1.
Watertown Republican (Watertown, WI), June 14, 1876, 3.
"Wayfinding: Marshall House." https://www.alexandriava.gov/historic/info/default.aspx?id=101305.
"Welcome to the Kings Arms." https://kingsarmsburton.co.uk.
Western Democrat (Charlotte, NC), June 13, 1865, 1.
"What Our Prince & Princess Saw of Buffalo Bill's Show." *Penny Illustrated Paper and Illustrated Times* (London, England), May 14, 1887.
Wheeling Daily Intelligencer (Wheeling, WV), December 21, 1877, 1.
Wheeling Daily Register (Wheeling, WV), December 30, 1872, 1.
Wheeling Daily Register (Wheeling, WV), January 3, 1873, 1.
"Wheelbarrow Idiocy." *Lake Charles Echo* (Lake Charles, LA), June 21, 1879, 6.
"The White House Building." https://www.whitehouse.gov/about-the-white-house/the-white-house.
Wichita Eagle (Wichita, KS), December 1, 1887, 1.
Wiggins, Sarah Woolfolk. "Lewis Eliphalet Parsons 1865." http://www.encyclopediaofalabama.org/article/h-1169.
"The Wild West Show." *The Era* (London, England), Buffalo Bill Center of the West; MS6, William F. Cody collection, MS6.3681.008.05 Oakley scrapbook. May 14, 1887.
"William Mungen." https://www.findagrave.com/memorial/8122776/william-mungen.
Williard, David C. "North Carolina in the Civil War." https://dev.ncpedia.org/history/cw-1900/civil-war.
Wilmington Daily Gazette (Wilmington, DE), June 4, 1873, 1.
Wilmington Journal (Wilmington, NC), January 17, 1873, 1.
"Winnsboro History." http://www.townofwinnsboro.com/winsboro-history.
"Wit and Humor." *Watertown Republican* (Watertown, WI), November 15, 1876, 6.
Wood County Reporter (Grand Rapids, WI), January 29, 1863, 1.

Wood County Reporter (Grand Rapids, WI), February 1874, 4.

Worthington Advance (Worthington, MN), May 14, 1875, 1.

Wright, Catherine M. "Danville During the Civil War." https://www.encyclopedia virginia.org/Danville_During_the_Civil_War.

Wyandot County Republican (Upper Sandusky, OH), January 7, 1869, 1.

"York County History, An Introduction." https://www.yclibrary.org/ychistory.

Young, Pat. "Book Review: Edward Pollard's *The Lost Cause: A New Southern History of the War of the Confederates*." https://civilwartalk.com/threads/the-lost-cause -a-new-southern-history-of-the-war-of-the-confederates-by-edward -pollard.140775.

About the Author

Randy Bishop is an award-winning high school history, economics, and marketing teacher who has also taught at the community college and university levels. Deeply involved in his local community, he is active in history preservation groups, including the Civil War Preservation Trust, Tennessee Civil War Preservation Association, and Parker's Crossroads Battlefield Association. His previous books include specialty-press guides to the history and preservation of battlefields in Tennessee, Kentucky, and Mississippi; a history of the Tennessee Brigade; and A Civil War Devotional. Bishop lives in Middleton, Tennessee.